MANUFACTURING BABIES
AND PUBLIC CONSENT

Manufacturing Babies and Public Consent

Debating the New Reproductive Technologies

José Van Dyck
Assistant Professor of Journalism
University of Groningen
The Netherlands

NEW YORK UNIVERSITY PRESS
Washington Square, New York

First published in the U.S.A. in 1995 by
NEW YORK UNIVERSITY PRESS
Washington Square
New York, N.Y. 10003

Library of Congress Cataloging-in-Publication Data
Van Dyck, José, 1960–
Manufacturing babies and public consent : debating the new
reproductive technologies / José Van Dyck.
p.   cm.
Includes bibliographical references and index.
ISBN 0–8147–8785–1. — ISBN 0–8147–8786–X (pbk.)
1. Human reproductive technology—Social aspects.   2. Human
reproductive technology—Public opinion.   I. Title.
RG133.5.V36   1995
362. 1'98178—dc20   94–30373
                                                              CIP

Printed in Great Britain

To the memory of my father

Contents

Acknowledgments   ix

**Introduction: Manufacturing Babies and Public
Consent**   1

**1   Mapping the Public Debate on New
     Reproductive Technologies**   9
     Introduction   9
     A Public Debate as a Field of Struggle   14
     Medical Authority and Feminist Criticism   27

**2   Reading Science, Journalism and Fiction as
     Culture**   35
     Introduction   35
     Science as Discourse   38
     Journalism as Discourse   44
     Science in Fiction, Fictions of Science   52
     The Role of the Critic in a Public Debate   57

**3   Constructing the Need for New Reproductive
     Technologies**   61
     Introduction   61
     The First Test-Tube Baby: 'Gee Whiz! A Miracle!'   62
     From Miracle to Cure: Establishing the Need
        for IVF   69
     From Cure to Plague   77

**4   Feminist Assessments of New Reproductive
     Technologies**   87
     Introduction   87
     Constructing a Countermyth   90
     Rejecting the Countermyth   99
     Imagining Reproduction: Feminist Fictions
        of Science   104
     Feminism between Margin and Mainstream   114

WITHDRAWN

5 From Cure to Commodity: The Naturalization of IVF   **119**
Introduction   119
Playing the Odds: The Numbers Game   121
The Natural Construction of Medical Facts   128
Reconsidering Oppositional Strategies   143

6 From Need to Right: The Legalization of Genetic Motherhood   **149**
Introduction   149
Anna Johnson versus the *Los Angeles Times*   152
The Naturalization of a Legal Definition   166
The Divided Feminist Body   171

7 From Legalization to Legislation: Race and Age as Determining Factors   **175**
Introduction   175
Postmenopausal Pregancies   178
Transracial Impregnation   184
Nature, Logic and the Public Debate   189

Conclusion   **195**

Notes   205
Bibliography   227
Index   235

Acknowledgments

I would like to express my gratitude to institutions and persons on both sides of the Atlantic who helped me realize this project. The American Association for University Women awarded me an international fellowship which enabled me to complete my library research in California. The University of Groningen, The Netherlands, generously allotted me precious research time while writing this book. I am particularly grateful to the staff, supporters and students of the Journalism Program for continuously recharging my motivation. The faculty of the Departments of Literature and Communication at the University of California, San Diego provided a stimulating intellectual environment. I would especially like to thank Valerie Hartouni, Roddey Reid and Stephanie Jed for commenting extensively on previous drafts. I have profited from the thoughtful criticism of the members of the 'Gender and Genre' group at the University of Utrecht, The Netherlands: Rosi Braidotti, Ruth Oldenziel, Lies Wesseling and Liana Borghi. I appreciate Maureen McNeil's careful reading of the manuscript and her insightful comments.

Over the years, I could always count on the love and kindness of many close relatives and friends. I would like to thank my mother, sisters and brothers for their incessant moral support while I was residing in the USA. Christina Accomando not only gave me valuable research assistance but she has also been an important discussion partner and friend. Marlowe Miller and David Keevil have inspired me with many good ideas. This book could not have been completed without the intellectual response, relentless support, editorial help and keen criticism of Ton Brouwers, my best and oldest friend.

JOSÉ VAN DYCK

Introduction: Manufacturing Babies and Public Consent

It contained all the ingredients of a Christmas story: on 25 December, 1993, a 59-year-old British woman gave birth to healthy twins. The babies were conceived in vitro in the clinic of doctor Severino Antinori in Rome; eggs from a younger donor were fertilized with the sperm of the British woman's husband and the zygote was implanted in her womb. That very same week, another odd birth occurred in the Pope's hometown: in Umberto I hospital a black woman bore a white baby, which was produced out of the semen of her white husband and an egg donated by a white woman. The new mother preferred a white baby because she did not want her child to experience racial discrimination while growing up. These two stories could be considered postmodern variants of an immaculate conception: both babies were conceived without sex, and produced with the help of advanced technology.

The conception and births of these babies invigorated heated debates across Europe and the USA. After the news about the 59-year-old mother broke in England on December 26, Antinori found his clinic invaded by British and American reporters from ITN to *Twenty-Twenty*, who wanted to interview him. Since 1988, the Italian doctor had allegedly administered in vitro fertilization (IVF) to more than 150 postmenopausal women. His oldest patient turned out to be a 62-year-old woman who was now pregnant. Talkshow hosts attacked Antinori and other doctors who 'played God' and 'defied nature.' Antinori was furious with the press and he angrily replied that all women, including women over 55, have a right to conceive with the help of modern technology. He finally had to call in the police to remove obtrusive reporters from his premises.

The scene in doctor Antinori's clinic strikingly resembled the siege of the hospital in Oldham, Britain, on the day Louise Brown was born in 1978. The birth of the first test-tube baby sparked moral, ethical and religious questions on whether

1

conception outside a woman's body should be allowed. The arguments launched in 1994 sound remarkably similar to those in 1978: IVF should not be used to transgress 'natural' limits of conception and family bonds, the medical risks for women are much too high, and the effect on children is bound to be detrimental. But whereas the debate in 1978 was triggered by a new invention, the recent commotion was the result of a particular application of IVF; in other words, in 1994 a storm of indignation over 'retirement mothers' broke loose, because a new consumer segment of the reproductive service industry had been tapped.

Fifteen years after the first test-tube baby, we have become quite used to the new technologies; their widespread use and availability are assumed matter-of-factly. When IVF was successfully applied for the first time, it was presented as a treatment for women who could not conceive because of blocked Fallopian tubes. Since then, variations and refinements of this technique have resulted in a wide range of possible applications. Gestational and genetic motherhood can now be split, resulting in a new range of reproductive options. A woman, for instance, can give birth to her own grandchild when her daughter is unable to conceive; a zygote conceived in vitro out of her daughter's egg can be reimplanted in the mother's womb. Twins conceived simultaneously can be conveniently gestated and born eighteen months apart. For those who can afford treatment, conception and pregnancy have become commercial transactions and professionally managed procedures. The application of these procedures has continuously shifted the boundaries of conception and reproduction. In fact, it is not the latest technological innovation that causes tumult, but the realization that the new technologies actually change familiar procreational contexts and traditional notions of motherhood, pregnancy and childbirth.

How could these technologies have become naturalized and legitimized in such a relatively short period of time? Fifteen years ago the very idea of conception outside a woman's womb triggered science fiction fantasies and scary speculations. Today, thousands of babies are 'manufactured' with the help of IVF and related techniques every year. The question how the technologies have turned from controversial practices into commonly applied procedures will be the central focus of this book.

Acceptance and dissemination of technology can be traced in a public debate surrounding these issues. In the course of fifteen years, IVF has elicited strong reactions, ranging from anxiety and fear to enthusiasm and abhorrence. Many groups and individuals have expressed their opinion with regard to the new technologies, each using their own specific arguments, images, facts and figures.

In the public debate on new reproductive technologies, two groups have particularly voiced their interested concern: medical researchers and feminists. The medical establishment and feminists became prime contenders in this debate on how the new technologies could enhance or harm woman's reproductive qualities. While medical scientists generally hailed the new technologies as unprecedented advancement, feminists were concerned about the way in which these techniques might take away a woman's reproductive autonomy and intrude upon her bodily integrity. Yet to regard the debate on new reproductive technologies as a power struggle between scientists and feminists would be far too reductive. Many voices stepped into the debate: ethicists, religious groups and politicians also expressed concern about the social and moral implications of the new technologies.

Despite initial controversy and subsequent agitated discussion, gradually a consensus emerged on the application and implementation of IVF and similar techniques. Consensus is always the result of a process of debating. A public debate - the exchange of meanings among a general audience - is a historically evolving process of signification. Over the past fifteen years, many people have exchanged arguments in the discussion on the new technologies. Recently mounting discussions on postmenopausal mothers and transracial impregnation can only be properly understood if they are viewed in the context of previous discussions on IVF, infertility and motherhood. A public debate is a process in which hegemony is never permanent; hegemony is contested by competing systems of representation, arguing from different ideological viewpoints. The aim of this study is to trace how dominant definitions in this field have emerged, or, in other words, how public consent has been manufactured.

A public debate evolves in a specific political and cultural context; for this study I have concentrated on discussions in the

USA and Great Britain. During the 1980s, the political and cultural climates in these countries, especially with regard to women and reproductive rights, had many points in common. Both Reagan's and Thatcher's zeal to deregulate the medical industry, to turn back the clock on rights of underprivileged groups, and to cut back on social programmes, disproportionally affected women and the poor. In both countries, women's reproductive autonomy eroded substantially. The abortion debate resurged in the USA, and culminated in a marginal victory for abortion rights activists in 1989; calls for 'foetal protection' and 'foetal rights' came at the expense of a woman's right to bodily integrity. In both countries, we have witnessed crumbling health systems that neglect comprehensive prenatal care, but promote technology that 'saves' premature babies. We have also seen a political climate emerge – especially in the USA – in which the legal system forces the use of contraceptive devices upon women on welfare, while wealthy, infertile couples are encouraged to conceive with the help of very expensive technology.

But despite the similarities in these social and political climates, there are also important differences between Britain and the USA in terms of reproductive politics.[1] In North America, the fear for the consequences of reproductive technologies has been channelled particularly into a concern about commercialization; legislators and judges sought to protect individuals from commercial exploitation. In Britain, by contrast, the main concern seemed to keep the state from meddling with the development of the new technologies and leave regulation to the market. Even though the distinction between these countries is a profound one, the parameters underlying the public debate on both sides of the Atlantic were strikingly similar. Yet rather than looking for distinctive national contexts, I will try to sketch the international range of this debate.

In the course of fifteen years, national borders have become less important obstacles in the promotion of reproductive technologies; as soon as certain techniques are outlawed or applications are banned in one country, it is not uncommon to see an exodus of women to countries where treatment is still allowed. 'Reproductive tourism' was in fact the case in the recent discussion on postmenopausal pregnancies: the 59-year-old

British woman had gone to doctor Antinori's clinic because Italy's laws were more liberal than Britain's in this respect. As a result of this incidence, both Italian and French members of parliament called for legal restrictions on IVF treatment, and the British secretary of Health even proposed a European ban on treatment for women past natural childbearing age.

Besides the political climate, it is also important to look at the cultural context in which the debate evolved. As I will explain in Chapter 1, I will not regard the new technologies as an exclusive medical or scientific issue, since such framing would obscure the essential ties between science and culture. An interdisciplinary approach, also known as the 'cultural studies of science,' foregrounds the intrinsic relations between science and culture.[2] Cultural practices and formations are inherent to scientific knowledge, as scientific articulations often draw upon cultural resources and vice versa. New reproductive technologies are not mere technical instruments or inventions, but their production and dissemination is contingent upon the norms and values prevailing in that society.

By the same token, feminist contributions to this debate cannot be viewed separately from the cultural matrix from which they arise; an exclusive focus on feminist positions would veil the reciprocity between oppositional and dominant voices. In my preferred approach, the cultural studies of science, gender is not merely a point of interest but a central concern. Other social factors, such as race, class and age are equally included in this perspective. A public debate on new reproductive technologies is not simply a discussion between scientists and feminists about the creation and application of technological gadgets; it is a debate between a number of interested parties on a social transformation which raises crucial questions of power and power sharing.

A public debate is also intrinsically entrenched in a discursive context. Meanings always emanate from a specific discursive setting. Knowledge on in vitro fertilization has been dispersed through many different publicitary channels, from medical journal articles to newspaper articles and science fiction novels. In a cultural approach to science and technology, it is assumed that knowledge is produced and disseminated in culture at large, and not just through the discourses that are conventionally reserved for communicating science. In Chapter 2, I will explain why in this study I concentrate on the public debate as it proliferates in three particular discourses: science, journalism and fiction. My preference to juxtapose scientific, journalistic and fictional texts does not stem from a mere coincidental personal preference; science, journalism and fiction represent three (institutional) discourses which play a major role in the distribution of public meanings. Moreover, the nature of these discourses has considerably changed in the course of fifteen years. The postmodern narrativation of knowledge has resulted in a gradual convergence of previously separate discourses - a decisive factor in the understanding of a public debate as a process of domination and opposition.

Naturally, the public debate on new reproductive technologies did not start in 1978 and end in 1994; carving out a temporal frame is always a symbolic act as it positions the boundary markers for a discussion. In one form or another, conception outside a woman's womb has been a point of interest to scientists, journalists and fiction writers for centuries. And the latest discussions, in 1994, will certainly not put an end to this debate. In order to expound an argumentative pattern in the public debate on new reproductive technologies, I will distinguish five more or less chronological stages.

The first phase, between 1978 and 1984, starts with the birth of Louise Brown, the first so-called test-tube baby. In Chapter 3, I will describe how the 'need' for IVF was constructed in those years; infertility appeared to become an obsession for scientists and journalists alike, and IVF was promoted as its sole cure. Chapter 4 focuses on the years between 1984 and 1987, when feminists started to vocally oppose new reproductive technologies. Feminists at first seemed to represent a uniform viewpoint, fiercely rejecting all technologies. Yet within a few years, feminist positions on this issue splintered, resulting in a number of differently nuanced standpoints. The years between 1987 and 1991, as illustrated in Chapter 5, are characterized by a growing acceptance of routinely used techniques. Reproductive technologies are promoted both as commodities and 'natural' procedures. During that same period, it becomes increasingly difficult to properly distinguish between feminist and dominant meanings of IVF, since these groups start to strategically deploy each other's discourses, arguments and metaphors.

After 1991, 'naturalized' and commodified reproductive services lead to remarkable legal claims about motherhood. In Chapter 6, I will extensively analyse the journalistic coverage of a court case in California, in which the judge preferred genetic ties over pregnancy and childbearing, thus changing the definition of motherhood in the USA. The analysis will show how this legal redefinition is grounded in earlier stages of the debate, and is in fact the outcome of previously contested meanings of motherhood and pregnancy. Finally, in Chapter 7, I will return to Britain and explain how the discussion on retired mothers and transracial impregnation resulted in heated debates for and against government regulation and legislation. Feminist opposition is barely traceable at this stage of the debate, as their differentiated positions and arguments seem to have been absorbed by mainstream voices.

While the proposed chronological order of different stages may facilitate the understanding of a complex debate, it is impossible to draw sharp lines between consecutive stages. In the process from the creation of a need for IVF, via naturalization to legalization and legislation, these phases obviously overlap and blend. Yet the distinctive stages appear useful in the demarcation of particular trends in the public debate, and help to identify crucial moments in the negotiation of meaning, the production of images and the construction of arguments. The analysis or 'map' of this debate ideally provides more insights into how public consent was manufactured, and how dissent has affected definitions of procreation, motherhood and the female reproductive body. In mapping the public debate, I hope to offer a more complete understanding of how these technologies have been disputed. It eventually raises the concern whether current formats of a public debate suffice, or whether the parameters of discussion should be changed to involve a larger group of people and allow more critical voices. With regard to feminist critics, this analysis may pose important questions of how to strategically articulate dissent; without the backing of a uniform group, feminist critics have to search for openings in the public debate to affect social changes.

1 Mapping the Public Debate on New Reproductive Technologies

What was once an act of private 'love,' of intimacy and secrecy, is now a public act, a commercial transaction and a professionally-managed procedure.

(Sarah Franklin, 'Postmodern Procreation')

The issue, then, is not whether these technologies are good or bad, but how we should think them and how they will think us. . . . Culture exists in the way analogies are drawn between things, in the way certain thoughts are used to think others. Culture exists in the images which make imagination possible, in the media with which we mediate experience.

(Marilyn Strathern, *Reproducing the Future*)

INTRODUCTION

The drive to invent technology which can be used to control human fertility is not particularly typical of this time and age. Pre-industrial societies have sought means to regulate reproductive practices, using everything from infanticide to contraceptives, and from abortion to ovulation rituals. But the development of what is called the new reproductive technologies has expanded at an accelerated speed the options of humans to manipulate the process of reproduction. In the past decade, techniques such as in vitro fertilization (IVF), and spinoffs such as Gamete Intra Fallopian Transfer (GIFT), Zygote Intra Fallopian Transfer (ZIFT), and Embryo Transfer (ET), have become regular procedures in reproductive medicine and

9

medical practice.[1] Increasingly, women rely on doctors and medical technology to 'assist' the reproductive process, part of which is occurring outside the woman's body. New reproductive technologies have turned from innovative, experimental techniques into accepted and even routine procedures. Despite low success rates, IVF is presented as a mere 'play-ground for beginners' in view of feasible revolutionary developments that have yet to come. The range of applications and possible variations of reproductive technology has captured the imagination of scientists and novelists alike. New variations of IVF are reported regularly, promising to make this technique more efficient, effective and affordable.

The first articles on preliminary testing of IVF appeared in 1968; research and practice in this area gained momentum after 1978, following the birth of the first so-called test-tube baby.[2] Gradually, the emphasis in scientific articles shifted from scientific research to applications of IVF. In her citation analysis of scientific articles, Anne Burfoot (1990) illustrates how 'IVF began as a pure research problem and evolved into a specific human application and then returned as a human application with appeal to scientists in general' (68). Fifteen years after its first successful application, IVF is accepted both as a research discipline, a specialized medical field ('reproductive medicine') and as a common medical procedure. Notions of 'routine,' surfacing both in medico-scientific journals and in general news media accounts, signal the acceptance and approval of these techniques among a large, general audience.[3] Infertile women can rely upon technology to promptly fulfil their desire to have a child that is genetically their own. IVF has become the unproblematic, transparent solution to an opaque, complex medical problem: some news magazines even recommend to women that they might as well not bother to find the cause for their fertility problems, and 'go straight to one of the high-tech procedures.'[4] If we were to believe the glowing stories in medical journals and media accounts, the technological fix holds the promise of being more efficient than 'nature itself.'

New reproductive technologies have also become a common subject in popular culture, indicating that they are part of the cultural consciousness. Representations of advanced IVF technology appear in Hollywood films, prime time soaps and science fiction; happy surrogate mothers figure in television series, while infertile protagonists unravel conspiracies of IVF clinics against women in medical thrillers.[5] These products of popular culture reflect and construct contemporary images of infertility and reproduction; they may glorify the advancements of modern science, but they may also function as projections of fear which are generated by potential social changes that are the result of these technologies.

Together, all these images in science, media and popular culture constitute public knowledge that people have about the new technologies. Both images and technologies are produced within a capitalist consumer culture: reproductive medicine has become a 'service industry,' offering for purchase a wide range of techniques, options, products and expertise. In medical journals and news media accounts, we can read that these 'services' are offered because they are in great demand. IVF is not just promoted by doctors who want to sell their product, but they are said to be 'needed' by consumers who apparently regard the new technology as a readily available option. The demand for medical technology is reflected in arguments of economic feasibility, and the need for it is expressed in terms of demand.

But the equation of need and demand, in relation to technology, is a logical fallacy. The vast market for IVF treatment is proposed as a 'natural' consequence of a growing need. The invention and development of technology, however, is not a self-evident, inevitable process. New reproductive technologies were not simply developed because they were desperately needed; after all, infertility is not a life-threatening disease. The need for technology is never simply 'there' but is always created – a process which is ideological rather than technical. In a consumer society that idolizes marketing and selling concepts, the creation of need is an intricate process of image-building and storytelling. In order to become accepted, technology needs a story, not only to sell itself, but also to justify the time, expenses and efforts invested in a new invention.

Usually, narratives of science and technology explain why particular inventions are needed and how they serve ideological, humanistic or divine purposes. Creation of need is often based on projections of hope or fear. The Strategic Defense Initiative (SDI) was not developed to protect US citizens from nuclear waste falling from the sky, but to thwart *possible* long range missiles launched by a *potential* enemy. The Human Genome

Project does not invent any cures to genetic disorders, but it is lavishly funded because researchers hope to find particular strings of genes that *may* account for certain illnesses or deviancies. In a similar vein, IVF has not been developed to treat the cause of infertility, but because it *may* allow couples to have a child 'of their own.' As a rule, scientific projects are not generated by an urgent medical problem or a natural disaster, such as a new virus or a famine. On the contrary, there are numerous examples of problems which seem to offer no incentive whatsoever for the invention of technology. Scientific projects are political and social arrangements, embedded in a society that gives rise to, or disapproves of, their legitimacy.

The assumption that technology is beyond ideology or culture betrays itself in the common perception that science and technology are exempt from social evaluation or political assessment: it just is. But the advent of technology can never be an explanation in itself. Fertility practices arise from changing economic or social conditions, and not from technological advancements. As we learn from Rosalind Petchesky's assessment of the abortion debate, the impact of technology is determined by the way it is diffused in culture.[6] Petchesky (1984) defines cultural diffusion as the process of 'how ideas and practices get transmitted from one class or group to another and how these ideas get accommodated and transformed under different circumstances' (49). The effectivity and widespread distribution of techniques is contingent upon the idea that these techniques are badly needed by everyone, not just by a few groups or individuals. In other words, acceptance of technological devices is intrinsically related to the social norms and economic conditions upon which their validation is based.

Social norms concerning reproductive technologies have gravitated from an ambivalent evaluation towards a firm embrace of these techniques. Gradually, the dominant meaning has evolved that IVF and related technologies are 'blessed' instruments to 'remedy' the 'problem' of infertility, and to which infertile women are 'entitled' because everyone has a 'right' to a genetically linked child. As this normative definition evolved, the technological developments themselves affected the terms of debating. Through IVF, it became possible for women with blocked Fallopian tubes to conceive and gestate a genetically linked child. The necessity or urge for a genetic baby rapidly became part of the story of IVF, and the term 'surrogate motherhood' entered the realm of debate. The technical possibility to split genetic and gestational motherhood opened up a new barrel of social, legal and ethical questions: Can motherhood be split? Who owns the fruits of joint reproductive labour? Should there be any limits on genetic or gestational motherhood? Some cases of split motherhood resulted in court rulings or legislative proposals. Legal and legislative definitions are considered explicit ratifications of a public consensus; they emanate from gradually evolving social norms concerning reproductive freedom, parenthood and the function of the female body.

This process of acceptance, and the related change of social arrangements in reproduction, can be traced in the public debate on new reproductive technologies of the past fifteen years. Still experimental and highly controversial in the late 1970s, IVF has become a routine procedure in the 1990s. But when and how did this change occur? What is the story underlying the popularity of IVF? What were the changing social values and norms that turned IVF into a 'needed' medical practice, and even a service to which women claim to have a 'right'? Even when a procedure becomes technically routine, that does not mean it is also socially accepted as a treatment. Abortion, for instance, has become a routine procedure, but it is still a controversial medical practice in the USA, while in other countries, such as Ireland, it is still outlawed. The French so-called abortion pill, RU486, is not even allowed to move beyond the experimental stage, since it is banned from the US market. Deployment of technology is dependent on a consensus about the appreciation of its use; consensus building is at the core of a public debate.

Public debates are processes of signification, in which meanings, definitions and concepts are discussed and wagered. Many voices partake in this debate, arguing from different interested positions, each trying to put their marks upon the debate. Doctors, researchers, feminists, investors and many others have a stake in this debate; they all vie to promote a particular meaning of new reproductive technologies. The trophy of a public debate is to turn a particular interpretation into an accepted fact which seems beyond the stage of negotiation. This construction of common sense is crucial because it informs 'official' definitions, such as legal rulings concerning (the 'right' to) motherhood and reproductive freedom. A public debate in fact provides the normative consensus that supports legal or political decisions and regulates social practices. Reconstruction of this debate may help clarify how common sense became common sense, and in what ways various interest groups contributed to the discussion.

A PUBLIC DEBATE AS A FIELD OF STRUGGLE

The term 'public debate,' which is at the centre of this study, needs to be discussed in more detail. Public debate is not synonymous to what Jürgen Habermas (1984) has labelled the 'public sphere': the space of political participation, debate and opinion formation.[7] According to Habermas, important political or social transformations only take place in institutionalized contexts, such as the court, the parliament, and especially the media. He contrasts the public sphere to the private sphere, which is restricted to the family – the symbolic domain of reproduction. The two spheres are linked together through the role of the individual, who is a consumer in the private sphere and worker or citizen in the public domain. Habermas observes a decline in the importance of the citizen's role in late capitalist societies and laments the decreasing space in the public sphere – particularly the commercialized mass media – for voices contradicting or resisting normative consensus.

Habermas's concept of the two separate spheres has been sharply attacked by feminist critics, because he ignores gender as a significant factor underlying the artificial separation of these spheres. Traditionally, women were concerned with the private domain, and restricted to tasks of reproduction and care; their only power was their power as consumers. Yet in both spheres women were dominated by men. As the public sphere tended to become more commercialized, and the citizen turned into a consumer, gender became an even more prominent factor in the determination of roles. Women's participation in the work force increased; women became both workers and mothers, consumers and citizens.

The emerging reproductive industry serves as a specific case in point to illustrate how the private and public sphere intermix.

The advent of IVF and similar techniques accentuated women's distinct reproductive role, and thus her function in the private sphere. At the same time, however, new reproductive technologies turned out to be an important issue in the public sphere, as they were fiercely debated by politicians, judges, priests and journalists. As private concerns were transformed into public issues, women's roles changed accordingly: they became the prime consumers of reproductive services, which were also publicly debated issues. Women's new ambivalent role, as Nancy Fraser (1989) poignantly argues, has become pivotal in the struggle with the state and other institutions over social meanings of 'woman' and 'man' and the interpretation of (re)productive roles.[8] Since the means of communication to discuss social changes have always been controlled by men, women struggle to 'redistribute and democratize access to, and control over, discursive resources' (135). Women increasingly seek access to public channels that were formerly closed to them.

A public debate is thus no longer restricted to the public sphere, as private concerns – intimate procreative decisions – are affected by public discussions on whether to implement reproductive technologies.[9] Habermas locates the construction of public consensus exclusively in institutional contexts, particularly the mass media. Voices of individuals or groups who are not organized through institutions are excluded from, or marginalized in, the debate. This view is shared by Edward Herman and Noam Chomsky (1988), who state that the manufacturing of public consent occurs within the institutional context of the news media, whose main function is to 'inculcate individuals with the values, beliefs and codes of behaviour that will integrate them into the institutional structures of the larger society' (1). Participation in a public debate is regulated by those who control news media organizations – a 'free market' system which does not allow for dissenting voices. Indeed, Chomsky and Herman postulate that American media ostensibly permit spirited debate, criticism and dissent, but only insofar as these remain within the premises and presuppositions that constitute elite consensus.[10] Dissenting voices can only be expressed through local, non-corporately owned channels and alternative publications.

Chomsky and Herman convincingly prove the overwhelming bias in coverage by the mainstream press of politics in Central

America and the wars in Cambodia and Vietnam. Yet I do not share their assumption that ideological consensus is solely shaped by the institutional forces of mass media. Especially with regard to a public debate on an issue as complex as new reproductive technologies, the 'propaganda model' for manufacturing public consent proves much too simple. My objections to Chomsky's and Herman's approach concern three points: their concept of power as it is displayed and exercised through institutions, their view of (news) media as the exclusive site for a public debate, and their conclusion that dissenting voices can only be heard through alternative channels.

Even though Chomsky and Herman deny that power is a monolithic force, they unambiguously peg it down to an identifiable elite group who controls the institution(s). For an analysis of a public debate, I would much rather adapt Michel Foucault's definition of power as a disparity of forces that is exercised from below – not from above, as Chomsky and Herman as well as Habermas contend. Contemporary methods of power, according to Foucault (1980) are methods whose 'operation is not ensured by right but by technique, not by law but by *normalization*, not by punishment but by control, methods that are employed on all levels and in forms that go beyond the state and its apparatus' (89, emphasis added).[11] Normalization, a keyword in Foucault's theory, works as a powerful means of control, because it presumes and provides the distinction between what is normal and what is deviant. Norms manifest themselves through definitions of the abnormal, rather than the normal; the marking of deviancies implicitly provides the limits of the acceptable. For instance, for IVF to become accepted as a commonplace instrument, it should be assumed that female infertility is a deviant state of health. If accepted as normal, the 'solution' to infertility, in the form of IVF, may become a 'natural' option; social norms ensuing from new technological possibilities may subsequently inform legal decisions. Because of their subtlety, norms are more powerful than laws as a regulating mechanism because they do not have to be enforced.

But who has the power to determine which norms will be accepted and transformed into legal entitlements? It is not easy to point at specific groups which control the public agenda. Societies are stratified into differentiated social groups with unequal status and power, defined along lines of gender, race and class. With regard to the discussion on new reproductive technologies, we need to take into account that the expenses of IVF can only be paid for by wealthy consumers, while minority and poor women are disproportionally excluded from medical care. The implementation of reproductive technologies is thus determined by factors of race and class. In a public debate, not all voices are equally authorized to speak. Some of the contestants in the debate are more powerful than others because they have access to public channels more easily. Only medical scientists who are qualified can publish in a professional journal; only specialists can be quoted as experts or authorities in newspaper articles. In fact, a public debate is prefixed by the extent to which its participants are allowed to express their arguments.[12] Individual utterances are communicated through institutionalized forms of expression, which require a particular qualification or expertise to be authorized to speak. Yet, legitimation or allocation of authority to speak is not static; it involves a dynamic process in which dissenting voices, whether coming from individuals or from groups, can obtain more power or authority. Opinions and arguments are voiced in a field of struggle – not in contemplation but in competition.

If power is understood as a multiplicity of force relations embedded in a social structure, the distribution of power is interwoven with questions of interest. Various groups have a stake in the debate on new reproductive technologies. The interest to control human fertility has been an issue as old as control over land and food supplies. For centuries, fertility control has been an area of negotiation between individuals, particularly women, and authorities, such as the state, the church or the medical establishment.[13] Individuals and authorities may have conflicting interests in gaining power over the reproductive process. Medical scientists, clinical practitioners and the medical industry may have a professional and commercial stake in the acceptance of reproductive technology. Women, on the other hand, may have a personal and political interest in protecting their reproductive rights and bodily integrity. The state, who has an interest in regulating population, may exercise power over women's fertility by implementing policies affecting reproductive and sexual behaviour. Neither of these interests are self-evident, nor are they clearly confined to one particular group of persons who share a particular ideology, gender or profession.

In a public debate, positions of interested parties cannot be easily categorized as consenting or dissenting voices. The manufacturing of public consent is much more complicated. In case of the debate on new reproductive technologies, the interests of researchers, women, doctors, or religious representatives may partly coincide, but simultaneously diverge. The Roman Catholic church, for example, opposes every form of human intervention in the 'natural' reproductive process, as it assumes procreation of human life to be the sacred goal in life. Doctors, while sharing the latter assumption, may disagree with the former. Commercial interests of medical institutions do not necessarily have to correspond with professional interests of doctors. In addition, the interests of participants sharing an ideological position may mutually diverge: feminists who are infertile may have a different view on the use of reproductive technologies than feminists who are fertile or who are childless by choice – personal interest may conflict with political interest. On the other hand, conflicting ideologies may sometimes result in conflating positions: both feminists and born-again Christians have opposed the use of IVF, but for very different reasons.[14] Dissenting voices are heterogeneous; new reproductive technologies are not just a uniform concern for feminists and religious fanatics.

Besides criticizing Chomsky's and Herman's monolithic view of power, I also object to their assumption that a public debate occurs primarily or exclusively in the (news) media. Public meanings are concurrently constituted in and outside media, in science, politics, popular culture, films, law, and so forth. Concepts of reproductive technologies may be expressed in various domains that affect each other. Results of IVF research which have appeared in a science journal may be recast in a popular magazine; we can read an article in a newspaper or magazine about a woman facing the choice between undergoing yet another painful cycle of IVF procedures or remaining childless; a judge assigning a newborn infant, whose mother did not provide the egg for the baby she carried, to the so-called genetic mother adds to the reconfiguration of reproductive technologies. The case of Angela Carder, a pregnant women from Washington DC who was dying of cancer and whose foetus was ordered to be delivered by means of Caesarian section, became the focus of an edition of *LA Law*, a popular television series.[15]

Even though the media play an important role in the construction of public consent, they cannot be viewed separately from other domains where meanings proliferate. Representations of IVF and related technologies travel from one domain to another; this interplay of representations may appear to us as a collage of (unrelated) propositions and opinions, yet they are always dialogic. All representations contain and inform each other, as they are at once reflections and constructions of social practices. Anyone entering the public debate on new reproductive technologies has assumed, to a certain degree, previous knowledge on the issue; no one is a *tabula rasa*, since representations published or aired in whatever context become part of the collective cultural consciousness. Meanings produced in (news) media, in other words, are part of culture at large; as Marilyn Strathern (1992) formulates concisely, culture 'consists in the images which make the imagination possible, in the media with which we mediate experience' (33).[16]

In addition, I do not want to analyse a public debate from the perspective of institutional power, as Chomsky and Herman propose, but from the viewpoint of discourse. Discourse, understood as a complex of signs and practices which assigns differential membership to a social or professional group, structures my understanding of a public debate.[17] The definition of discourse encompasses the 'signs' but also the 'practices' involved in language use. As Foucault has pointed out, the use of language is structured by a system of rules which forms modes of speaking; these structured formations may apply to both professional and social groups. Professional discourse is commonly used within institutions, such as (medical) science, law, journalism, politics or business. Besides institutional discourses Foucault identifies social discourses, and he maintains that they arise from social groups – feminists, environmentalists, or religious groups – who share an ideological point of view.

But the use of institutional or social discourse is not constrained to the realms from which they arise. Medical discourse, for example, may appear in feminist accounts, and feminist discourse may surface in mainstream journalism.

However, between institutional and social discourses exists an ideologically inscribed hierarchy. While institutional discourses are often assumed to represent a 'disinterested' or neutral position, social discourses are conventionally thought to represent an ideological viewpoint or 'special interest.' Institutional discourses have more authority in a public debate because of their supposed neutrality. Within an institution, the use of discourses appears heterogeneous, but is regulated by the unstated mechanism of discursive hierarchy. Inside a hospital, for example, the statements of a pregnant woman may conflict with those of an obstetrician. Evidently, the doctor's interpretation of the patient's illness carries more weight than the patient's own assessment. Whereas the patient may speak from her own viewpoint, the doctor may speak for the institution which prompts her or him to speak.

The exchange of opinions is regulated by a discursive practice which is characterized by hierarchy and authority: each voice occupies a position in a field of power. In order to map a public debate it is essential to acknowledge the pre-existing power relationships between various discourses – institutional and social. With regard to the discussion on reproductive technologies, the discourse of medicine and medical science is accepted as 'neutral,' whereas feminist or religious discourses function as counterdiscourses: they are defined in terms of opposition to the norm, tainted by interest. The assumed disinterestedness of medical discourse allows it to serve as a dominant, authoritative mode of interpretation. Yet, the binary opposition between (dominant) discourse and counterdiscourse is as appealing as it is deceptive. There is not, on the one hand, a discourse of power and on the other hand, a discourse that runs counter to it. Mainstream and oppositional voices, discourse and counter-discourse, exist *conjuncturally*, and are necessarily involved in a power struggle.[18] They operate in the same field of tension, often deploying the same strategies and tactics.

The propaganda model of manufacturing public consent is based on a binary, institutional view of power. Such a model is problematic because it narrowly defines a public debate as an ideological difference of opinion, which is debated in a homogeneous, institutional context: the media. Neither of these presuppositions apply to this discussion. IVF and related technologies are not favoured by one group and opposed by another; nor are they discussed in terms of support or rejection, but in terms of necessity, desirability, and (im)morality. Initially, IVF and related technologies were vehemently opposed by religious groups, particularly the Roman Catholic church and secular 'pro-life' groups, who were against any human intervention in the reproductive process. In the mid-1980s, religious opposition was eclipsed by feminist counter-voices, who claimed that the medical establishment had taken charge of the female reproductive body. Yet, feminist assessments of new reproductive technologies were not uniform; some feminists claimed that the advent of IVF could be liberating and desirable, while others argued that the IVF industry represented nothing less than a capitalist conspiracy against women. Feminists, like other groups, appeared to take many different positions. Hence, positions cannot simply be divided along axes of ideology, profession, discourse or gender.

Moreover, the discussion on new reproductive technologies has never proliferated strictly within the media, divided in mainstream and alternative press. Chomsky and Herman conclude that dissenting, critical voices can only be expressed through alternative channels; in their view, mainstream media systematically ostracize any views that are not in line with public consensus. However, the alternative publications in which dissent is expressed, do not exist in isolation; neither do mainstream newspapers completely ignore dissenting or radical opinions voiced through alternative channels. Indeed, feminist opposition to these techniques initially appeared primarily in feminist magazines, journals and pamphlets, while dominant medical views were prominently displayed by the mainstream press. However, feminist voices later also appeared in general newspapers and magazines, and were countered by contrasting meanings; previously alternative feminist publications have in the course of time also altered their discursive strategy to enter mainstream channels. I think it is important to analyse these differentiated forms of resistance in order to reveal the interrelation between various positions.

Mapping a public debate on new reproductive technologies thus entails focusing on the complexity of the negotiation of meaning. The issue is not whether these technologies are 'good' or 'bad' but how they have changed images of procreation, motherhood and the female body. This process of negotiation is characterized by attraction and rejection, strategic moves to encapsulate and subvert. The inscribed dominance of institutional discourses, for example medicine, does not mean that counterdiscourses, such as feminism, are bound to taste defeat. In capitalist cultures, discourse is a practice but also a transaction, regulated by the mechanism of the market. When an oppositional meaning gains a significant number of supporters, it will affect the social practice at stake. Meanings are launched to persuade people to 'buy into' a particular technological provision.

Paula Treichler (1990) makes a useful distinction between 'meaning' and 'definition' which is quite relevant in this respect. Though the terms are often equated, she notes that the word 'meaning' signifies 'to have as an opinion,' whereas a 'definition' purports to state what 'is.' Multiple meanings may thus coexist, but a definition, according to Treichler, is less democratic: 'A definition is a meaning that has become official and thereby appears to tell us how things are in the real world' (123). In a public debate, several meanings may simultaneously enter the arenas of discourse, and fight to become a definition. The construction of definitions is a complex cultural process in which meanings are deployed and mobilized in reaction to competing meanings.

Treichler provides an illustrative example of a public debate revolving around the definition of 'childbirth.' The meaning of childbirth as a medical procedure, necessarily taking place in a hospital, changed as a result of the establishment of alternative birth centres, which were collectively run by women who viewed childbirth primarily as a 'natural,' as opposed to a medical, event. When the initiative gained more support, the 'natural' meaning of childbirth – woman-centred and without the presumed intervention of doctors – started to challenge the official 'medical' meaning of childbirth. By comparing advertisements, policy statements, newspaper articles and other texts in which the confrontation between birth centres and regular hospitals is played out, Treichler shows how the alternative meaning slowly gained ground. More women started to prefer birth centres, insurance companies acknowledged their economic advantages, and hospitals began to adjust their delivery rooms to create a more 'woman friendly' environment as the competition with less expensive birth centres intensified. At the same time, medicine to a great extent incorporated the alternative definition of childbirth by labelling medicalized childbirth 'natural,' and fixing this alternative meaning to hospital delivery rooms. In her analysis, Treichler illuminates how the childbirth debate maps the 'intersections among linguistic constructions and professional authority, economic interests, institutional structures, politics, money, and ideological positionings with regard to health care' (131).

Treichler's example shows how feminist meanings can affect dominant social practices and challenge medical authority, but it also proves how vulnerable feminist meanings are to co-optation and reappropriation by dominant discourses.[19] In the past decades, we have seen similar struggles in the area of reproduction, such as abortion, prenatal care, the use of contraceptives and new reproductive technologies. In none of these cases do feminists automatically oppose the dominant view of medical doctors and scientists, on the contrary. In the abortion debate, feminists have been supported by the American Medical Association (AMA); both argued for safe and legal abortion, but for very different reasons.[20] In Roe vs. Wade, for instance, the AMA did not support a woman's right to choose, but argued for the recognition of abortion as an exclusively medical event. While the objectives of the AMA coincided with those of feminists, their interests were mutually incompatible.

A model that maps the manufacturing of public consent and dissent on new reproductive technologies as a debate between 'groups' or 'discourses' is therefore misleading. Mapping a debate entails not just locating these various positions, but also tracing how dominant and oppositional meanings evolve, how they clash in different domains of discourse, and how arguments change in reaction to one another. It requires an analysis of the relationship between existing social arrangements – including cultural authority, political activism, scientific expertise and economic incentives – and the construction of meanings of reproductive technologies. But if these are produced in so many different discursive arenas, it is imperative to first establish the central mobilizing issue.

As I have stated earlier, this debate revolves around questions of needs rather than technology.[21] Claims of need are expressed not in terms of technical feasibility, but in terms of social, psychological or physical necessity. The claim, for instance, that

IVF is technically possible is not sufficient to establish its need; the claim requires the implicit or explicit warrant that IVF is needed in order to make it possible for infertile women to have a genetically linked baby.[22] This need claim may be contested in various ways: one may question the assumption that (infertile) women should have genetically linked babies, or one may question the need to use IVF in order to have a baby.

Public debates often proliferate as a result of the contestation of implied assumptions, ideological warrants or unstated premises. Needs claims, in fact, both contain and contest other interpretations of needs. These interpretations emanate from very different assertions about the nature of a need. Infertility, for instance, may be defined as a natural deviance, a physical disability or a social construction; IVF may be defined accordingly as a technological intervention in the sanctity of life, a cure to a disease, or an instrument of control. Moreover, the paradigms of argument show similar incompatibilities: whereas some accept biblical texts to substantiate claims, others rely on empirical research to validate arguments, and again others accept emotions or experience to be sufficient evidence for their claims. Even though the various participants in a public debate do not share each other's idioms, vocabularies, or paradigms of argumentation, they still try to address the other's argument in order to persuade or convince; despite their seemingly incompatible natures, these interpretations effect one another, causing a pattern of changing meanings.

The discursive resources for these interpretations do not solely consist of rational considerations and arguments; they also consist of collective myths and communal assumptions about health, science and the reproductive process. Anne Karpf (1988) signals three myths specifically relating to these issues.[23] First, there is the pervasive image of the doctor as magician, God or Faust: doctors tend to be regarded either as selfless pursuers of scientific knowledge, or selfish wizards aspiring to control human life. The image of a group of scientists concocting conspiracies against mankind – breeding foetuses in a secret laboratory – is a frequently recurring theme in novels and movies. Secondly, patients are either looked upon as helpless victims of disease, or moral culprits who have called the illness upon themselves and others. In line with this argument, disease lends itself particularly easily and symbolically to fears of a threat to moral order, a divine judgement of collective misdemeanour. Each of these myths, according to Karpf, is entrenched in Western culture, and can be traced in medical reports as well as in forms of popular culture. Myths surface simultaneously in various social institutions and discursive realms, as they provide resources for arguments formulated by scientists, fiction writers, journalists and politicians.[24] Laboratory, clinic and myth are intricately interwoven in the process of signification; claims, arguments, images and myths are all part of the public debate on new reproductive technologies.

As the discussion gradually evolves, the talk about 'needs', noticeably changes into claims about 'rights,' implying assumptions of legal entitlement. The increasing availability of something – in this case a medical service – appears to provide the condition for claiming the right to acquire it. 'Rights' arise from the assertion that if techniques are readily available, people should have access to them. As I noted in the beginning of this chapter, recent accounts on IVF often use the notions of 'demand' and 'need' interchangeably. In the 'free marketplace of choices,' reproductive technologies tend to be transformed into commodities, and equated to regular material products. Such an equation implies that the process of production, distribution and consumption of IVF is the equivalent of making and selling cars or detergents. In a consumer society, the 'right' to be able to choose from a variety of products – at least for those who are able to afford them – seems unproblematically transferable to medical services. The implications of this equation are manifold.

The assumption underlying the alignment of material products and reproductive services is that individual or personal reproductive decisions have no consequences for collective social practices, or do not affect social arrangements. However, the choice for IVF or a similar technique has ramifications beyond the personal level of benefit or drawback. The use of reproductive technologies reinforces the ideal that parents need to have a child they can call their own, either because of genetic ties or through a gestational relationship. IVF and related techniques funnel considerable attention and expenses to the creation of a healthy baby – the resulting product – at the expense of the woman's health. Reproductive technologies always involve surgical methods and hormonal injections, which solely affect the female body. In addition, a considerable amount of money is allocated to the conception of a child, while elsewhere no funds are available to pay for nutrition programs for malnourished infants. The liberalist argument that fortunate individuals can spend money on products they desire, as long as their 'choice' does not harm others, does not alter the fact that both public and private funds have been allocated to develop these reproductive services in the first place – money that might have been spent differently. In other words, new reproductive technologies are not just like any other products, but they have the potential to profoundly affect social values and norms concerning motherhood and reproduction.

The increasing tendency to describe medical services in terms of the marketplace also obscures ideological ramifications of the new technologies for the status and role of women. The technical possibility to fertilize eggs outside the womb, or to monitor the foetus in the womb, is commonly explained by medical technicians as beneficial to women, because they optimize chances of getting a healthy baby. Advanced equipment, such as laparoscopy, ultrasound, and sophisticated methods, such as oocyte transplantation, have one thing in common: they are invariably focused on the moment of conception and the ensuing foetus. The womb is rendered into a gestating space, a female environment in which the precious foetus is supposed to mature. The invention and application of monitoring and surgical instruments is not ideologically neutral; the 'invisible' consequence of these technological advancements may be that specific female reproductive functions, such as gestation and childbirth, get less attention than the moment of conception and the product of reproductive labour. As a result, the foetus may gain status at the expense of a woman's reproductive body.

The influence and effect of medical definitions concerning motherhood and reproduction have been a consistent focus of feminist criticism over the years. The 'medical gaze' tends to erase the socialness of female sexuality and to monopolize the female body as a medical object of knowledge. Feminist critics and theorists have traditionally directed their anxieties at various levels of medical authority, ranging from doctors to the medical establishment, from hospitals to the American or British Medical Association, and from the actual instruments to the medical-industrial complex which produces them. In the past fifteen years, feminist criticism of medical science has shifted its emphasis from the institutions of medicine to the culture which legitimatizes and perpetuates its authority. This recent development deserves to be examined in more detail.[25]

MEDICAL AUTHORITY AND FEMINIST CRITICISM

Until the late 1950s and early 1960s, the dominant view on reproduction and childbirth was that both were private affairs, part of woman's biological fate. They were also private experiences connected with sex and subject to similar taboos. As medical power and intervention rapidly expanded in the sixties, reproduction and pregnancy came to be seen almost exclusively as medical matters; the number of Caesarian sections increased and hospitalized childbirth became the norm.[26] Concurrently, the advent of the contraceptive pill and large scale distribution of birth control devices in the 1960s, gave women more power to control their own reproductive processes. While on the one hand medical inventions advanced a woman's sexual freedom, they also infringed upon her reproductive freedom by making her more dependent on medicine. Over the last thirty years, the invention of medical-chemical expedients has caused a split between sexuality and reproduction. As Rosi Braidotti (1991) concludes: 'With chemical contraceptive techniques we could have sex without babies. With the latest reproductive techniques, especially IVF, we can have babies without sex' (59).

Until the 1980s, feminists generally targeted medical institutions as bastions of sexism: the gendered hierarchy between doctors and patients, and the virtual absence of female doctors and researchers helped explain the patriarchal focus of most scientific theories and practices. In her biography of Nobel-prize winning geneticist Barbara McClintock, Evelyn Fox Keller (1983) outlines her vision of a 'gender-free' science; women scientists, she contends, bring different ('holistic') values to the field of science. In the wake of Keller, Sandra Harding (1986) criticizes the absence and underrepresentation of women in science. She advocates a sort of affirmative action programme in the biological and natural sciences: more women should move into this male bastion of power and change the institution by imposing their gendered participation. Equal representation of women in science, according to Harding, will affect the 'male-centred paradigms and methods of inquiry' used in science.

Both Keller's and Harding's feminist critiques of science depart from the idea that knowledge production is the exclusive domain of scientists, and occurs only within the walls of this institution.[27] The assessment of science as an autonomous epistemological realm, however, appears to leave intact much of the conventional understanding of science as a privileged area of knowledge production, at once reinforcing its 'status aparte' and obscuring the embeddedness of scientific thinking in social and cultural structures.

A second form of feminist criticism of medical authority foregrounds the way in which women are represented as objects of medical knowledge. Emily Martin (1987), for instance, studied metaphors and images used in medical textbooks which describe women's reproductive organs and functions. Comparing these textbook analyses to responses elicited through interviews with North-American women of diverse ethnic and class backgrounds, Martin concludes that women have to a large extent internalized the harmful metaphors purported by medical discourse. She elaborates on the pervasive image of the body as a 'production machine' which assigns pregnant women the function of workers, and doctors the function of managers of pregnancy. Martin's ethnography of medicine, like Harding's theory, is based on Marxist notions of power and class; she assumes the inevitable oppression of women by doctors and denies women the power to partake in the production of meaning. In Martin's view, women are merely consumers of cultural signs – victims of medical discourse. Even though Martin recognizes that science is informed and structured by everyday culture, her model of cultural production and consumption leaves open the question of how theories of science can be reworked to actually change inscribed gender identities.

More recent feminist critics of science no longer focus on women in science, and they refuse to regard women as passive objects of medical research; in fact, they question the very distinctions between science and non-science, object and subject of knowledge, and medical and feminist authority. Unlike

Harding or Martin, Donna Haraway (1988) rejects the inscribed boundary between science and non-science; the production of scientific knowledge occurs simultaneously in and outside science, in culture at large. Haraway mocks paranoid images of 'them' (male scientists) against 'us' (female non-scientists) evoked by earlier feminist criticism of science, and warns of an even greater danger lurking behind the natural acceptance of scientific assumptions and modes of inquiry beyond the small circles of scientists. The immense impact of science's logic is evident when you look at pervasive images of science in mass subscription journals, television and popular culture.[28]

Haraway perceives of scientific practices and texts not as 'special' domains of knowledge but as cultural constructions. Immanent to this critical strategy is the denial of science's privileged status – its claim to neutrality and insistence on objectivity. Instead, Haraway argues, science should be viewed as 'a series of efforts to persuade relevant social actors that one's manufactured knowledge is a route to a desired form of very objective power' (577). Although you can distinguish between science and non-science, there are no separate, pure domains; daily scientific practice and language are part of the process of producing public knowledge.

In postmodern culture, Haraway claims, the distinction between subject and object of scientific research is also illusive; both live on as constructions in language, pretending that the 'natural' object and the 'knowing' subject can be properly defined. Whereas the human body was previously defined as the object of medical science, with the advancement of medical technology the contours of the physical body have become anything but clearcut. Haraway (1990) uses the cyborg – a cybernetic organism that inhibits all proper definition – as a critique of representation to illustrate the fading of these contours.[29] A cyborg represents the blurred boundaries between humans and machines, humans and images, resisting the very definition of the organic or 'natural' body. Technology now permits to keep a 24-week-old foetus alive outside the womb, to create human life in test-tubes, and simulate the 'maternal environment' with machines and computers. On the other end of the lifetime spectrum, machines prevent people from dying, keeping comatose bodies alive and stretch the physical existence of people suffering from terminal diseases. Without these machines, there would be no physical bodies. As extensions of human life, cyborgs symbolize the blurred boundaries between bodies and machines.

The dispersion of the body as an object of scientific knowledge is reflected in the diffusion of discourses on the body: distinctions between areas of knowledge production have become increasingly porous. Haraway extends the cyborg concept to the delineation of discourse itself, pointing out that knowledge is now produced as a result of 'cyborg-discourses.' The demarcation between 'pure' and 'applied' science is itself a construction; the presumption that medical science 'discovers' and medical technology 'applies' knowledge is misleading. Medical technology more often than not provides the condition for generating knowledge and creating medico-scientific theories.[30] In addition, medical science has merged with computer science and information theory, most notably in the areas of biotechnology and genetics. Computer calculations and models have enabled geneticists to design the theories of gene mapping and sequencing, and thus change the very nature of this discipline.[31] The dissemination of scientific knowledge of the reproductive body in so many specialized disciplines and fields complicates the identification of any proper discursive formation, as Foucault had still envisioned in his *The Archaeology of Knowledge*.

One of the main problems for feminist critics of science, according to Haraway, is to recognize and negotiate the classification of the object in the jungle of discourses. She considers it more important to show how scientific concepts are formed in several discourses concurrently, than to delineate new realms of scientific discourse. Constructs and concepts of science function reciprocally; scientific-human constructs have affected the imagination, evidenced by, for example, movies like *Starwars*, *Bionic Man* and *Jurassic Park*. Conversely, science fiction concepts have inspired the development of engineered devices or scientific theories.

Scientific constructs and concepts have also shaped images and configurations of the human body. The geneticist's assumption that the body is a collection of genes and cells elicits the view of the body as a compilation of exchangeable and replaceable parts. The perception of the body as a 'composition'

– in both the physical and textual meaning of the word – allows for a definition of woman in terms of her parts: reproductive capacities or the quality of her genes or eggs. The culturally defined concept of the ideal body provides the subtext for imagined bodies and actual medical practices. Cosmetic surgery would be less advanced or in demand if the idealized, reconstructed bodies of Elizabeth Taylor and Michael Jackson were not floating around. By the same token, IVF and other reproductive technologies would probably be less popular if the cultural norm to have 'a child of one's own' were not as pervasive. Technology and ideology are mutually connected; the public consensus underlying scientific concepts is achieved through articulation of the ideal.

In addition to recognizing how medical science and technology are inextricably bound up with cultural concepts, Haraway argues it is also crucial for feminist critics to unveil how the authority of medicine is perpetuated outside the realms of science. Whereas Martin examines the metaphors structuring women's bodies in medical discourse, Haraway focuses on how medically produced forms of evidence are frequently adopted in other discursive settings. The medico-scientific way of arguing is often used as a privileged mode of interpretation. Ultrasound pictures are presented in the court room to 'prove' the autonomous existence of a foetus, allowing lawyers to argue that foetuses have a 'right' to claim tort liability. Doctors in white coats frequently appear in television soaps figuring as baby-saving heroes, advocating the idea that foetuses should be kept alive at any price. Religious groups use ultrasound pictures as 'evidence' in their anti-abortion campaigns. The acceptance of medical authority as 'just' is pertinacious, but even more significant is the uncritical adoption of the medico-scientific way of knowing, which increasingly functions as a discourse of 'truth.'

Anti-abortion groups, for instance, tactically moved from using religious symbols to medical rhetoric, despite their vocal opposition to the medical establishment. Petchesky (1987) shows in her analysis of *The Silent Scream* how this propagandistic anti-abortion documentary continuously calls upon scientific-medical images to 'prove' that a foetus is 'torn apart' during an abortion. Borrowing the authority of medical discourse, the voiced-over narrative imposes a moral indictment on the visualized event. So-called objective medical evidence is exploited to reinforce the religious message, as Petchesky argues: 'The film's genesis seems to have been an article in the *New England Journal of Medicine*' (59).

Medico-scientific discourse is also deployed as an unchallenge-able form of evidence in legal discourse. Patricia Spallone's (1987) overview of government reports on new reproductive technologies – such as the Warnock Report in Britain – shows that all definitions used in these reports are based on jurisdiction in medical practice. The Warnock Committee defined reproduc-tion as the proper domain of medicine and evoked medical 'evidence' to the exclusion of other material or texts in establishing a definition of new reproductive technologies. An American equivalent of this legal reappropriation of medical authority is discussed by Valerie Hartouni (1991). She describes how, in April 1981, a senate Judiciary Subcommittee sought to extend the Fourteenth Amendment of the Constitution (protection of life) to foetuses. To substantiate this definition, backers of the Amendment 'solicited testimony from embryol-ogists, chemists, geneticists, and biologists' who are purportedly 'objective, morally neutral, and untainted by the world' (34). Evidence is not presented in the form of elaborated opinion, but as a medically established 'fact,' preferably stated as a laboratory report or an article in a prestigious medical journal.

The tendency to define reproduction as a primarily biological or genetic process occurring within a corporeal vessel is enhanced by the power of medical knowledge to count as the only legitimate way of knowing. This authority is constantly reproduced outside science, not only in the domains of politics and law, but also in popular forms of culture. Reproduction is primarily addressed in popular culture as a medical or medical-legal issue, and is hardly ever depicted as a political or personal issue. Celeste Condit (1990) concludes from her analyses of popular television series such as *Cagney and Lacey*, *Hill Street Blues*, and *St. Elsewhere* that abortion is overwhelmingly represented as a medical problem. This depiction clearly reverberates the Supreme Court's definition which in turn is based on medical documents and 'expert' testimony.

Since the production of scientific knowledge occurs in so many discourses in and outside the scientific realm simultaneously, it makes sense to divert feminist criticism in as many directions as possible. Haraway (1989) urges feminist critics to consider any area of knowledge production, including media and popular fiction, to analyse how scientific authority comes to be constructed and perpetuated.[32] In addition, she insists it is not sufficient to expose the mechanism of domination and authorization; it is also imperative to reveal points of feminist resistance, spaces where medical authority can be and actually is counteracted or subverted. But in light of previous claims about waning distinctions between science and non-science, subject and object, and between the boundaries of discourse, can we still speak of feminist criticism?

The problem inherent to 'criticism,' whether feminist or otherwise, is that it presupposes an unambivalent context, a point from which one can criticize. Yet the disintegration of a clearly defined object of knowledge and the subsequent discontinuity of discourses is naturally accompanied by a similar disintegration of a stable context. Like other poststructuralist feminist critics, Haraway argues that there is no transcendent (feminist) viewpoint, no outside-text, from which the 'subject' might be theorized or 'science' might be criticized.[33] The absence of a unified viewpoint from which to theorize gender, race, class or, for that matter, science or discourse, complicates any notion of 'feminist criticism' or 'feminist analysis' of science. The term 'analysis' presupposes a distinction between an object and a knowing subject, while 'feminist' presumes an unambiguous ideological viewpoint. As Haraway argues, feminism does not offer a theoretical oasis, a clearcut framework from which meanings can be inferred. There are multiple views on constructions of gender, and they are all located in the specific circumstances from which they emanate.

This seemingly pluralist notion of feminism(s), though, is not the end of feminist criticism; on the contrary, it opens up many opportunities to contest and create meanings. The challenge for feminists, according to Haraway (1991), is to act not as passive critics or observers, but as active participants in the construction of meaning:

> Feminism is, in part, a project for the reconstruction of public life and public meanings; feminism is therefore a search for new stories, and so for a language which names a new vision of possibilities and limits. That is, feminism, like science, is a myth, a contest for public knowledge. (82)

Every meaning generates and is generated by public knowledge. Mapping a public debate on new reproductive technologies is thus as much an act of reconstruction as it is an act of contribution to the debate.[34] The double meaning of mapping as 'charting' and 'producing a symbolic landscape' implies that mapping is both a reflection and reinscription of reality. As a feminist critical practice, the activity of 'mapping' cannot be located outside a discussion, but becomes necessarily part of it.

My mapping of the public debate aims at tracing how certain meanings of infertility, IVF and the reproductive body have come to dominate public discourse, and how they have been disputed by feminist and other interpretations. Identification of multiple meanings in the contest for what may count as public knowledge will move beyond separating the good sheep of 'correct' meanings from the bad goats of bias and misuse. Feminist meanings are not constructed apart from other meanings, they are not a 'special interest.' All responses to new reproductive technologies, whether from researchers or feminists, will be regarded as interested positions – nodes of power in the field of struggle.

The manufacturing of public consent, as I have argued in this chapter, cannot be viewed separately from the cultivation of dissent; both dominant and opposing meanings are produced within the various discourses that constitute this debate. Of all possible discourses from which meanings of new reproductive technologies arise, I will focus on three particular areas of knowledge construction: science, journalism and fiction. It may have become clear that I prefer to regard these areas not as institutions, but as discourses. Science, journalism and fiction represent three discourses with varying cultural authority to establish common sense knowledge. In order to map a public debate, it is necessary to theorize how these discourses inform the meanings that structure consent and dissent.

2 Reading Science, Journalism and Fiction as Culture

A fact is nothing but a statement with no modality and no trace of authorship.

> (Latour and Woolgar, *Laboratory Life*)

A fact seems done, unchangeable, fit only to be recorded; fiction seems always inventive, open to other possibilities, other fashionings of life.

> (Donna Haraway, *Primate Visions*)

Factual and fictive discourses are not immutable essences but are historically varying types of writing. They do not remain within their fixed boundaries.

> (Barbara Foley, *Telling the Truth*)

INTRODUCTION

In March of 1978, David Rorvik caused an uproar in the worlds of scientists and journalists by publishing a book called *In His Image: The Cloning of a Man*. The book describes the process of cloning, through IVF, in a secret far-off laboratory. Rorvik, a science journalist, was purportedly invited to observe the creation of a genetic replica of the alleged sponsor of the project: a millionaire called Max who wished to remain anonymous. The book, which was published as a nonfiction, journalistic account of a scientific experiment, was picked up rapidly by the news media, and Rorvik became the centre of media attention. With some rare exceptions, journalists obediently reported Rorvik's claim without challenging its truthfulness.[1] *In His Image* sold 100 000 copies in its first print, and the paperback rights were sold immediately after publication.

The gullibility of reporters and their eagerness to uncritically turn Rorvik's story into a news item, becomes understandable if we take into account how the ingredients of his book perfectly fit in with prevailing images of scientists and their work. Rorvik's story plugged into already widespread myths about scientists: the scenario of a group of scientists secretly concocting a device to control human life; the scary yet imaginable myth of parthenogenesis, symbolizing man's total control over human reproduction, and thus over one's origins. *In His Image* was just one of the many science fiction fantasies embroidering on these myths.

When the book turned out to be a hoax, Rorvik's publisher Lippincott appeared hesitant to immediately change the book's label to fiction. The publisher's reluctance was understandable from a commercial point of view; the book was successful because many people believed the cloning experiment to be true, and changing the label to fiction might annul the initial soaring sales. Indeed, Lippincott argued that Rorvik had sufficiently legitimized his nonfiction claim by writing a disclaimer on the last page of the book; here he stated that *In His Image* was a call for social awareness, an attempt to bring home to a wider public significant issues about reproductive technologies which would otherwise not be aired. According to Lippincott, the disclaimer was a clear enough signal to the reader, who should be able to recognize Rorvik's objective. The publisher thus justified the nonfiction label as a writing and publishing strategy.

June Goodfield (1981), writing for the American Association of Advanced Science, considers Rorvik's choice of the nonfiction format and his publisher's argument regarding the disclaimer, to be 'irresponsible.'[2] Goodfield argues that *In His Image* is just one example of a 'host of marginally scientific productions' which, in purporting to be factual but smoothly gliding towards the fictional, might harm the image of scientists. She laments the increasing obfuscation of genres that blurs the distinction between scientific claims to truth and fictional claims to fantasy; she also argues that journalists have the obligation and responsibility to uphold this distinction, and thus to avoid the muddled borderline between fact and fiction. For Rorvik, however, the obfuscation of genres appeared to be an effective tactic: if his book aimed at eliciting reactions from scientists, journalists and readers, the only way he could make them think about the possible ramifications of new reproductive technologies was by publishing his account as nonfiction. Labelled as fiction, the book might not have had the same impact, since fiction is generally taken less seriously as a form of criticism.

Goodfield, in her negative judgment of Rorvik's 'contaminating' act of writing, presupposes an unambiguous distinction between the discourses of science and journalism on the one hand, and fiction on the other. Science can and may only be reported factually in genres of nonfiction, whereas fictive representations belong to another domain of discourse. Yet as Foucault, Lyotard and other theorists of postmodernity have argued, the production of knowledge in this time and age can no longer be regarded the exclusive function of science. The encounter of science with (mass) culture takes place within the multiple contexts of everyday life, where discourses of science, journalism and fiction increasingly intermix. Science's overlap with advertising and information, and science journalism's convolution with commercial and fictive discourses exemplify this blurring of boundaries.

However, the postmodern discontinuity of discourses should not be deplored – as Goodfield does – as the devaluation of norms, principles and clarity. In fact, discourses have never been distinct, but have always varied according to their historically differentiated contexts.[3] The limits between discourses are never established for once and for all; these limits are themselves the provisional outcome and the stakes in the battle for signification. Rather than policing the boundaries, postmodern 'reality' prompts us to develop alternative ways of thinking about the relation between the still dominant hierarchy of institutional discourses and hybrid categories of text and genre. The institutional discourses of science and journalism are self-legitimizing because they insist on the exclusive validity of traditional discursive frameworks and hierarchy; science and journalism's claims to truth and objective knowledge can only function through a negation of possible claims to truth and objectivity in other discourses.

Recent theories of the 'postmodern condition' have consistently centred on the production of scientific knowledge in discourse. The shift from an epistemological to a poststructuralist critique of knowledge can be traced in fields as diverse as anthropology, literary theory and theology.[4] Constant throughout these studies of postmodernity is the recognition that as boundaries between discourses dissolve, the production of knowledge becomes nomadic. Science and journalism are commonly regarded as institutional discourses that are characterized as domains of 'factual' and 'objective' knowledge. Yet the discourses of science and journalism, for one thing, are not as easily distinguishable as they might appear, and neither are the borderlines between science and commercial discourse clearly marked. Fictive discourses are often informed by the 'factual' language of science, while journalistic discourse thrives on the use of narrative. If the relations between discourses become complex and porous, the underlying discursive hierarchy may be obscured. This hierarchy of discourses, which functions on the basis of inscribed authority of 'factual' and 'disinterested' discourses over 'fictive' and 'opinionated' ones, always needs to be taken into account. Statements about reproductive technologies are expressed strategically, so the way in which they are inscribed is an important factor in the constitution of meaning.

Many critics, including social constructivists, have asserted the impregnability of scientific discourse, thus sustaining its authoritative position. In a cultural analysis of the public debate on new reproductive technologies, the discourses of science, journalism and fiction cannot be separated, although they may be distinguished. Without neglecting the preinscribed hierarchy between the discourses of 'fact' and 'fiction,' I will consider science, journalism and fiction equally as cultural inscriptions of knowledge. This (postmodern) reality of permeable discourses not only prompts a recontextualization of discourses, but also an adjustment of reading conventions. From a cultural studies approach, the 'mapping' of a public debate thus implies a reconsideration of the critic's position.

SCIENCE AS DISCOURSE

The discourse of science has long been regarded as a privileged domain of knowledge construction, reserved to professional participants of the scientific debate. It was not until the 1970s that sociologists started to take the habits, practices, and activities of scientists as an object for their fieldwork; particularly social constructivists like Bruno Latour and Steve Woolgar articulated the social embeddedness of a scientific community that had formerly seemed elevated from public life. One of the constructivists' greatest merits is that they have highlighted writing, or the production of discourse, as a crucial activity which functions to establish the authority of scientists.

Latour and Woolgar (1979) were among the first to systematically observe the work of scientists in a laboratory, and to scrutinize the practices and daily routines of researchers. Their foremost conclusion was that much of the scientist's work revolves around the construction of facts: the process of negotiating the status of a claim or hypothesis. A scientist is an investor in credibility, whose 'objective [is] to persuade colleagues that they should drop all modalities used in relation to a particular assertion and that they should accept and borrow this assertion as an established matter or fact, preferably by citing the paper in which it appeared' (81). Writing articles for scientific publications constitutes the core of scientific activities, as they establish the authority of scientists to have a particular observation accepted as fact.

Latour and Woolgar emphatically point at the socialness of science: scientific practice is defined by social and economic conditions and is therefore subject to ideological impediments, political directives and market fluctuations. Yet the textual reflection of science discourse is such that it erases all traces of its socioeconomic context. Woolgar (1988) explores some inscription devices scientists use to 'argue' the establishment of facts, and he concludes that the end product, the scientific article, omits indications of enabling conditions, deliberation and materialization. Woolgar specifically distinguishes four rhetorical devices which direct readers in the interpretation of a scientific article: preliminary instructions, externalizing devices, pathing devices, and sequencing devices.

Preliminary instructions are those indications in the text that instruct the reader how to evaluate its meaning; for instance, the designation of the genre ('research report') the listing of institutional affiliations (accreditation), and the division into subheadings ('introduction', 'methodology,' 'discussion') summon the reader's interpretation of the academic journal article as scientific discourse. Secondly, Woolgar distinguishes 'externalizing devices': rhetorical strategies which reveal the assumption that scientists simply discover objects that are out there, while the agent of discovery is merely transient. Scientists seem to react to given problems, diseases or circumstances. The rhetorical convention to invoke other observers ('we'), to use the passive voice ('it must be concluded that') and to attribute agency to data ('the data suggest that') are examples of externalizing devices. Thirdly, the establishment of a past state of affairs, or the custom of referring to previous research, constitutes what Woolgar calls 'pathing devices.' Embedding new scientific results in the tradition of formerly established knowledge reassures the homogeneity of scientific argumentation, and consequently, the rules of consensus-building. Finally, Woolgar mentions the use of 'sequencing devices' as a rhetorical strategy to present the results of scientific research as facts. The sequential organization and the framing of a scientific article allow the scientist to present a constructed process as a 'natural' chain of events.

These four devices – preliminary instructions, externalizing, pathing and sequencing devices – organize science discourse 'as to sustain and reinforce the objectivity of its objects, and systematically to diminish the contrary (constitutive) view' (79). The constraints of science discourse, according to Woolgar, are such that non-scientists who do not share the same rules of formation are not allowed to criticize science. Sociologists or ethnographers of science describe science discourse from the point of view of the 'other'; they point out the socialness of science by spotlighting the involvement of agency in the construction of a scientific debate. He laments that sociologists' criticism does not affect scientists because they do not accept the same conditions of debating. But despite Woolgar's proposal to 'reconstitute the moral order of representation, not only to explore alternatives to the dominance of the rhetoric of science, but also to dispute its right to define what counts as an alternative,' his analysis shows no signs of actual attempts to reassess the hierarchy of discourses (105).

The implication of Woolgar's stance is that science discourse does not allow any social criticism which goes against the immediate interests of scientists. But scientists debate amongst themselves the 'rightness' of scientific facts, and even though proposed research results can only be disputed by assuming the same conditions of arguing, dissenting opinions or alternative constructions or facts are not simply excluded from academic journals. The *New England Journal of Medicine* and other prestigious journals regularly feature articles that contradict formerly claimed research results. In addition, these journals allow space for disagreement and tentative scientific claims in genres like 'Letters-to-the-Editor' and 'Research reports.' Science results are often discussed and evaluated in 'discussion sections' of articles; even though these sections are reserved to discussion of scientific results, evaluation of the social usefulness of new techniques or methods often surface in these spaces.

I therefore disagree with Woolgar and other ethnographers of science that science discourse cannot be criticized unless the critique is formulated in its own terms, on its own conditions. The problem with this theory is that it regards the reading instructions prescribed by the discursive format to be compulsory – rhetorical devices coercing the ethnographer to interpret and argue within the scientist's rules of formation. Woolgar's critical practice, in my view, is disempowering and counterproductive, since it actually accredits and reinforces the authority of science discourse by suggesting that its terms of debate are impregnable. In so doing, he acquiesces in science's definition of what may count as knowledge.

Moreover, Woolgar locates the centre of the scientific debate in one particular textual genre: the academic journal article. But science journals do not comprise a homogeneous category of texts, characterized by equal standards of knowledge construction and argumentation. With regard to the debate on new reproductive technologies, prestigious journals like the *New England Journal of Medicine* in the USA and the *British Medical Journal* are recognized as authoritative sources of knowledge formation. Research results published in these journals are commonly quoted as facts by other scientists and journalists. Yet the scientific debate is not restricted to highly specialist articles that are closely scrutinized by peers and evaluated according to the strict protocols shared by members of the scientific community; the same mode of constructing authority is simulated in the 50 000 or so (semi-) scientific publications that flood the market each year, containing over one million articles. These 'info-science' products, as I would like to call them, range from very specialized professional journals seeking to inform and update peers, to general journals aimed at informing an interested audience, and to info-magazines geared towards selling services and technology to a large audience. Some info-science journals published by professional organizations look exactly like established academic journals, but are actually nothing but trade journals. The American Fertility Society, for example, issues a journal called *Fertility and Sterility*, which is a hybrid of scientific articles, information and editorial commentaries. The line between science, journalism and advertising discourse is definitely blurred in so-called newsletters, such as *Medical News* or *Fertility Assistance*, which report the developments regarding new reproductive technologies to their members – customers of infertility clinics – but are actually direct mailings issued by fertility centres.

Science discourse should not be solely located in the academic journal article; the cultural authority of science is not just established in respected scientific journals, but even more so in the variety of publications that seek to adopt their rhetorical devices in order to acquire a similar aura of credibility. Articles in 'newsletters' like *Fertility Assistance*, for instance, assume textual features which clearly fit Woolgar's classification of externalizing, sequencing or pathing devices. These journals invariably claim the usefulness and success of IVF research as scientific facts, deploying rhetorical techniques associated with professional, peer-reviewed science journals. To a less than informed or critical reader, info-science journals probably represent the same kind of factual knowledge than academic journals, while these publications are obviously infested with commercial or ideological interests. All discourses of science, whether published in 'respected' or info-science journals, equally add to the configuration of meaning, even though some are regarded as more 'trustworthy' or factual than others. In fact, so-called respected professional journals often rely on these info-science publications to disseminate and popularize their claims among a wider audience.

Scientific claims to truth are thus concurrently disseminated through professional journals, trade publications, and popularized accounts. As Greg Myers (1990) has convincingly argued, scientists publish, or assist in the publication of, various accounts of science because they aim at various goals. The choice of a publication medium may offer either an immediate professional reward or an indirect advertising reward. Popularizations are regarded as investments in public recognition, while articles in professional journals are investments in credibility. Myers analyses a number of scientific texts, ranging from grant proposals to magazine articles, yet he correctly avoids the trap of regarding articles in scientific journals as 'primary texts,' and popularizations as 'versions' of professional publications. He doubts this common accreditation of status and states that each 'version' has a politics of its own, and should therefore be read in the context of its particular discursive framework. In grant proposals the complex process of negotiating the need for research is aimed at fundraisers, in scientific articles the act of negotiation is directed toward peers, and in popularized versions the negotiation of claims addresses a general audience. But all three versions are exercises in persuasion and mutually affect the understanding of science. The arenas of negotiation differ according to their respective goals of fundraising, establishing professional credibility and public recognition. Only by pointing out the relationship between these different exercises in persuasion one can reveal the constructedness of science.

Whereas social constructivists like Woolgar find the discourse of science immutable and impregnable to outside criticism, Myers simply denies that science stays within the boundaries of its described discourse. He disputes the idea that science is exclusively constructed within the privileged borders of the science journal, and rejects the inscribed hierarchy by equally acknowledging other constructions of scientific authority. Myers's position represents the cultural studies approach to science, which is both an extension and a distinctive alteration of constructivist theories. Proponents of cultural studies of science, rather than sanctioning the limits of scientific discourse, prefer to contest its boundaries.[5] The traffic between science and culture is two-way to the extent that there is no inside or outside of science. The position of the social constructivist as an 'ethnographer of science' – someone who can criticize science from another platform – is problematic. To assume such platform is to affirm the limitations of science discourse, and thus the distinctive hierarchy between the discourse of science and other formations of knowledge.

This position of the critic as an ethnographer of discourse is also found frequently in poststructuralist theories of communication and journalism. Most communication theorists assume a sharp line between journalism and other professional discourses. The popularization of science in journalism is commonly understood as the 'accommodation' of scientific knowledge to journalistic accounts, as it passes from one rhetorical situation to another.[6] In line with Myers's argument, I regard journalistic accounts of science as autonomous acts of persuasion, strategically phrased to disseminate a particular view. From a cultural studies perspective, journalism is not a separate discourse, subordinate to science and obediently distributing information to a general audience. Journalism, like science, is heterogeneous and permeable; the discourses of science and journalism are produced conjuncturally, and increasingly contain one another.

JOURNALISM AS DISCOURSE

Until the 1970s, science remained relatively 'untouched' by news media, and scientists were rarely bothered by journalists demanding access to scientific processes or openly criticizing scientific projects. When calls for democratization affected politics, education, journalism, culture and other areas, science ineluctably became one of the last institutions to be subjected to public scrutiny. As the centre of public debates gravitated towards the media, at the end of this decade, scientists became less reluctant to open up discussion to the public eye.[7] A heightened media awareness caused scientists to pay attention to the rhetoric of public communication. In addition, social pressure also affected the institutional power of journalism: the news media turned from a mouthpiece of established authorities into a platform for discussion.

As institutional discourses, science and journalism have a lot in common. Because of its relevance to the debate on new reproductive technologies, I will narrow the focus of this discussion to medical science and the reporting of medicine. Both institutional discourses contain centripetal forces of commerce and ideology; the commercial stakes in medical institutions as well as news organizations are not seldom square with professional requirements. Journalism and medicine are both self-regulating professions, defending editorial and clinical freedom, but largely depending on market fluctuations. Most significantly, the ideal of objectivity is inscribed in both discourses, and has materialized in professional routines, normative practices and textual conventions.[8]

I have described previously how the ideology of objectivity in science is reified in the rhetorical devices which erase traces of agency and the process of constructing, thus assuring the 'disinterestedness' and 'impersonality' of scientific knowledge. We can distinguish similar discursive norms in the news media, aimed at anchoring the rules of balance and fairness, which function as mechanisms to ensure objectivity. In journalistic accounts of science, for instance, the convention to balance off two perspectives on an event erases any trace of construction: rendering the interpreting subject invisible, the representation leaves the impression of a factual, observable reality. The ideology of objectivity inscribed in journalistic practices perpetuates the special status of objective knowledge and information. As John Fiske (1992) summarizes: 'The journalistic power to define certain narratives as factual and others as fictional is the equivalent of that of scientific rationalism to define its reality and exclude others: both are examples of top-down informing of a reality and of a believing subject' (50).

Naturally, both science and journalism have a vital interest in upholding this normative discursive power. The shared interests of these two institutions may partly explain why their discourses have gradually blended. In the 1970s, journalists approached scientists with a hybrid sense of awe and suspicion. The hierarchical ordering of these institutions was firmly entrenched in Western culture; journalists were supposed to merely report scientific results if scientists chose to make these public. Scientists generally formed an exclusive community and were often regarded by journalists as adversaries who resisted the public's right to information. Dorothy Nelkin (1987) labels this pattern of journalistic recognition of science, typical of the 1970s, the 'awe and mistrust' frame. Despite a sense of mistrust, the awe for scientists and their work remained prevalent throughout this era. However, scientists became more and more aware of the importance of their public image, as they saw their funding affected by stories in the lay press. Nelkin observes that science and research centres became increasingly vulnerable to external pressures: 'For once information enters the arena of public discourse it becomes a visible public affair and the way is open to external investigation and regulation' (159).

The perception that the public image of science serves not only as a tool to affect fundraising, but also as a mechanism for influencing the demand for science or technology, typifies the changed relationship between scientists and journalists in the 1980s. Information has become a valuable commodity to scientists, or more precisely, to investors in scientific knowledge. As a result, scientists have increasingly come to seek control over science discourse as it dissipates into the news media. Most laboratories, universities and research centres hired public relations officers to handle information to the press, and to promote the public image of their institutions. Editorial policies of science journals were adjusted to provide journalists with advance copies of important articles, thereby allowing them to publish their newspaper reports the same day as the journal article appeared. Scientists were trained to talk to the press and to give interviews, as well as to anticipate press coverage while writing their publications. 'Information control' is a euphemism used by public institutions and commercial enterprises to indicate their ambivalent attempt to guard off public scrutiny and at the same time maintain an image of accessibility.

Signs of raised awareness of the impact of journalism appear in science journals at the beginning of the 1980s. A 1983 article in the *New England Journal of Medicine (NEJM)*, for instance, seeks to provide guidelines for medical researchers on how to handle the press.[9] The guidelines do not solely aim at funnelling information scientists convey to the press, but also at instructing scientists how to manipulate their information to influence funding sources and Congress. The *NEJM* advises medical researchers to anticipate publicity and play along with journalists. Instead of using 'medicalese,' researchers should try to use 'journalese,' meaning they ought to use simple language, striking metaphors and analogies, avoid medical explanations, and provide examples of beneficial applications instead of abstract theories or experiments. Recognizing what interests the news media and the public constitutes the game in which information control is at stake; the author of the *NEJM* article compares the tactics of journalists to those of scientists: 'Just as scientists have tricks to induce genes to express themselves, journalists use a bag of tricks to acquire information. Knowing them will reduce surprises and perhaps allow you to foil them' (1172). The discourse of science, according to the guidelines in the *NEJM*, should be adjusted to accommodate the discourse of journalism. Scientists apparently start to recognize the lay press as an important arena of knowledge construction, which forces them to reconsider their own formative rules of discourse.[10]

Conversely, journalists in the 1980s have increasingly turned to scientists as sources of information. There is more information about science in the press today then there has ever been in the past. The hunger for information concerning medical science seems particularly insatiable. Nelkin, who has traced trends in science reporting since the late fifties, notices how the 'awe and mistrust' frame of the 1970s changed in the subsequent decade into a renewed 'marvel of science' frame. Stories of breakthroughs, successes and an unconditional admiration of scientists as altruistic, disinterested heroes dominate mainstream journalism. Promotional enthusiasm tends to overwhelm undercurrents of ambivalence towards science; scientists seem to deserve a sense of awe even if they claim controversial theories as 'scientific facts.' In this respect, journalistic perceptions of science coincide with public attitudes and biases. Nelkin charges that the interests of both journalists and scientists skew critical coverage so that science is typically represented as progressive and beneficial; the result of this erroneous portrayal is that it neglects both the tentative nature of scientific inquiry and its political context. As the hybrid term 'science journalism' indicates, journalism frequently assumes the form of an institutional advertisement.

The attribution of authority to scientists is reflected in a gradual inclusion of science discourse in mainstream news media, such as *The New York Times*, *Time*, or *Newsweek*. Science reporting has become more technical and includes abundant scientific details and photographic evidence. If we compare news media reports on science between 1970 and 1990, it is apparent that journalism has adopted science discourse as its model for reporting.[11] Journalistic accounts of science today contain more 'visible' proof, such as pictures and detailed graphics. Since science has provided journalists with irresistible visuals to illustrate their stories, technology itself has shaped the very object of reporting. Enlarged, full colour microscopic photographs of eggs and cells frequently lard news magazine reports on the newest results in IVF research. The very availability and eager inclusion of these visible 'proofs' of science's 'advancement' change the very nature of journalism discourse. The mutual need to enhance the appearance of objectivity and the entangled interests of scientists and journalists have worked to promote a science coverage dutiful to scientific interests while inhibiting a truly critical appraisal of science by journalists.

A merger between science and journalism discourse can also be traced in the rhetoric that is increasingly deployed by journalists to cover science. Research results and technological inventions are often presented as 'facts of life,' events covered as indisputable facts. The discourse of journalism tends to authorize itself by assuming scientific features: it presents processes as facts – inevitable outcome of scientific experimentation – and it presumes the absence of a narrating or observing subject. The rhetorical strategies used by journalists are virtually similar to the devices that Woolgar identified as typical of science. Journalists, like scientists, tend to present themselves as 'witnesses of reality,' deliberately erasing the social and political context of scientific practice. They assume the cultural authority of scientists by borrowing similar rhetorical devices and paradigms of argumentation – including visual proofs – to confirm science's presentation of reality as 'truth.'

Journalism discourse does not pretend to be void of subjective knowledge, yet it purports to be able to separate facts from opinion. In most 'serious' or quality newspapers, like *The New York Times*, the conventions of news reporting require that 'facts' are stated on the front page, while opinions appear on the editorial pages. The obvious hierarchy between fact and opinion is reflected in the lay-out of the newspaper. On the face of it, the newspaper appears to present a pluriform platform of discussion, particularly geared toward accommodating divergent ideological voices. Information on the newest IVF-related technique may surface on the special science page, but may also be framed as a 'health' or 'human interest' story. A story about some innovative genesplicing technique may appear on the front page or on the business page; the implications of this technique may be discussed in an editorial or Op-Ed piece. Unrelated stories and the scattered appearance of unrelated facts and opinions leave the impression that journalism discourse is a pluralistic representation of voices. Yet, there is an unarticulated hierarchy between different utterances. Science results printed on the science page are often unmarkedly represented as facts, carrying more weight and credibility than science results discussed in 'Letters-to-the-Editor,' 'Op-Ed' or 'Comment' pieces, which are usually earmarked as subjective perspectives from individuals or special interest groups. The discourse of journalism is thus used almost imperceptibly to cast a veil of objectivity and credibility; journalists inscribe the norms of acceptability and deviation by marking some positions as factual and others as opinionated.

Many critics of (news) media, like for instance the French communication theorist Louis Quéré, contend that the format and conventions of journalism discourse work to promote and enhance dominant norms, and marginalize or exclude voices critical of these norms.[12] In his theory of postmodern manifestations of journalism, Quéré claims that both journalism and science discourse are successful at hiding their interested, partial perspectives behind a screen of objectivity and naturalness. The obligatory use of authorities as sources, the rules of balance and fairness, the requirement of finding a story's news angle, and the convention of translating abstract issues into simplified, personal or human stories leave little room for critical assessments of power. Journalism, Quéré argues, does not allow a different view because it purports to provide a witness report of reality.[13] Like Woolgar, Quéré discloses how power is hidden and how it is exercised by a discursive mechanism. Their critical missions resemble Dorothy's role in *The Wizard of Oz*: they open up the curtain to reveal the rhetorical wizardry used in the prolongation of power. Yet in doing so, they reinforce the illusion that knowledge is exercised from a clearly defined epicentre and constructed through (institutional) discourses.

While such a critical strategy may bare the mechanism of knowledge construction, it also perpetuates science's and journalism's exclusive claim to determine what may count as 'fact.' The cultural authority of journalism to define what counts as fact is based on the presumed immutability of its discourse. Yet historically, journalism has never been an unchangeable category; the borders between journalism and other discourses have often been redefined. In the 1960s, so-called New Journalists questioned the boundaries between journalism and fiction by foregrounding interpretation and personal impressions in their reports, and by using literary devices to frame a journalistic account.[14] In the past decade, journalism has clearly become more narrative. Postmodern science discourse, both in scientific journals and in newspapers or news magazines, can be characterized by a narrativation of knowledge; if we compare journalistic accounts of the late 1980s to science coverage of the

1960s and 1970s, one of the most striking features is the abundant presence of narrative elements.

Most poststructural theorists consider the narrativation of knowledge to be a degradation of norms and clarity.[15] However, the increased use of narrative may be be viewed as an asset rather than a drawback. Narrative in journalism can be exploited to include voices oppositional to or critical of dominant norms and values. As storytellers, journalists construct meaning by ordering and framing sources or documents, and by positioning themselves in relation to reported events.[16] The narrative conventions of journalism – however normative and prescriptive – are never impenetrable or unchangeable, and can be deployed to construct alternative meanings. Journalistic practices, routines and conventions may be challenged by individual journalists who interpret the norms of objectivity differently.

Writing from a clearly marked position, feminists for instance, may manipulate journalistic discourse to subvert the authority inscribed in rhetorical devices aimed at anchoring objectivity. Changing the interpretation of which 'authorities' to use as sources – hence authorizing other voices to speak – and rearranging the hierarchical order of voices, feminist journalists have exploited narrative to subvert conventions of discourse.[17] Analysis of feminist journalistic accounts may help determine what kind of rhetorical strategies feminists can effectively use to contribute to a public debate while at the same time criticizing the conventional rules of formation that deter alternative meanings. Criticism is not enabled or prohibited by a specific mode of discourse, but can be deployed to question the ideological imprint of discursive conventions. Journalism, like science, is not innately unsuitable to voice meanings that contravene mainstream perceptions.

The narrativation of journalistic discourse becomes even more apparent when we do not restrict analysis to the standards of 'quality' news reporting, such as *The New York Times* or *The Times* in Britain. Features that are usually associated with fiction – personal narratives, metaphors, images and dialogue, to name just a few – surface in all journalistic texts. Accounts of new reproductive technologies appear frequently in popular news magazines, such as *Time* and *Newsweek*, and in tabloids, for example *The National Enquirer* in the USA or the *Daily Mail* in

Britain. Tabloid stories of 'miracle conceptions of two sextuplets' are naturally not considered to be factual, but the way they are reported remarkably resembles 'serious' journalistic accounts in their use of discursive techniques: popular images, myths and stories are presented as 'facts' by quoting medical experts in addition to anecdotal and personal stories. Significantly, the stories in *Time* or *Newsweek* are not much different in their method of construction: the story of the '59-year-old woman who becomes a mother with the help of IVF,' is equally supported by quotes of experts, doctors and nurses. In fact, magazines like *Time* and *Newsweek* depend on tabloids like *The National Enquirer* to define themselves against these kind of 'fictive' stories, and to present their own stories as 'factual' information.

Presenting drama and fiction as information is an increasingly popular trend in Western culture; the abundant supply of 'infotainment' and 'news shows' epitomize the penetration of entertainment by journalism discourse. Michael Schudson (1991) appropriately labels this phenomenon the 'newsification of popular culture.'[18] Institutional discourses, such as entertainment, politics or religion, show the tendency to contain features of journalism discourse: just as science has adapted the conditions of journalism logic, as I have pointed out earlier, other institutional discourses incorporated the rhetoric and formats commonly used by news media to enhance their own authority to report 'facts.' David Altheide and Robert Snow (1991) theorize the pervasiveness of journalism discourse in the 'postjournalism era' of the 1980s as the reflection of a changed social order, an order in which appearance and public image have surpassed the experience of reality.[19]

Most poststructuralist theorists, notably Lyotard, have lamented the porousness of discursive domains, because they claim it renders ideological inscriptions of hierarchy and power invisible. Yet the obfuscation of discourses could also be seen as a positive rather than a negative attribute. The diffusion of boundaries facilitates the view that both science and journalism are part of culture, instead of functioning as privileged institutional discourses. As many of the pillars of journalism's discursive edifice appear unstable, it is important to undo manifestations of discursive authority of their confining outmoded skin. But simply 'undoing' or 'unmasking' journalism's or science's claims to objectivity and impartiality is not sufficient as a critical practice. By recontextualizing discourse – juxtaposing those areas of meaning production which are commonly viewed as incompatible domains – we might see how these texts are equal inscriptions of narrative knowledge.

Regarding science and journalism as narrative constructions is thus a deliberate attempt to reveal how fictional devices inform these 'factual' discourses. To designate any vision of science and technology as 'fictional' we should extend critical inquiry to the discourse of fiction. Fictional accounts of science have played a significant role in the construction and dissemination of scientific ideas. In addition to reading science as fiction, we should thus consider fictions as serious (factual) constructions of knowledge.

SCIENCE IN FICTION, FICTIONS OF SCIENCE

As I explained in the beginning of this chapter, the commotion caused by Rorvik's *In His Image* was less the result of a hoax than of his publisher's refusal to reclassify the book as fiction. Scientists and journalists would presumably have been reassured if the book could have been dismissed as fantasy. Marked as fiction, Rorvik's warning of the possible abuse of reproductive technologies would not have had to be taken seriously. The discourse of fiction, particularly popular fiction, is commonly looked upon as an innocent sanctuary, a harmless source of entertainment or aesthetic pleasure that does not affect the construction of truth and reality. Scientists who dismiss a claim often do so by labelling it fiction, not on the basis of its content, but on the ground that the claim was not constituted by the scientific paradigm of argumentation.

Science and fiction have more in common than scientists might like to admit. Science projects have been and still are inspired by imaginary concepts or speculations of a possible future. Images or ideas underlying science projects are always propelled by ideological fantasies or projections. Huxley's *Brave New World*, for instance, inspired scientist John Rock, who set out looking for a 'cure' for infertility and 'invented' the contraceptive pill. The idea(l) that a human body consists of genetic coding strings, which may be freely manipulated and endlessly reproduced, is not just an extremely popular theme in science fiction movies and books; it is actually the underlying rationale for a four-billion-dollar government sponsored project.[20] Just as fiction informs and incorporates the scientific, the scientific instructs and converges with the fictional.

Science discourse, which purports to be exempt from narrative knowledge, betrays its groundedness in collective fictions most explicitly through the metaphorical systems that structure its language. An adequate understanding of the metaphoricity of the language of science is crucial to a critical assessment of scientific knowledge; metaphors are consciously selected by scientific communities, and since they are grounded in common perceptions of the world, they are easily disseminated to other discourses.[21] In medical discourse, the dominant perception of disease as a (collective) threat to human life has produced a barrage of military metaphors which have lost their metaphorical signification, and are now used routinely. Scott Montgomery (1991), for instance, cites examples from medical journals which denote illness as an 'enemy,' the body as 'land' and medical scientists as the 'defending army.' He gives numerous examples of metaphors found in medical journal articles which are used non-metaphorically: disease 'strikes' as a virus 'invades' the body, 'spreads out' and forces the body to develop an 'immune system' to 'fight' the disease. Imaginative concepts thus structure the formation of scientific knowledge, losing their metaphorical signification in this context. Conversely, fiction is also structured by scientific language. The best science fiction novels rival science articles in technical precision and ingenuity; descriptions of medical or technical procedures in science fiction are sometimes barely distinguishable from those in science journals.

To an even greater extent, science journalism relies on the inclusion of fictional features in its discourse. Both television and print reporters use imaginary descriptions, narrative, and strategic visuals to tell their stories, yet they fiercely reject the 'fictiveness' of their products. Journalists' ability to produce 'facts' actually depends on an implicit or explicit rejection of fiction writers to claim that same cultural authority. Rorvik's book is a case in point: journalists and scientists were appalled at the deceptive use of the nonfiction label, and angrily redirected Rorvik to 'his own domain' – the domain of fiction. Deliberate attempts to reveal the permeable boundaries between journalism and fiction have always elicited strong reactions from journalists.

As Barbie Zelizer (1992) points out in her book on the coverage of John F. Kennedy's assassination, journalists reacted furiously to Oliver Stone's film *JFK*. According to American news celebrities like Dan Rather and Ted Koppel, Oliver Stone had 'tampered with historical truth' by mixing actual footing of the Kennedy murder with fictional shots; it was this particular rhetorical strategy that offended journalists who had witnessed the event in 1963. Ironically, most networks had already aired fictionalized portrayals of Kennedy's life and death – 'authorized' biographical documentaries. In addition, none of the three mainstream networks object to the use of so-called simulations or recreations in their national news programmes. Indeed, while journalists may freely borrow fictional devices, fiction writers are blamed for unashamedly drawing from 'factual' sources. As Zelizer concludes, journalists' criticism towards Stone's movie revolved around their claim to cultural authority: 'In contesting the versions of events that reporters have set forth, *JFK* has also contested the journalistic authority their versions imply. This makes reporters' public criticism of *JFK* not only predictable but essential to their integrity as an authoritative interpretive community' (213).

Transgression of the borderlines between science and fiction, or journalism and fiction, is thus a discursive strategy used by both mainstream and oppositional voices. Genres that locate themselves in the borderlands of fact and fiction may call in question the distinctive character of each discourse. The documentary novel, for instance, is a mixed genre that derives its status from the incorporation of journalistic or historical features, and its popularity from the inclusion of fictional characteristics.[22] It is precisely this combination of discursive features that gives the documentary novel its impact, yet these hybrid genres can only exist by virtue of the assumed separation of the factual and the fictive. While cultural authority takes shape at the interface of discourses, the use of mixed genres is not a critical strategy in itself; it may also be used to reconfirm existing limits or hierarchies. As I have pointed out earlier, medical newsletters and other info-science publications position themselves in between science and journalism to actually reify conventional boundaries. Apparently, scientists and journalists have great stakes in affirming their authority to establish facts; despite the obvious obfuscation of discourses, they ceaselessly accentuate the contours of their 'proper domains' by refuting any power to fiction as an area of knowledge production.

Popular culture and fiction cannot assert propositions that are taken as seriously as those in other modes of discourse. However, fiction's ability to propose new realities poses a peculiar correlative to its impotence. It may be precisely this paradoxical nature of fiction that makes it suitable as a critical or subversive discourse. Therefore, it comes as no surprise that a considerable number of feminist authors have taken fiction seriously as a site of knowledge construction. Over the past decades, feminist authors have shown a significant preference for popular literary forms, such as science fiction, detective fiction, utopian/ dystopian fiction, romance and fantasy, to voice their oppositional views to dominant ideologies of science. Anne Cranny-Francis (1990) considers this preference of feminist authors for generic forms of fiction to be an understandable and appropriate political practice. It makes sense for feminists to use the popular fiction format because it exploits the 'popular' in the two most obvious senses of the word: it reaches a large and diverse audience, and it allows unfamiliar ideas to be presented within a familiar and much loved format. Feminist embrace of popular fiction – the 'lowest' of literary genres in the hierarchy of discourses – may prompt a reassessment of this genre as a viable site of ideological struggle.

The popular novel also seems an appropriate genre for questioning the hierarchy and authority of discourses because of its dialogic nature. While all discourses are in fact dialogic – able to absorb other discourses and allow other worldviews – the novel invites collision or confrontation between different views.[23] The narrative subject in fiction has more power than the narrative subject in journalism to select, frame and rearrange fragments of other discourses. Narrative plotting in fiction is a way of negotiating meaning from the mass of information which confronts us. Discursive hierarchy, engraved in the discourses incorporated in the novel, may thus be explicitly questioned or rebutted by the narrative subject.

The awareness of the politics of form is a frequently recurring theme in feminist popular novels, foregrounding the conceptualization of fiction itself and questioning the status of fiction in relation to other discourses. This meta-commentary often consists of implicit proposals on how to read the several discourses that are incorporated in the novel. One of the important functions of feminist popular fiction, according to Cranny-Francis, is that it challenges the 'natural' discursive hierarchy:

> [S]ocial changes are the result of changes in dominant discursive formation, of the renegotiation and reconfiguration of the discourses describing society at a particular time. Feminist genre fiction is an intervention in this configuration, an attempt to subvert the dominance of patriarchal discourse by challenging its control of one semiotic system, writing, and specifically genre writing. (17)

Although I share Cranny-Francis's enthusiasm for genre fiction as an appropriate venue for expressing feminist critique, I do not subscribe to her claim that popular fiction is the only or most suitable means to voice feminist opposition. Just as I refute Woolgar's complaint that science does not allow critical voices, and Quéré's claim that journalism is wholly unsuitable as a discourse for a (feminist) critical practice, I am hesitant to accept Cranny-Francis's contention that genre fiction as a discourse is pre-eminently fit to serve this goal. Indeed, popular fiction lends itself to reconfigurations of reproductive and social arrangements yet the deployment of this genre in itself is no guarantee for a critical, feminist assessment of technology.[24] Feminist criticism is not limited to fictional genres, but can be found in all discourses, at the intersections of discourses and in the dispersal of fiction into other domains.

Feminist criticism, as I have argued in the previous chapter, cannot be located in one discourse, just as it cannot be restricted as coming from one group of people. It is not a counterdiscourse that is easily identifiable in one location, genre or publication. Instead, both dominant and oppositional meanings may be traced in fiction. The convergence of discourses should not be deplored as the erosion of stable standards, but may be accepted as an essential feature of postmodern culture. All voices, whether dominant or oppositional, strategically manoeuvre themselves to find a space in the plethora of discourses. While cultural authority is to a large extent predisposed by the hierarchy of discourses, contributors to a public debate may contest this authority by challenging established discursive arrangements. Discursive and rhetorical coatings are integral factors in the construction of public knowledge; as a consequence, all public discourses – whether science, journalism, fiction or some hybrid form – should be regarded as vehicles in the construction of consent and dissent, as long as the underlying discursive disposition is understood as a shaping factor.

THE ROLE OF THE CRITIC IN A PUBLIC DEBATE

Emerging out of the interface of feminist theory and cultural studies, my approach thus prioritizes a recontextualization of discourses. Pivotal to a critical analysis of the public debate on new reproductive technologies is the act of *redefining the body of texts* that constitute a debate. In order to map the public debate on new reproductive technologies, I have selected texts from science journals, journalistic publications as well as fictional accounts. The juxtaposition of scientific treatises, journalistic accounts and fiction will reveal how each of these texts is inextricably bound up with other narratives, and how each of these texts incessantly incorporates and generates others. In a public debate, all voices are articulated in relation to one another; a reassemblage of these utterances may reveal how, and to what extent, voices contain and construct each other.

The cultural practice of recontextualization has been called different names. Ormiston and Sassower (1989) label this activity 'creating a labyrinth of narratives.' The labyrinth metaphor refers to the activity of assembling a cohesive whole out of the numerous stories on a particular subject; it is up to the critic, then, to sort out her or his way through the various domains of knowledge by unravelling their idiosyncratic discourses and rhetorics.[25] Donna Haraway (1992) uses the term 'webbing' to designate the activity of realigning a number of related texts from very different sources.[26] She prefers the 'webbing' metaphor because it implies both an act of reconstruction – knotting loose story threads into a cohesive network – and a creative act of production.

The critical practice I will deploy in the following analysis has much in common with Haraway's definition of 'webbing.' Yet I prefer 'mapping' as a structuring metaphor because the term seems better suited to indicate the activity of analyzing a public debate. 'Mapping' means both 'charting' and 'producing a symbolic landscape.' With regard to the public debate on new reproductive technologies, I have assembled and charted a number of different texts, ranging from medical to trade journals, from general to special interest magazines, and from bestseller thrillers to feminist science fiction. From the numerous texts that have been produced on the new technologies, I have gathered those which have been distributed by publishers, libraries, public organizations or institutions.[27]

But mapping a public debate is easier in theory than it is in practice. In order to obtain a wide variety of texts on new reproductive technologies, I had to pursue my quest in divergent places. Research acquainted me with a number of different libraries; it took me from the medical to the social science library, and from the humanities to the science collection. This kind of search journey alerts one to the politics involved in institutionalized collections, archives, and categorization systems; each text is already defined by the way it is classified in a library, and is ascribed a meaning due to its grouping with other books. The physical dispersion of texts over so many different collections sets up a substantial barrier to this kind of interdisciplinary research.

My search journey took a surprising turn when I discovered the archive of the Global Network for Reproductive Rights (GNRR) in Amsterdam. The GNRR is an autonomous institute representing groups and individuals from all five continents who work to support the reproductive rights of women. For more than ten years, documentalists of the GNRR have carefully saved clippings from a variety of sources and put them into files categorized by subject headings, such as 'in vitro fertilization,' 'genetic engineering,' 'infertility,' and so on; sometimes these categories were subdivided, e.g. 'male/female infertility,' but they were never organized by textual or academic features. This non-academic categorization of texts revealed obvious yet commonly invisible continuities between medical journal articles, newspaper clippings, flyers, newsletters, trade journals, feminist magazine articles and front page announcements.[28] Hence, the GNRR literally facilitated the act of 'networking,' or reassembling texts which emanate from distinctively different discursive settings.

But 'mapping' does not just mean gathering and juxtaposing texts from different sources. Along with assembling a web of narratives, an adjustment of reading strategies is indispensable. As readers, we are conditioned to read each text according to the rules of formation inscribed in its discourse. These rules of formation are particularly coercive in the discourses of science and journalism. In relation to science discourse, Greg Myers (1990) proposed to simply refuse scientists' conditions for making sense, and instead assume methods of interpretation that are commonly used by historians or literary critics. Readers of an academic journal article are not supposed to infer political implications from this text, or apply literary interpretation strategies to make sense of its content. With regard to journalism, Fiske (1992) argues that both form and content of journalism discourse work to position it within what he calls the 'scriptural economy which attempts to discipline its readers into deciphering its texts rather than reading them' (59). While deciphering pertains to subjecting oneself to the 'truth' inscribed in discourse, reading entails a negotiation of meaning between text and reader. Critical readers, particularly feminists, cannot take for granted the packages of rules which are handed to them as ready-made strategies for reading and which help only to uphold the status quo.

Reading is not a passive act of consumption but an active search for meanings; by reading fiction as a source of social and political transformation, while interpreting science discourse as a rhetorical or imaginative construction, one questions the 'natural' hierarchy of discourses. Or, as Haraway (1989) puts it eloquently: 'Mixing, juxtaposing, and reversing reading conventions appropriate to each genre can yield fruitful ways of understanding the production of narratives in a society that privileges science and technology in its construction of what may count as nature, and for regulating the traffic between what it divides as nature and culture' (370). The public debate on new reproductive technologies is a contest for the language to announce what counts as public knowledge. The role of the critic in this contest is to struggle against the dominant definitions and meanings that appear as 'natural' and 'factual' but which cannot be accepted gratuitously. By defying inscribed reading codes, the critic is able to provide a different context for the interpretation of statements or facts, and to bare alternative meanings. To extend Haraway's metaphor, out of a variety of textual material the critic weaves her own account – a patchwork of texts laced up to form a new artifact, while the origins of individual constitutive parts remain clearly traceable in the creative product. To map a public debate is thus also a creative act, as it translates seemingly incompatible discourses into a cohesive symbolic representation.

From a cultural studies perspective, a critic is thus both reader and writer, who is also a participant in the debate. A cultural critic is not out to attack a specific powerful group which dominates the construction of (scientific) facts, but intends to become a player in the debate. In my analysis of the public debate on new reproductive technologies, I will show how this debate has developed, how positions on the issue have emerged and changed, how various voices have contested and incorporated each other, which rhetorical and discursive strategies they have used to persuade one another, how some strategies may elicit others, and so forth. I do not want to reveal a 'mode of construction' for every account that has been published on IVF or related techniques; the sum of my analyses should provide a modest proposal to redefine the scope and nature of a public debate.

To the many stories of science, I will add my own story, which will in turn become part of the debate – one more interpretation in the field of struggle. Mapping a debate entails that I will be assigned shifting positions of critic and contestant, reader and author, consumer and producer of meanings. My effort will not result in a uniform map reflecting 'the' debate on new reproductive technologies but rather a creative reconstruction. This map is at once a reflection and reinscription of the debate, both analysis and construction of meaning. The role of the critic is one of disentangling consent and discovering dissent, to show how power structures are constructed and subverted.

3 Constructing the Need for New Reproductive Technologies

> The whole idea of designing our descendants, of fabricating the next generation, of making reproduction synonymous with manufacturing is already in the picture.
>
> (*Newsweek*, 7 August, 1978)

> . . . [IVF] will give new hope to women who have been unable to conceive because of tubal difficulties . . . It may give researchers an important new laboratory tool for devising ways of coping with genetic diseases, testing new methods of contraception and, perhaps most important of all, studying close up one of nature's most awesome and still baffling processes: the first stirrings of life.
>
> (*Time*, 31 July, 1978)

INTRODUCTION

The first 'serious' proposition that human fertilization might be attained in vitro appeared in the journal *Science* in 1944.[1] At that time, however, biologists and gynaecologists rejected this proposal as a science fiction fantasy. In the 1950s and 1960s, the idea of human conception occurring outside the woman's body was picked up again by the British medical researchers Robert Edwards and Patrick Steptoe. In the ensuing decades, Edwards and Steptoe took the lead in reproductive medicine; they pioneered techniques such as the use of laparoscopy for the retrieval of oocytes, and first proved the possibility of spermatozoa penetrating eggs in a petri dish. A report on the first successful application of in vitro fertilization in animals appeared in 1972.[2] While research on human IVF was terminated in the United States in the mid-1970s, clinical research in Britain continued. This resulted in 1978 in the birth of Louise Brown in Oldham, a town in north-west England. For Edwards and Steptoe this birth meant the crown on decades of experimentation.

A human being conceived in glass – suddenly a science fiction fantasy had become reality. All over the world, the birth of Louise Brown triggered medical curiosity and moral outrage; it gave rise to astonishment and secrecy, and was reported as a miraculous, yet conspicuous phenomenon. The successful application of IVF in humans spurred doctors, scientists, theologians and politicians to formulate a position on the ethical permissibility of this innovative technique. Scientists, journalists and fiction writers disputed each other's authority to define the significance of this technological advancement, provoking agitated discussions. After the first excitement and controversy subsided, the question of applicability came into focus: who actually needs the new technologies?

Within a few years, infertile women became the centre of attention. Originally designed as a remedy to women who suffered from tubal damage, the applicability range of IVF was quickly expanded to all kinds of female and male infertility. In this first stage of the public debate, between 1978 and 1984, IVF was significantly constructed as a cure to a disease; the dominant meaning of infertility becomes that of an illness which strikes a particular group of women. But how was this myth constructed?

THE FIRST TEST-TUBE BABY: 'GEE WHIZ! A MIRACLE!'

The unprecedented conception and birth of Louise Brown, on the 25th of July, 1978, was officially reported to the medical community in *The Lancet* on August 12, almost three weeks after the actual birth.[3] Steptoe and Edwards report the delivery by Caesarian section of a 'normal healthy infant girl'; following the announcement of the delivery is a description of the patient's medical history, the cause of her infertility – blocked Fallopian tubes – and the subsequent application of an experimental procedure: in vitro fertilization. The description of the actual procedure is remarkably short and general, not allowing for any technical specifications of the IVF process. Leaving the reader with a promise that they will 'publish further medical and scientific details in [these] columns at a later stage' the authors finish up the report.

The report of Louise Brown's birth in *The Lancet* is framed as a 'Letter-to-the-Editor' – a peculiar format for such a momentous breakthrough. Most commonly, important scientific discoveries are displayed as research reports in professional journals, to allow co-specialists in the field to scrutinize the validity of the results, and examine the implications of this research with regard to the practice of medicine. Framing research reports as a 'Letter-to-the-Editor' speeds up the publication process, yet it has less weight than a peer-reviewed article. A 'Letter' format also does not allow for a detailed explanation of the procedure. Edwards's and Steptoe's concise description of the IVF-induced pregnancy – 'established after laparoscopic recovery of an oocyte on November 10, 1977, in-vitro fertilisation and normal cleavage in culture media, and the reimplantation of the 8-cell embryo into the uterus two and a half days later' – simultaneously reports and obscures the actual working of the IVF process. The only technical details reported in *The Lancet* are symptomatic facts, not procedural facts. Reassuring details of normal blood pressure and lactogen levels of the patient, Mrs Brown, veil the absence of information on the procedure itself.

At the time of Louise Brown's birth, Steptoe and Edwards were established enough as scientists to be counted as authoritative; both researchers had published on IVF on a regular basis in the 1970s.[4] Extensive referrals to their previous publications in the birth-announcement in *The Lancet* serve as 'pathing devices' leading up to the momentum of the first successful application. The birth of Louise Brown is presented as the 'logical' result of decades of experimenting and testing. Yet two reasons might have accounted for Edwards's and Steptoe's choice to postpone publication of an extensive research report: they either did not know any scientific details at that time, or they were reluctant to bring them into the public sphere.[5] The absence of a clear protocol or methodological framework raises the question of whether Louise Brown was the result of an experimental coincidence rather than a carefully developed technique or experiment. Edwards's and Steptoe's caution and probable anxiety may form another explanation for their reticence with regard to publishing scientific details. Even though their research was condoned, the laws in this area were not particularly clear. The two researchers had secretly conducted their experiment in order to avoid premature moral and ethical questions surrounding extracorporeal conception.

Despite Steptoe's and Edwards's attempts to keep the experiment a secret, Louise Brown's peculiar birth had become public property long before the publication in *The Lancet*. The story of Mrs Brown's unusual pregnancy had leaked to the press via a hospital staff member, weeks before the expected delivery. Reporters offered hospital staff large sums of money for the name and address of the first test-tube baby. Journalists dressed up as manual workers masqueraded as plumbers and window cleaners to gain entrance to the hospital. When the news broke that the baby had been born, police was called in to clear away photographers from hospital windows. The siege of Oldham General Hospital by journalists became a media event in itself.[6] Finally, the Brown's sold the exclusive rights for photographing the baby and interviewing them to the *Daily Mail* for an estimated 580 000 dollar.

Banner headlines accompanied the event – the British baby became front page news in most national and international newspapers. Louise Brown was coined 'Baby of the Century' and 'Miracle Baby,' the mythical connotation of which was at least partly administered by the refusal of doctors to provide scientific details concerning IVF.[7] When the first official medical report appeared eighteen days later in *The Lancet*, the birth of Louise Brown, as well as the possible ramifications of IVF, had already been widely debated in the news media. The refusal of Steptoe and Edwards to give comments to the press, and their order – which was extended to the hospital staff – not to relinquish any information on the well-being of the parents or the baby, infuriated most journalists. Reporters complained that scientists hampered their professional duty to correctly inform the general audience. Obviously, the attempts of scientists to hide Louise Brown from the press had the opposite effect: it only raised the suspicion of journalists that the two doctors were concocting a conspiracy.

The competition between researchers and journalists to bring out the first report of a scientific endeavour is symptomatic of the underlying struggle to control the terms of discourse. Rivalry between doctors and journalists to report the significance of IVF is also reflected in a *Time* cover story.[8] Since the journalist cannot include any pictures of the parents, nor commentary from the doctors or the parents, he has to resort to other narrative techniques to report Louise Brown's peculiar birth. Published on July 30, 1978, the article describes the commotion caused by Steptoe's and Edwards's experiment. Even though the *Time* story is rubricated as 'medicine,' there is actually very little medical information to be found in this article. A minuscule drawing shows the consecutive steps of conception in a petri dish, but the illustration provides as few insights in the IVF procedure as the one sentence in Steptoe's and Edwards's letter in *The Lancet.*

As information is scarce, the inadvertent absence of technical details and the subsequent struggle to obtain these, become the focus in *Time* – the process of getting the story replaces the process of IVF. Lamenting the reluctance of the two doctors to disclose information to the press, the journalist expresses his frustration at the policy to keep hospital doors hermetically sealed. Even though the *Time* reporter is sympathetic towards the doctors' inclination to keep their ongoing experiment a secret, he resents the fact that both doctors and hospital staff are inaccessible for comments. Journalists, he argues, have as much a responsibility as scientists: the duty to inform the general public. The responsibility of doctors to help women to become pregnant is implicitly equated to the plight of journalists to inform the public.

Thus equalizing their professional missions, the *Time* reporter suggests that scientists should collaborate with journalists because they pursue a common goal. To enforce his claim, he articulates his power to popularize or pulverize the image of science. Despite the lack of medical details, he labels IVF a 'scientific breakthrough' and a 'miracle.' Even though the miracle of wonder cannot be adequately explained by the reporter, he calls the procedure a 'scientific blessing.' Steptoe and Edwards are represented as the unconditional, divine heroes of medical science. Referring to them as model professionals and citizens, Steptoe is depicted as an 'eminent scientist,' a 'pioneer in the use of laparoscopy,' and an 'impeccable dresser who is a 'fine organist,' and 'enjoys watching cricket' (65). The juxtaposition of professional and personal qualities strengthens the impression that a civilized person like Steptoe must be a trustworthy scientist. The inherent benevolence of technology is projected on the scientist as a person; personification of science is a powerful rhetorical tool journalists can deploy to shape the definition of a new technological invention.

But journalists can also use this narrative power to the disadvantage of scientists, as this *Time* article clearly shows. The unconditional heralding of Steptoe is alternated with stories of monsters and devils. If scientists exclude journalists from their experiments – if they leave them 'scrambling for information' – the only thing left for journalists to do is to speculate on what is happening in the laboratory. The absence of factual scientific information elicits scary fantasies, as the reporter argues. To illustrate his threat, he first relates how Huxley's *Brave New World*, Mary Shelley's *Frankenstein*, and George Orwell's *1984* have created frightening prospects, and subsequently quotes how mass newspapers embroider on science fiction images like baby farms and clone hatcheries. Gratefully absorbing the hyperboles of the British tabloids, the reporter of the 'quality' press concludes that 'the Brown venture fell short of ushering into a brave new world.' By varying images of scientists as heroes and as possible Frankensteins, the *Time* journalist demonstrates his power to transform the meaning of new reproductive technology by manipulating the image of scientists. Simultaneously adhering to the authority of science to define, and contesting this power, the journalist engages in an act of translation which is also one of transformation. The implicit warning seems to be that if scientists refuse to work with journalists, journalists will work against them.

A blending of the discourses of science, journalism and fiction reveals the rivalry for the power to define. According to *Time*, 'responsible journalists' tend to endorse science, and provide 'accurate' information in order to avoid distribution of speculation and myth. In fact, journalism needs authoritative sources to be able to inform 'correctly.' But as the report also implies, the pact is mutually beneficial – scientists need 'good' publicity to sell their research and avoid 'bad' image-building, that is, uninformed speculation. As illustrated by this article, the process of representation becomes part and parcel of the myth itself; the interaction between scientists and journalists is exposed as a power play – the power to tell the news, to define the meaning of IVF, and to shape public images of science and scientists.

The struggle between scientists, journalists and (science) fiction writers to define the meaning of reproductive technologies, is also foregrounded in Pamela Sargent's science fiction novel *Cloned Lives*, published a year before the announcement of the first IVF baby. In this novel, a group of five scientists are secretly experimenting on the cloning of one of them, Paul Swenson, a Nobel laureate. All scientists involved in the experiment are weary of publicity because IVF and cloning are, at that moment, very delicate political issues. And when efforts are made to hide the nature of a scientific experiment, they take on a sinister quality – at least that is the way it is perceived by journalists. While five clone-foetuses are maturing in artificial wombs in the laboratory, a reporter turns up claiming to have unravelled the scientists' secret and threatening to make the experiment public. Jason, the journalist, starts bargaining with the scientists to obtain a scoop:

> 'Just what sort of story do you want?,' Hidey asked.
> Jason stopped rocking and smiled slightly.
> 'What I'd like is an interview with you people, pointing out why you're doing this, what you hope to find, what motivated you. You could tell me how you went about the experiment and I could try to simplify things for the general public. It could be a sympathetic piece, a nice feature story in addition to being headline news. Or you can refuse to talk to me and I might have to start speculating about what you're trying to hide.' (61)

Jason motivates his demand claiming that his 'journalistic brethren' could do a lot worse than he, if they were to write the story. They could publish 'Faust stories' and tales of 'mad scientists' who breed foetuses in a lab. He shows off his power to frame the story any way he wants, and thus to manipulate the results of the cloning experiment.

The deal Jason offers is clear: if the scientists grant him this scoop, he will promise to be a 'responsible journalist,' an ally in the process of constructing public consent. As a journalist who does not have access to the desired scientific information, he has the power to make or break the image of scientists and their work. All five scientists consider Jason's proposal to be blackmail, but they do not have much choice. The next scene in the novel remarkably resembles the siege of Oldham General Hospital, as described graphically in *Time*. Reporters trample the laboratory in order to get a glimpse of the incubated clones. The news of the cloning, and the excessive coverage of the birth of the clones, turns out to be devastating for the five children. For the rest of their lives, they have to fight off their images as 'test-tube babies' and 'clones'; the press has turned them into non-authentic humans, curious products of technology.

Whereas in *Time* magazine science fiction authors were represented as distributors of speculation and myth, in Sargent's novel journalists are accused of false image-building. In the author's perception, the selfish interests of reporters – to get the news at any cost – invariably leads to misinformation about the work of scientists. The interpretative frames that journalism offers prohibit an adequate picture of scientific research. As this scene in *Cloned Lives* seems to imply, the discourse of journalism is intrinsically inappropriate to report on science, since journalistic configurations are defined by news value and journalistic conventions of framing. But the impact of this new technology goes beyond the news angle and the short attention span of reporters; news stories are thus not the appropriate means to present thorough, balanced assessments of possible ramifications. Sargent's novel seems to argue that science fiction is a more suitable discourse than journalism to map possible consequences of new reproductive technologies.

Towards the end of the novel, the work of fiction writers is related to that of scientists. Kira, one of the five clone children who has grown up to become a prominent biologist and doctor, tells her brother Jim, who is a poet and novelist, that an important task lies ahead of him:

> His task might become something new; in addition to depicting, refining, and interpreting human experience within a linguistic and dramatic structure, he might also become the creator of scenarios that people could construct and experience for themselves. Such an art would be demanding, calling on every resource of an artist. It would require new structures, new rules and limitations, new purposes. (332)

Fiction writers have as much a responsibility as scientists to constantly probe the ramifications of new technology, Sargent's novel seems to conclude. She regards fiction to be a pre-eminent tool to reflect on human consciousness – allowing the construction of possible futures to raise moral awareness upon which responsible choices should be based. Fiction, rather than journalism, may help people imagine and interpret reality as it is construed outside the 'linguistic and dramatic structure.' The meta-discursive commentary in *Cloned Lives*, conveyed through the main character of the novel, suggests that (science) fiction has the discursive power to create different maps of reality, an imaginative quality that is necessary to give direction to science, but which other discourses lack.

The advent of the first test-tube baby gives rise to divergent representations of reproductive technology: from IVF as a 'miracle' and 'revolutionary technique' to speculations about the possibilities of science to remake nature. Simultaneously, we can identify a discursive struggle for the power to define – scientists, journalists and fiction writers all claim the authority to define, and the responsibility to request or withhold information. But amidst stories about miracles, doctors as heroes, and journalists as blackmailers, the real information gets lost; between controversy and magic, the actual technological-medical process of IVF, and the reason why it might be applied, remain remarkably absent in the storytelling. At this first stage of the discussion, new reproductive technologies are cautiously approached as an issue on which various views are possible. The birth of Louise Brown appears to elicit perturbed and agitated reactions; moral, ethical and religious objections to artificial reproduction receive close attention.

FROM MIRACLE TO CURE: ESTABLISHING THE NEED FOR IVF

Three years after Steptoe's and Edwards's first success, IVF was still regarded as a magical procedure. Its actual working remained obscure, even to specialists, and research was both costly and controversial. Religious and political objections to 'science fiddling with nature' prohibited unrestrained experimenting with new reproductive technologies, and research could only be funded privately, particularly in the USA. As a result, hundreds of small, specialized clinics where IVF was developed and administered, opened across America, Europe and Australia. Lack of federal funding did not discourage the pharmaceutical and medical industry from investing consider-able amounts of money in these research and treatment centres, which indicates the expected market potential of IVF procedures. Privately funded clinics, which became known as 'infertility clinics,' boomed between 1978 and 1985.[9] Their commercial success was primarily due to the ability of doctors and managers to market IVF as the only possible 'cure' to infertility.

During the same period that the IVF industry started growing, we can notice an increasing emphasis on infertility as a problem. Newspapers, talkshows, magazines, health rubrics and so on, eagerly embraced the topic. In her analysis of popular representations of infertility in British magazines and newspapers at the beginning of the 1980s, Sarah Franklin (1990) shows how IVF is construed as a fortunate technical-medical solution to a physical problem. Franklin argues that infertility, while being a social construction, has been overexposed in the media as a medical disability. Images of 'desperate infertile couples' are juxtaposed with stories of 'happy couples' who have won their fight against infertility with the help of modern medical science. But the media did not construct this image out of the blue; while IVF becomes a commercial activity at the centre of a new market place, the medical industry significantly helps construct-ing the 'disease' that justifies the need for advanced technology.

Despite the amounts of money spent on research and experimental treatment, the results of IVF remained invariably disappointing. By December 1981, only three more cases of IVF-administered live births had been reported in the world; yet in vitro fertilization was depicted in both medical journals and media as the promising technology of the future. A 1981 article in *Fertility and Sterility* may illustrate how medical discourse is used to construct the social need for IVF, while also rebutting religious objections.[10] *Fertility and Sterility* is a professional journal, issued by the American Fertility Society, a privately sponsored special interest group of obstetricians and gynaecol-ogists working in the area of reproductive medicine. *Fertility and Sterility* resembles an independent scientific journal, like the

NEJM, in that it features research articles written according to academic protocol. On the other hand, *Fertility and Sterility* contains business news, editorials on issues such as ethics of medical practices, and special reports on success stories in the field.

The 1981 article, titled 'In Vitro Fertilization: the Challenge of the Eighties', reviews two years of IVF research at the University of Melbourne, Australia, and is framed as a regular scientific report aimed at conveying results of clinical research to co-professionals. Like any article in a medical journal, the report starts with a summary, after listing the accreditations of the authors. The core of the article conventionally consists of five sections: introduction (explaining indications for treatment), methods, technical problems, results and discussion. However, the framing of this report as a medical review – the connotation of which is objectivity and neutrality – only thinly disguises its underlying argumentative, commodifying nature.

The results of IVF treatment, as reported in this article in *Fertility and Sterility*, are undeniably poor. Out of a total of 402 treatment cycles involving 186 patients, six pregnancies are reported, five of which result in miscarriage and one in a live birth. Despite the admitted low success rate, the article describes the only birth as a 'very exciting and important milestone scientifically' (702). The word 'success' is mentioned in almost every paragraph, rendering self-evident the conclusion that this technique is the promise of the future. Disappointing results only lead the authors to claim that further basic research is mandated:

It is clear that there still remains an enormous amount of work to be done before in vitro fertilization can be offered as a regular service to the patient, but at present the success that is being achieved is providing momentum for continuation of this work. (704)

The rhetoric to describe the results of the research program seems more befitting an advertisement than a medical journal, as it simultaneously commodifies and markets IVF technology.

While IVF is glorified in this article, the definition of infertility is almost unmarkedly expanded to guarantee the required outlet for this 'regular service.' As I noticed in Steptoe's and Edwards's report on Louise Brown's birth, IVF was initially administered to women who could not conceive because of blocked Fallopian tubes. Relocating the site of fertilization to the petri dish, doctors were able to 'bypass' the tubal blockage which prohibits natural fertilization of the egg to occur. In *Fertility and Sterility*, the medical indication for IVF treatment turns out to encompass all kinds of infertility causes:

> About 60% of patients in the program have varying degrees of tubal damage, but . . . many of these patients have at least one patent tube. The other 40% have problems with abnormal semen, sperm antibodies, endometriosis, and so-called unexplained infertility. (699)

Even though blocked Fallopian tubes are the only 'logical' reason for applying IVF, other indications are simply equated to tubal blockage as if they were mere variations of the same 'disease.' Yet, 'abnormal semen' locates the cause of infertility in the male partner, while 'unexplained infertility' is the collective term for suspected psychological causes of infertility. The implication that IVF treatment should be beneficial to all kinds of infertility does not make much sense, except from a commercial point of view. The sentence following the above quoted indication reveals the underlying implication of a broadened definition of infertility:

> It is worth mentioning that in vitro fertilization and embryo development has been achieved in all these groups of patients, including unexplained infertility, and when one realizes that the list summarizes virtually all causes of infertility, exclusive of intractable anovulation and those patients *without a uterus or a husband*, one realizes the real potential of this work. (700, emphasis added)

'The real potential of this work' – market potential, that is. Expanding the list of medical indications for IVF treatment, and thus broadening the definition of infertility, obviously opens up an enormous reservoir of possible clients for infertility centres. More significantly, the expanded medical definition is based on a social norm of who is allowed to become a mother: the equation 'women without a uterus or a husband' implicitly excludes women who deviate from the norm, either physically or socially.

The physical absence of a womb is equated with the 'physical' absence of a husband, in casu single women and lesbians. Women who show signs of behaviourial deviance are effectively labelled as 'non-authentic' women.

The apparently huge reservoir of possible IVF clients simultaneously proves and creates the need for treatment. Emphasizing the need to alleviate long waiting lists of patients, an observation recurring in most other medical reports on IVF research, the authors claim a sociomedical need for this kind of treatment.[11] Economic or commercial arguments never overtly enter the arena of scientific discourse, but are disguised as medical arguments; the definition of infertility is thus authorized by the medical assumption that many patients await treatment. The demand for a particular kind of treatment apparently justifies its need. Using Lyotard's words, the initial question whether technology is acceptable or needed becomes equivalent to the question whether it is saleable.[12]

But the discourse of medicine, in this article in *Fertility and Sterility*, turns out to be insufficient to justify the need for expensive and controversial IVF treatment. The discussion section of the article – a section which is commonly used to discuss earlier presented medical data – is fully exploited to rebut social, ethical and religious objections to IVF. The success of this type of research, the authors argue, has polarized the non-scientific community in their views on whether IVF is ethically or morally justified. To meet these objections, the authors claim that IVF treatment does not interfere with nature, but simply assists a (faltering) natural process. The petri dish in which fertilization occurs, is nothing but an 'artificial Fallopian tube,' something quite similar to an 'artificial kidney used to maintain life' (704). IVF treatment, according to the authors, is more like helping God to even better attain his procreative goal. The argument that IVF allows scientists to tamper with embryos is rebutted indignantly: the authors claim that they are well aware of the ethics involved in this issue, and that they will be 'happy to come to the conference table and discuss solutions to this problem' (705). Most importantly, the authors argue, science is a humanistic enterprise; the duty of scientists working on the fringe of human knowledge is to 'unravel and unveil' the secrets of human life. The conclusion that 'science provides a dynamic revelation of the marvellous world in which we live' is supported by a Theodor Roszak poem. ('And unless the mind catch fire, the God will not be known . . .' 705)

Holding on to their medical authority, the authors open up the debate to other than scientific contestants, in this case religious objectors. As they let moral and ethical arguments enter medical discourse, the very nature of the narrative changes; religious discourse and even poetry are invoked to support the (scientific) claim for IVF treatment. This conflation of medical, religious and fictional discourse divulges the inherent hierarchy between the discourses: religion and fiction are deployed in the service of science. Using the narrative framework of the medical journal article, the discussion section becomes the site where the authority of science is expanded into the realms of religion and fiction. In the merger of discourses, we can observe how one discourse 'colonizes' another while it is evidently dependent on the other for its own legitimation. Religious objections are counteracted in medical discourse by appealing to the assumed desire of humankind to cure diseases with the help of technology. Even more so, medical science itself is ultimately presented as a divine activity, aimed at assisting God to unveil the secrets of nature.

The article in *Fertility and Sterility* is not a unique example of a medical article which exploits the medical discursive format to anticipate religious objections. An article in the *Journal of Reproductive Medicine*, which reports on the first experimental research with Gamete Intrafallopian Transfer (GIFT), shows a similar rhetorical pattern.[13] Following the description of infertility indications, the GIFT procedure, and the success rates per patient and per cycle, the authors discuss medical advantages of GIFT over IVF. One of the major advantages of GIFT, according to the authors, is that the embryo is never outside the woman's body, since fertilization occurs after the egg and sperm are replaced in the Fallopian tube. The fact that 'the embryo is never extracorporeal suggests that orthodox religions, such as Roman Catholicism, will accept GIFT,' the researchers argue. Not a medical, but a religious argument is used to acclaim the effectiveness and marketability of this reproductive technology. The authors conclude the article expressing their hope that this new procedure will find its proper role in the treatment of infertility. Acceptance by religious standards appears to enhance the viability of this technological variation on the market.

Ethical and religious objections to reproductive technologies are discussed in virtually every journal article on IVF between 1978 and 1984.[14] Ethical objections are similarly anticipated and accommodated in medical discourse as religious objections. The first application of Embryo Transfer (ET), a technique which had previously been used to generate prize herds from single pairs of cattle, was first successfully applied in 1983, when two women became pregnant and delivered healthy babies.[15] Researchers from the Harbor UCLA Medical Center called a press conference to coincide with the announcement of their success in *The Lancet* of July 23. The *Journal of the American Medical Association (JAMA)* subsequently reports on the technique in its column 'Medical News.'[16] The column is a hybrid of a medical report and an interview with the researchers involved. After a detailed explanation of the procedure itself, doctor Richard Seed (what's in a name?), one of the inventors who filed patent applications for instruments and methods employed in ET, emphasizes the indispensable need for corporate funding in the development of new reproductive technologies. He likes to think of the ET procedure 'in terms of industry, where large numbers of process grants have been granted.'

The first successful Embryo Transfer is also reported in *Fertility Assistance*, a newsletter issued by the Institute for Fertility Assistance in Ann Arbor, Michigan.[17] Newsletters like the *IVF Report* and *Fertility Assistance* are regularly published by infertility centres to report the latest developments in reproductive medicine, research and treatment to clients or prospective clients of IVF treatment centres. *Fertility Assistance* resembles a newspaper in format and lay-out: double vertical columns, headlines, and subheadings characterize the articles. As a newsletter, the discursive format veils the function of this text as a marketing tool by borrowing the features of journalism discourse. The illusion of objectivity invoked by the newspaper lay-out is further enhanced by the article format and content, which has all the features of a regular newspaper article. Announcing a 'giant step forward' in alternative reproduction, the lead heralds the birth of two healthy babies as a result of the first successful embryo transfer. Neither the babies, nor the women who bore them, but the heroism of industrial investors is the focus of this article. The research program at Harbor UCLA

Medical Center was funded by Fertility and Genetics Research Inc., a Chicago based company. This corporation, which has taken the initiative to patent the technique, confidently predicts 'several thousand births in the United States each year.'

Having adopted the journalistic format, the author questions in a perfunctory fashion the involvement of a commercial company in the development of medical processes. Acknowledging that 'many have objected to this, saying that turning pregnancy into a profit-making business could harm research,' the argument is hastily rejected by the company's Chairman of the Board, Mr Sucsy. He first compares infertility treatment to kidney dialysis, which is also a patented technique, and subsequently argues that the involvement of industry in research increases efficiency and guarantees quality control. The journalistic routine of balance, signifying the 'objectivity' of the report, is thus applied to promote the interest of a for-profit industry as a nonprofit, general interest.

In addition, the same journalistic device of balance is deployed to counteract religious objections to ET. Father Donald McCarthy of the Medical-Moral Education Center in St. Louis is first quoted as saying that the marital act is the 'only fitting context for sharing the divine act of human creation.' But in an extensive reaction, Chairman Sucsy explains that ET is more natural than IVF. Echoing the kind of argument used by scientists in *Fertility and Sterility* to defend the GIFT procedure, Sucsy supports his claim that Embryo Transfer is 'closest to natural conjugal procreation' by saying that it allows conception to take place in the body. Downplaying the commercial interest of his enterprise, Sucsy gets assigned the last words of the article: 'Each time we create a family unit, we are inching our way toward a better world.'[18]

The conventions of journalism, anchoring the ideals of balance and fairness, are fully exploited to sell a specific technique to a targeted group of interested buyers: infertile couples. Commercial companies borrow the legitimacy of journalism discourse to give their products an altruistic sheen, and acquire an aura of 'truth.' Religious objections and objections to the commercial nature of reproductive technologies put forward in the article do not serve to balance off opposing sides of the issue, but to give the initial pass for rejecting any objection to reproductive technologies. Journalism, like science discourse, is deployed by special interest groups to commodify and market IVF and related technologies, while simultaneously expanding and emphasizing the need for them by pointing to the large number of infertile couples desperately waiting for treatment. It is interesting to notice how the discourses of science, information and advertising blend, almost beyond recognition, in the newsletter format: reproductive technologies are authorized by medical scientists, who use the discourse of journalism to promote a commercial interest.

FROM CURE TO PLAGUE

The definition of infertility, used as an indication for IVF treatment, is almost invisibly expanded in medical journals from women with blocked Fallopian tubes to all women and men with (potential) fertility problems. As religious and ethical objections are swiftly appropriated by medical discourse, I have shown how (info-) science publications exploit rhetorical conventions of journalism to disseminate a particular view on IVF to a wider audience. But science is not the only discursive site at which the market for IVF is constructed; a similar construction of need can be witnessed in the news media, where the phenomenon of infertility takes on unlikely proportions. As the analysis of a 1984 article in *Time* magazine will reveal, journalists use the 'logic' of medical evidence and the power of metaphors to launch a specific interpretation of infertility as a relentless plague. In doing so, they simultaneously help create a potentially lucrative market for IVF technology.

Six years after the birth of Louise Brown, *Time* again dedicates a cover story to IVF. This 1984 report purports to review the state-of-the-art in infertility treatment, and the various feasible future applications of new reproductive technologies.[19] Contrary to what its headline suggests, the article focuses on the 'disease' rather than its technological remedies. The first sentence of the lead sets the tone for the rest of the story: 'Already science has produced an array of artificial methods for creating life, offering solutions to the growing problem of infertility.' Childless couples are waiting for science to bring them hope, and their numbers are rising 'dramatically.'

A special side story illuminates the extent of 'the saddest epidemic,' as its headline suggests. The incidence of 'child-lessness' – a term which is used interchangeably with infertility – has 'jumped 177% between 1965 and 1982' and 'now affects one in six American couples' (46). These statistics, supposedly used to prove the seriousness of the epidemic, are based on a report from the National Center for Health Statistics. But the numbers are not in the least conclusive: depending on the kind of definition used to mark infertility and the kind of statistical analysis deployed to determine the extent of infertility cases, the outcome will vary. For one thing, it does not become clear from the *Time* article whether people who are childless by choice are included in these numbers. And even if infertility is uniformly defined as the 'failure to conceive after one year of unprotected intercourse,' the definition allows for many interpretations.[20]

A 1985 article in *The Lancet* cautiously expounds on the arbitrary analysis of infertility cases, which complicates a systematic description of infertility patterns: previous analyses (like the one from the National Center for Health Statistics) have been based on literature reviews rather than on a single comprehensive data base.[21] Moreover, each IVF centre reports on infertility using its own unique method of diagnosing, classifying and treating infertile patients. 'The lack of unifor-mity, the differences in the extent of the investigation of each partner, the variation in selecting patients for treatment, and differences in follow-up, make it impossible to compare these data,' concludes *The Lancet*.

Since an unambiguous medical definition of infertility appears to be unfeasible, the evidence for an epidemic seems highly unlikely. The figure 'one out of six,' which, after being first quoted in *Time*, starts to live a life of its own as a medical fact, turns out to have little basis in medical research. The preliminary 1981 survey from the National Center for Health Statistics got widespread recognition and attention; when the Center published the definite results of a nationwide survey three years later, it appeared that infertility had actually declined since 1965.[22] The statistics that contradicted the myth of the infertility epidemic never received any media attention, in contrast to the 'mythical' numbers which can still be found in news media accounts today.[23] These misleading statistics are not just quoted by popular news magazines, but also by medical journals which try to legitimize their expensive search for new infertility treatments.

It is not until 1987 that the myth of the infertility epidemic is officially contradicted in both Britain and the United States by medical research. A study in the *British Medical Journal* by eleven general practitioners, examining the medical records of all women on their lists born in 1935 and 1950, finds no significant increase in infertility cases.[24] In addition, the survey shows a significant rise in voluntary childlessness, as well as a one hundred per cent increase in demands for specialist referrals. The conclusion that four-and-a-half per cent of the general population can be properly defined as infertile contradicts previous statistical projections of eight to ten per cent published in the *Journal of the American Medical Association*, and the 'one out of six' suggested by the National Center for Health Statistics in 1983.[25] Neither of these studies denying the myth of an infertility epidemic received the big headlines which accompanied the announcement of the 'plague.' In 1988, the Office of Technology Assessment (OTA) officially denies an epidemic has anywhere near existed in the USA.[26] The journal *Nature* discusses the implications of the OTA report for IVF clinics and research centres.[27] The most important conclusion is that the number of infertility incidences has remained stable over the past fifteen years; if the percentage of infertile couples has not changed, the numbers seeking treatment have increased substantially, and 'infertility therapy has become big business in the U.S.,' according to *Nature*.[28]

The use of statistics is a popular journalistic device to make stories look objective, scientifically sound and beyond interpretation. However, statistics are always interpretations of data, and even these data are the result of a predisposed method of inquiry. The limitations of gathering, analysing and evaluating data are well known among scientists and journalists, who are all perfectly aware that a simple percentage like 'one out of six' can never even remotely 'prove' a phenomenon as complex as infertility. The impact of *Time*'s 'scientifically backed up' claim lies mostly in the discursive format, which favours the invocation of authoritative sources over complex evaluations. The presentation of statistics directs the reader into accepting these numbers as 'facts,' thus discouraging any active involvement in the construction of meaning. Few readers will look for (contradictory or affirmative) sources besides the ones presented by the journalist, to dispute the interpretation of infertility as an epidemic.

As an argument appealing to logic, statistical evidence would not have been as convincing if it were not accompanied by powerful images and analogies. Disquieting metaphors illustrate the construction of infertility as a disease in *Time* magazine: scientists are fighting a 'cruel and unyielding enemy,' an 'epidemic' and even a 'plague.' Military, medical and biblical images all intertwine to emphasize the severity of the problem and the heroism of doctors.

Biblical connotations and metaphors saturate the story, and serve to both accommodate and rebut religious objections to IVF and related technologies. The 'plague' metaphor allows doctors to be heralded as saviours of human life. Six years after the advent of the first test-tube baby, Steptoe's and Edwards's clinic is revisited by the *Time* reporter, who depicts researchers and doctors as 'saints' and 'assistants of nature.' One observer in the waiting room of the clinic observes: 'They [infertile women] depend on Mr Steptoe utterly. Knowing him is like dying and being a friend of St. Peter's.' Technical details of IVF procedures are more abundant than in the 1978 *Time* report, but they are significantly phrased in terms of religion and nature. Doctors 'harvest eggs,' which are 'gently waiting' in dishes, while sperm is 'washed' to become more likely to 'penetrate' in order to achieve the 'transcendent moment of union.' Infertility clinics, according to *Time*, 'help nature along by administering drugs' so that a woman feels like a 'pumpkin ready to burst.' IVF becomes metaphorically aligned as a natural concept, which in turn warrants the author's claim that it will soon become a 'standard part of medical practice.' This report in *Time* magazine absorbs religious objections to IVF and transforms them to fit a dominant definition in a similar fashion as previously observed in medical journals.

Religious imagery is thus deployed to strengthen medical discourse; as a structuring metaphor, the 'epidemic' is even more distorting than the 'plague,' presumably because it is barely recognizable as a metaphor. An epidemic presupposes the rapid transmission of a disease – commonly a contagious virus – among a certain population or community. Evidently, infertility cannot be 'spread' and neither can it be contagious, but the very use of the term implies differently. And like any plague or epidemic, this one naturally appears to have its vigilantes who somehow deserve to be punished by the disease:

> Doctors place much of the blame for the epidemic on liberalized sexual attitudes, which in women have led to an increasing occurrence of genital infections known collectively as pelvic inflammatory disease . . . Other attitudes are also at fault: by postponing childbirth until their mid- and even late 30s, women risk a barren future . . . Other surveys have found that such athletic women as distance runners, dancers and joggers can suffer temporary infertility. Stress can also suppress ovulation; women executives often miss two or three consecutive menstrual periods. (50)

According to this description in *Time*, the dramatic 'infertility epidemic' has commenced with the women's liberation movement, which incited women to assume men's jobs and neglect their naturally assigned duties: the procreation of human life. The focus in this passage shifts unmarkedly from infertility treatment to infertility cause, as the emphasis shifts concurrently from medical aspects of the disease to aspects concerning lifestyle. The implication that women's behaviour has disrupted the 'natural' order of things, is amplified by the assumption that women's collective disobedience has called the disease upon them. These shifting emphases in the reporting of infertility strikingly resembles mainstream coverage of AIDS in this era, which also tends to highlight the deviant character of the victims rather than the problematic aspects of the illness itself.[29] The use of medical images in relation to the intense use of religious imagery seems to account for the reinterpretation of 'cause' as 'blame.' More significantly, 'cause' is exclusively interpreted in terms of 'blame,' and not in terms of treatment.

These images press the reader to perceive of women as both the perpetrators and the victims of this terrible disease. Paradoxically, the same paragraph from which the above quote is taken, reveals that male deficiencies account for infertility forty per cent of the time, the same percentage as deficiencies in females, whereas problems with both members of the couple account for the remaining twenty per cent. However, the equally high percentages of male infertility causes lead the

Time journalist to conclude that infertility is a woman's disease and not a man's problem. The exclusive interpretation of female causes, while being equal to those of men, appears to be self-evident; apparently, women are predisposed to be afflicted with reproductive defects, and therefore, treatment also applies exclusively to this group. Since they are the cause of infertility, they are destined to suffer for the collective curse they have called upon them: 'Doctors are also beginning to use IVF as a solution to male infertility,' the *Time* journalist observes in the side-story, as if it were a mere footnote to the main text. This casual comment, however, betrays the powerful norm that women are unconditionally to blame for reproductive mishaps and irregularities; this implied assumption makes it acceptable that even when men are to blame, women must bleed.

Resonating the expanded definition of infertility in medical journals, *Time* represents IVF as the cure-all for infertility, regardless of its (differentiated) cause. But is the myth of infertility – a disease solely inflicted by and affecting women – created by journalists? Or are these assumptions shared by medical researchers and do they also show in medical journal articles? What do journalists add to the story of infertility? As the article in *Time* clearly reveals, causes for female infertility are defined in terms of behaviour or life-style. Male infertility, however, is primarily inferred by biological or environmental factors. 'Low sperm counts' according to *Time*, are commonly caused by 'varicose veins on the left testicle' and 'chemicals such as insecticides' (50). The explanation of the roots of the epidemic is differentiated in terms of gender: while women's decrease in fecundity is caused by self-inflicted behaviour, men's fate is destined by biology or environment, two things over which men have no control. These explanations in *Time* can be retraced in scientific research; in medical journals I found research reports that examine cigarettes, alcohol, drugs, and even caffeinated beverages as the cause of decreased fertility in women.[30] Assumed factors that affect male fertility include 'exposure to environmental toxins' and 'genetic and hormonal abnormalities.'[31]

The 'popularization' of IVF and infertility in *Time* has neither distorted nor sensationalized medical research. Instead, the language of journalism, however inflated and disturbingly filled with fear, has emerged fully shaped by medicine itself. Neither journalists nor scientists can be pinpointed as creators of this myth; the reason why this explanation is so powerful is because its (scientific and journalistic) assumptions are rooted in dominant social norms and values: as the assumptions seem self-evident, the explanations sound only natural. The *Time* journalist obviously does not question the biased research assumptions because they are the norm; the journalist's exclusive interpretation of female causes of infertility can go unnoticed because the reader is supposed to share this norm. The images conveyed in *Time* and medical journals do not innocently reflect dominant norms: they concomitantly enhance and shape the very norms by which they are informed.

The shaping power of medical and journalism discourse becomes evident when we further examine the construction of the infertility myth. The article in *Time* suggests that this cruel disease does not affect women indiscriminately, but targets a particular group of females; evidenced by the descriptions and pictures illustrating the article, infertility 'strikes' primarily white, affluent women, mostly working in well paid positions. The journalistic interpretation in *Time* is mirrored by equally biased assumptions in medical research. Numerous reports state that infertility strikes upper class women who 'want to have it all' – that is smoke, drink (coffee), work, exercise, have sex and still have a baby! Contrary to this popular representation, however, incidences of infertility occur mostly among the nonwhite, the poor and poorly educated.[32] Nonwhite women are one and a half times more likely to be infertile than their white counterparts, while the dominant picture we get in *Time* and other news media is that of minority women and women on welfare as 'breeders.' As Valerie Hartouni (1991) aptly sums up:

> Both text and subtext are straightforward: white women want babies but cannot have them, and black and other 'minority' women, coded as 'breeders' within American society (and welfare dependents within Reagan's America), are having babies 'they' cannot take care of and 'we' do not want. (46)

In the scientific explanation of infertility, factors of race and class are conspicuous by their absence. The image of infertility as a 'disease' that strikes particularly white, middle class women not just reflects the pronatalist and racist agenda of conservative politics; it also reflects the vital commercial interests of the medical industry. Can it be a coincidence that primarily affluent, usually white couples can afford IVF treatment?

The cogency of the infertility myth, as presented in *Time*, is constituted by its apparent groundedness in irrefutable 'medical facts' and statistical numbers. The journalist obviously selects those statistics and research results which enhance a perception of a disease that affects primarily white, affluent women; facts which might challenge or contradict an unambiguous interpretation are clearly ignored. In contrast to the 1978 article in *Time*, new reproductive technologies are no longer framed as a controversial 'miracle,' or as posing a 'moral dilemma' which allows for several views. In 1984, the *Time* reporter deploys medical claims to support and authorize a definition of infertility as an exclusively medical problem, to which IVF is the only logical and sensible solution. Through the deployment of metaphors and analogies, future investments in new reproductive technology are rendered self-evident. The persuasive power of this article is precisely in the narrative ordering of 'facts': the cause of infertility leads to a natural acceptance of the proposed cure. The presentation of infertility in IVF is symptomatic and symbolic for other representations in mainstream media accounts.

Ethical, moral, and religious objections to IVF – still viable at the beginning of the debate – have to yield to medical definitions of reproduction as the discussion proceeds. Rather than being excluded from the debate altogether, opposing voices are instead appropriated by dominant definitions. In fact, the medical definition gains in persuasiveness by adapting other discourses and absorbing other arguments. Both in medical articles and journalistic accounts, religious and ethical objections to IVF are smoothly aligned with appeals to humanistic and spiritual values.

In the first stage of the debate, it becomes clear that different voices structure the discussion on new reproductive technologies. The stories do not work as isolated incidences, but as a curriculum; they contain and construct each other. The interpretation of IVF and reproduction is discussed in medical journals, news media accounts and fiction; in this contest, the medical meaning becomes increasingly privileged over others. The discourses of journalism and science are effectively used in the construction of 'facts.' A rhetorical analysis yields insight in the vital interests that are at stake: the interests to establish a normative definition of IVF as a much needed technology. The creation of a (potential) market is evidently one of the prime results of this first round in the battle for signification. Voices critical of IVF, particular ethical and religious objections, are smoothly incorporated in scientific accounts that claim the indispensability of this new technique. Yet as the second round commences, a more vocal opponent comes into play: the voice of feminists.

4 Feminist Assessments of New Reproductive Technologies

A regulated percentage of each household – say one-third - would be children. But whether, at first, genetic children created by couples within the household, or, at some future time, children were produced artificially or adopted, would not matter . . . [W]e must be aware that as long as we use natural childbirth methods the 'household' could never be a totally liberating social form. A mother who undergoes a nine month pregnancy is likely to feel that the product of all that pain and discomfort 'belongs' to her.

(Shulamith Firestone, *The Dialectic of Sex*)

It was part of women's long revolution. When we were breaking all the old hierarchies. Finally there was that one thing we had to give up too, the only power we ever had, in return for no more power for anyone. The original production: the power to give birth. Cause as long as we were biologically enchained, we'd never be equal. And males never would be humanized to be loving and tender. So we all became mothers. Every child has three. To break the nuclear bonding.

(Marge Piercy, *Women on the Edge of Time*)

INTRODUCTION

While objections to IVF in the first stage of the debate came mostly from the religious side, between 1984 and 1987 particularly feminist voices galvanized the discussion. Yet feminist assessments of new reproductive technologies predate the actual birth of the first so-called test-tube baby. Two important feminist predictions on the consequences of artificial reproduction for women were published in the 1970s: Shulamith Firestone's *The Dialectic of Sex* (1970) and Marge Piercy's *Women on the Edge of Time* (1975). Both Firestone and Piercy envisioned reproductive technologies to be liberating instruments, which could help women achieve a non-sexist society. Their views have had substantial impact on feminist contributions to the debate on new reproductive technologies in the 1980s.

In her theoretical blueprint for a revolt against the nuclear family, Firestone assumes that biological motherhood lies at the heart of woman's oppression. In *The Dialectic of Sex*, she contends that if technology replaces the chores of pregnancy and childbirth − hence erasing the differences between men and women − the hierarchy between the sexes will be nullified. Firestone unambiguously celebrates the promises of new reproductive technologies, tools which in her view facilitate the liberation process of women and free them from their constraining reproductive roles in society.

In her utopian antidote to Aldous Huxley's *Brave New World*, Marge Piercy explores the imaginative territory laid out in Firestone's theory. She envisions a culturally androgynous society, based on feminist values, where the reproductive process occurs outside the body; genetic material taken from human males and females is stored in 'brooders' where it is fertilized and where embryos are grown until they are ready for birth. The new technologies in Piercy's novel help erase all reproductive differences between men and women; by the same token, the bond between genes and culture is deliberately broken, and genetic engineering aims at effacing racial inequalities. In Piercy's utopia, abolishing difference is the solution to sexism and racism; technology that may help achieve this goal thus becomes a desirable tool in women's striving for liberation. In contrast to Firestone, Piercy also anticipates a potential repressive usage of the new technologies, as she lets her protagonist Connie see a glimpse of a possible totalitarian state, a society dominated by men and technology, which may emerge if Connie does not stop the experiments of scientists in the mental hospital to which she is confined. This potential horror scenario, however, functions as a warning to her overall positive interpretation of a full implementation of new reproductive technologies.

What is significant about both Firestone's and Piercy's early feminist speculations is that they perceive of a woman's capacity to reproduce as the problem, rather than the way in which reproduction is valued and organized within society. In other words, because they find a woman's function as childbearer a hindrance to equality, they are inclined to erase her specific reproductive role rather than change the perception and validation of it. Both Firestone and Piercy present physiological and genetic difference as a problem to which reproductive technologies are *the* solution. Their representations have elicited conflicting responses, causing division and mutual disagreement among different groups of feminists.

Between 1984 and 1987, feminists acquired the public image of being radically opposed to all reproductive technologies. The most vocal group of feminists indeed perceived of IVF and similar techniques as a direct threat to women's reproductive freedom. Regarding the technologies as pre-eminent instruments of male control, this particular group of feminists defined the issue exclusively in terms of gender – a struggle of women against men who have power over science and medicine. However, feminist assessments of new reproductive technologies were far from homogeneous. Other groups have acclaimed the benevolence of technology for women, or argued for a more balanced evaluation of science and technology.

As feminist assessment of patriarchal power changed, the emphasis of criticism shifted from the institutions of power to the interrelation between medicine, politics, law, and their discourses. The dualistic construction of gender was replaced by a stratified concept, in which gender is intrinsically interwoven with other factors such as race and class. Concurrently, feminists started to reconsider the textual and discursive strategies in which their critique was expressed, and the publications and discourses which mediated their views. The awareness that representation is intrinsically part of an ideological struggle results in a growing interest in the politics of representation.

Despite the diversity of feminist responses to the new technologies, their common concern was the protection of women's reproductive rights. I think it is essential to both historicize and contextualize feminist assessments. The different groups of feminist writers articulating critique or dissent are particularly concerned with positioning themselves in the public debate. Consequently, oppositional voices should be analysed in relation to dominant definitions of new reproductive technology; yet feminist assessments should also be studied as a dialogue among partial ideological allies negotiating the parameters and terms of debate. A range of voices arguing from different feminist positions raise the question of what 'feminism' actually entails. Feminism, like power, is not a monolithic force; rather, it is an assemblage of views which partially overlap but also diverge.

CONSTRUCTING A COUNTERMYTH

While reproduction, in the early 1980s, was becoming a privileged trope for the logic of expansion and investment, a group of feminists started to vocally oppose what they called the 'capitalist takeover' of the reproductive process. In 1984, at a women's studies conference in Groningen (The Netherlands), the Feminist International Network on New Reproductive Technologies (FINNRET, later FINNRAGE) was founded, to function as an organized discussion platform.[1] Members of FINNRAGE actively started campaigning against the implementation of all new reproductive technologies, because they considered them to be an unequivocal threat to the lives and rights of women. Their manifesto, *Test-Tube Women*, edited by Rita Arditti, along with Renate Duelli Klein and Gena Corea, was published in 1984. Most of the thirty-six essays also appeared, in slightly different forms, in feminist journals or newsletters.[2]

The introduction to *Test-Tube Women*, written by the three editors, sets the political agenda for a feminist protest. Shulamith Firestone's contention that the new technologies might contribute to women's liberation is vehemently dismissed: new reproductive technologies are the instruments of oppression, and not the instruments to fight oppression. Arditti regards science and technology as harmful to women, in large measure because the technological instruments are in the hands of men, and will thus be used to control and oppress women. The editors also reject the possibility of a feminist contribution to science; science is inherently patriarchal, so the only thing women 'in' science can do is act as 'spies': 'to distribute what they learn as widely as possible to the feminist media worldwide' (5). The tone of the introduction to *Test-Tube Women* is such that it pits men against women, producers against resources, the powerful against the powerless. Women are the 'targets' of technological manipulation, victims of systematic oppression: 'We are not in control, neither at the professional level as scientists or doctors, nor at the personal level as consumers' (2). While scientists are constructed as evil men, women are simultaneously constructed as helpless victims, thus reifying social relations along gender lines.

This binary opposition and the tone of anger and suspicion structures most contributions to this collection of articles. Jana Halmner, in her polemical essay 'A Womb of One's Own,' develops the theory that the scientific-medical control of men over women has resulted in a full-fledged conspiracy.[3] Arguing that the world is dominated by men, Halmner expects new reproductive technologies to be used as instruments in the pursuit of absolute male dominance, turning women into guinea pigs for experimental research. To achieve their goal, medical scientists have conspired with journalists and politicians, using the media to inculcate their ideas to a wider audience: 'In the promotion of reproductive technologies, relations between professional groups, the state and the media are not limited solely to scientists and medical men. Social scientists are also implicated' (443).

In Halmner's as well as other contributions to *Test-Tube Women*, women are the vulnerable targets of a male brotherhood that is out to colonize women and take over their reproductive power. Images of 'breeding brothels' and 'egg farms' abound; a complete 'war on the womb' and 'hormonal bombardments of the ovaries' are used to describe the IVF process. The way these images are deployed, remarkably reminds one of the metaphors used in *Time* Magazine. Halmner projects emotions of fear and inevitable catastrophe on the concept of technology. Depicting women as unconditional victims of a scientists' conspiracy, she almost mirrors the construction of women as victims of an 'infertility plague' in *Time*. Both depictions render women helpless and unable to escape their collective fate.

While some feminists regard patriarchy to be at the heart of this conspiracy, others hold capitalism responsible for the evils of reproductive technologies. Renate Duelli Klein, another FINNRAGE-member, targets the patriarchal system in her

critique, published in a feminist journal.[4] Acknowledging the
benevolence of IVF to some infertile women in a perfunctory
fashion, she claims that reproductive technologies in general are
disastrous for women, and argues that feminists should regard
IVF not as a personal or medical problem, but as a political
issue. Klein adds to the conspiracy myth by claiming that it is
male scientists – 'technodocs' as she persistently calls them – who
hold all power with respect to both technology and politics, and
who use this power against women. She even claims to have
'proof' of this conspiracy, which is mainly concocted at academic
conferences from which women are excluded:

> Thanks to international research done by women we now
> have extensive proof of the worldwide capitalist 'brotherhood'
> of science, medicine and technology . . . Reproductive
> technology experts meet at international conferences and
> mark their territory by showing who has the best technique,
> who will have the next successful breakthrough and, finally,
> who will be the ultimate winner in the race toward the total
> domination of nature; toward the total elimination of women
> once the artificial womb has been perfected; towards the
> moment when men (sic) will play God and be the sole
> procreator of the human species. Will Frankenstein become
> reality once man can create man? (93–4)

Here again, rhetorical devices favoured by *Time* are similarly
deployed in the construction of a feminist countermyth: the
threat to 'eliminate' women by scientists who pretend to play
God (but who are in fact devils), is clearly reminiscent of the
depiction of Steptoe and Edwards in *Time*. Renate Klein
resuscitates Frankenstein horrors to draw the worst possible
scenarios for women's future; these images should prove her
contention that in any case women will be ruled out from power.
    The only possibility of fighting the conspiracy, according to
Klein and other FINNRAGE-members, is for women to go out
and 'find as many facts as possible' on reproductive technologies.
By this she means that feminists should move into the bastions of
science to increase their knowledge of technology. She
emphasizes the need for making these collected facts widely
available through mass media, in order to 'translat[e] the
mystifying jargon of scientific literature into a language that we

can all understand' (96). By learning the language of science, women would be able to confront scientists on their own turf. Klein apparently conceives of medical discourse as a 'secret' language which needs to be deciphered and subsequently translated into ordinary language; initiation into 'their' language will allow women to fight patriarchal constructions of reproduction on 'their' own discursive terms. Klein's proposal to 'steal' the language of scientists, and use it to women's advantage, reveals her assumption that the discourse of science is indeed distinct from everyday language, and that it is inaccessible to anyone but scientists. Yet her proposal reinforces the elevated, specialist status of science discourse; rather than viewing science as part of culture at large, Klein confirms its institutional and discursive privileged position.

Along with the other editors of *Test-Tube Women*, Klein also seems to imply that were new reproductive technologies in the hands of women, they would be used to their benefit. This assumption is radically opposed by Maria Mies, another feminist detractor of the new technologies. In a paper published in the grass-roots feminist journal, *Women's Studies International Forum*, she explains how 'highly priced technology is employed for the mastery over and political control of people.'[5] According to Mies, it makes absolutely no difference whether men or women control the new technologies. She renounces Shulamith Firestone and other feminist thinkers who argue that technology, if in the hands of women, can be liberating. Technology is invariably capitalist, so the very thought of a feminist use of reproductive technology is, in Mies's view, an illusion. Men deploy reproductive technologies in the service of capitalism and use women as a resource to multiply capital.[6]

Like Klein, Mies defines reproductive technologies as a threat, and a political problem; in Marxist terms, IVF and such are invariably aimed at stimulating (over)consumption, at the expense of nature and powerless groups. The only remedy in Mies's view is to 'opt out of capitalist logic,' implying that women should resist all use of reproductive technologies. Feminists should not even argue with advocates of these techniques, since their logics are mutually exclusive: 'We shall never beat them on their own ground and with their own logic' (5). However, Mies actually accommodates the logic of the argument she so fiercely rejects. In her article, she lists eight reasons why technology in general could be useful. For instance, Mies admits that technology could mitigate heavy human labour, shorten working time, and eliminate poverty in the Third World. She subsequently refutes any of these eight arguments by repeating that Western capitalism will result in nothing but colonialism and exploitation.

Mies's litany of repetitive rebuttals results in the conclusion that women under this system will remain 'imprisoned in the home as housewives.' Thus arguing, Mies holds what she considers the 'conglomerate' of politicians, medical industrialists, and journalists accountable for the harm that reproductive technologies cause to women – unwitting victims of state apparatuses. Paradoxically, this feminist attempt to redefine reproductive technology dangerously approaches the dominant definition itself. In fact, by using similar argumentative strategies and metaphorical constructions, feminist discourse fosters its own colonization. It simply endorses the dualisms used in mainstream journalism and science journals, and therefore makes itself vulnerable to co-optation. The assumed opposition between capitalist-male perpetrators and anti-capitalist female victims perfectly fits the binary frameworks that mainstream news media use to represent the issue.

Not surprisingly, the *Wall Street Journal* picks up the 'counter-attack' launched by Klein, Mies, Corea and others to expatiate upon the controversy.[7] The opening sentence of this 1985 article represents a common journalistic convention to frame discussions in terms of war: 'Radical feminists are targeting a new enemy: artificial birth methods.' Describing Gena Corea as the 'leading polemicist of this feminist viewpoint,' and quoting the founding of FINNRAGE as a 'declaration of war,' the issue of reproductive technologies is reduced to a fairly predictable power struggle – it simply mirrors the 'battle between the sexes' in other areas of public discourse. As the rhetoric of war commonly attributes equal power to each side, the assumed threat of feminism to the medical-political establishment is blown out of proportions by the journalist of the *Wall Street Journal*:

> But the radical-feminist attack goes further, taking off from a longstanding hostility in some quarters towards medicine in general, and towards obstetrics and gynaecology in particular.

Feminist critics charge that these fields have historically tended to abuse women's bodies (and possibly cause considerable infertility in the process) with needless Caesarian sections, hysterectomies and other damaging options.

The journalistic narrative used in the *Wall Street Journal* easily incorporates the terms and rhetoric launched by Mies, Klein, Corea and others; dominant myth and countermyth appear to constitute each other's mirrors. Because feminist counterdiscourse presupposes the hegemony of its 'other,' the dominant surreptitiously turns out to have penetrated the counterdiscourse which sought to attack it.

This particular feminist definition of new reproductive technologies as a male capitalist conspiracy against women, configures what Barthes (1972) would call a 'myth on the left.' Left-wing myths, like Stalinism, are inessential because they borrow the form and signifiers of dominant myths, and reduce these signifiers to a litany.[8] Countermyths are ineffective because they always define themselves in relation to the oppressors; the very definition of women as victims of 'malestream science,' as illustrated by the *Wall Street Journal*, is quickly absorbed by mainstream journalism. Another reason why countermyths are never effective, according to Barthes, is that they usually consist of 'stolen language,' which takes on the form of a mathematical formula so it seems like it cannot be argued. Mies's repetitive argument that reproductive technology is inherently an extension of capitalist power blocks all other (feminist) assessments of reproductive technologies, not allowing for any differences in interpretation.

Radical feminists often claim to act 'in the name of women' in their vocal and sometimes even militant resistance to the new technologies. The 'war' between the sexes, as provocatively stated by the *Wall Street Journal*, gains significance when, in the mid-1980s, IVF centres start to be attacked by feminist groups. A German underground guerilla named 'Rote Zora,' commits numerous 'subversive' acts, ranging from bombing IVF clinics to burglarizing these clinics to destroy equipment and steal documents and files.[9] In December of 1987, the police arrests two members of the 'Gen-Archiv,' a feminist documentation centre seeking a state ban on all reproductive technologies; the two arrested women were accused of 'terrorist activities.' The burglaries and bombings of IVF clinics in Germany coincide with violent attacks on abortion clinics in the USA by religious anti-abortion groups; strategies preferred by radical feminist groups peculiarly correspond to those managed by religious fanatics. Yet while the first group fights to defend women's reproductive power, the latter disputes the right of women to make their own reproductive decisions.

Radical feminist voices not only presume a unanimous feminist stance on the issue of reproductive technologies, they also assume an unambiguous and simplified distinction between scientists and feminists. The perception of all scientists as representatives of male power engenders the reductionist view of all women as powerless victims. In other words, the rigorous definition of the issue in terms of gender entails an unyielding containment of women as a homogeneous group, and precludes differences among feminists' assessments of reproductive technologies; in addition, it reduces scientists to a caricatural monstrous enemy, an image which may have inspired the bombings and attacks on IVF clinics.

Because of the presumed antagonism between feminists and scientists, feminists initially address their concerns almost exclusively to a sympathetic audience. Special meetings and conferences are organized frequently in the mid-eighties to discuss strategies and define feminists' common cause with regard to the new technologies.[10] Most articles by FINNRAGE-members are published in radical feminist magazines, distributed among a small, but internationally oriented, readership. Not all feminist opponents of IVF consider it strategic though, to publish solely in their own journals. Few feminists choose to channel their argument against reproductive technology to an audience that is not primarily interested in feminist issues but that is professionally interested in relating science to social issues.

A science journal that regularly offers a forum for voices critical of science and technology is *The New Scientist*. In a 1986 edition, the push for IVF is analysed by two authors who clearly identify themselves as feminists: Anita Direcks and Helen Bequaert Holmes both work for women health organizations.[11] The article provides a well researched and documented review, which not only critically evaluates IVF as a technological device, but also the way it is marketed by both medicine and journalism.

Pivotal to their discussion is the comparison of IVF treatment to DES, the drug that was routinely administered in the 1950s as a measure to prevent miscarriage, even if the need for this drug was not medically indicated. Like IVF, Direcks and Holmes argue, DES was promoted as a 'wonder drug' that resulted in 'wonder babies,' and both therapies received equally big headlines in the press. In both cases, journalists uncritically endorsed the promising and glowing reports published in medical journals, despite a lack of common criteria for assessing the success of treatment. Researchers doubting the effect of DES were largely ignored and never given much credit; the acceptance of the drug as standard treatment came to justify its need until, two decades later, it was proven to cause cancer and hormonal abnormalities in children born of mothers who used the drug during pregnancy.

The comparison allows the authors to reveal a serious deficiency in the representation of IVF in medical journals and the lay press: both present this kind of infertility treatment as a 'mechanical' procedure, deliberately omitting or minimizing the large quantities of hormones and drugs that are administered to women. Neither medical accounts, nor journalistic articles pay much attention to extensive drug therapy, surgery and anaesthesia involved in IVF. Extending the comparison, DES was initially prescribed to women with one specific physical problem, just as IVF was first prescribed to women with blocked Fallopian tubes, but was at a later stage ordered as a preventive medicine to many pregnant woman, regardless of symptoms or history of miscarriage. In addition, Direcks and Holmes draw attention to the implications of routinizing any treatment which has not yet proven to be without serious side-effects. The omnipresence of technology increases the imperative to use it, and reinforces the suggestion that it is safe and harmless, even when its future ramifications are yet unknown. Or, as the authors phrase their question rhetorically: 'In 1986, subfertile sons and daughters are putting their names on the waiting lists for in vitro fertilization. What does the future hold for their sons and daughters?' (55).

The comparison of these two types of treatment both subverts and accommodates dominant medical discourse. Just as researchers have likened IVF to heart bypasses or artificial kidneys to claim this technology's benevolence, Direcks and Holmes use the analogy to DES to 'prove' the detrimental effects of IVF. In doing so, they subversively shift the emphasis from the mechanical part of infertility treatment to its chemical component, highlighting the politically strategic omission of extensive drug and hormone therapy from regular accounts of IVF procedures. Direcks and Holmes, in *The New Scientist*, thus use the narrative conventions of the medical article genre to counteract the dominant image of IVF as an innocent and medically sound therapy. However, the same analogy also accommodates medical discourse, because it can be contradicted on purely medical grounds. Providing statistical evidence of disastrous longterm effects of DES use, they imply that similar defects will be revealed in 'IVF children' years from now. This speculative vision can easily be dismissed by arguing that treatments proven to be harmful in the past cannot be projected onto other kinds of treatment in the future. Therefore, Direcks and Holmes's prediction of apocalypse forms the spitting image of scientists' uncritical heralding of limitless possibilities of the new technologies. Even though their critique of science succeeds in foregrounding important underexposed aspects of infertility treatment, Direcks and Holmes fail to affect the terms of debate set by the medical community. Rather than change the perception of IVF as a purely medical (or medical-political) concept, they seem to underwrite the predominant definition of infertility and its treatment as medical concerns.

In that respect, few feminist authors seem to question the discursive conditions set by the dominant discourse of medicine. Like Corea and company, Direcks and Holmes also add to the construction of a countermyth, identifying IVF as an unconditional threat to women. The binary oppositions that structure their argumentative frameworks (men/women, science/nonscience, threat/stability) construct men as pro-technology and women as opponents or victims of technology. Even though there are significant differences among feminists in their assessments of IVF, Corea, Klein, Mies, Direcks and Holmes insist that *all* women should oppose *all* technology. They univocally perceive of IVF as a technological arrangement, stipulated by patriarchal-capitalist institutions, and they thus remain within the argumentative structures laid out by mainstream science and journalism discourse.

REJECTING THE COUNTERMYTH

A second group of feminists exploring the impact of IVF and related technologies strongly disagrees with the political definition of reproductive technology articulated by 'radical' and 'Marxist' feminists.[12] In 1985, this group of feminists starts calling for a personal assessment of technology, one which allows individual interests and situations of women to play a role in the definition of reproduction. In response to the countermyth, this group calls for the acknowledgment of varied personal and social experiences that women have with reproductive technologies. Some feminists also try to infuse the experiential definition of IVF in dominant scientific views on reproduction. While similarly insisting on reproductive rights of women, these feminists argue against a definition of dissent exclusively in terms of politics.

Writing in a 1985 issue of *Trouble and Strife*, a radical British feminist journal, Naomi Pfeffer angrily reacts to 'radical' feminist attitudes towards reproductive technologies.[13] She argues that these feminists have failed to understand the actual significance of the techniques because they are ignorant about infertility. In her opening paragraph, Pfeffer states that FINNRAGE members have consulted the views of all women except for the infertile themselves. Feminist critics of IVF tend to talk about 'we,' implying all women but excluding infertile feminists, according to Pfeffer. FINNRAGE supporters even accuse infertile women of being 'vulnerable' to manipulation by the medical industry, and thus being 'complicit' – ready to sell out women's power over their bodies in return for a baby of their own. Pfeffer fiercely rejects this type of victimization: infertile women are neither 'desperate,' as mainstream media want to depict them, nor 'powerless,' as the 'radical' feminist media try to define them.

She also contends that the 'radical' feminists' call for women's political solidarity is at odds with the needs of many infertile women, and reproaches Arditti, Corea, and others for ignoring personal differences among women. Their exclusive political definition leads them to rigorously dismiss any possible advantage of technology which might be of personal benefit to infertile women. Rather than hysterically campaigning against reproductive technology, feminists should scrutinize treatment facilities and discriminatory policies used by infertility clinics. Pfeffer accuses 'radical' and 'Marxist' feminists to have more eye for scary science fiction scenarios than for the reality of exploitative and substandard treatment presently offered by infertility programs. Reproductive technologies have to be evaluated systematically on their merits as well as their disadvantages; Pfeffer thinks a balanced assessment will serve to avoid further alienation of infertile women who are 'struggling to take control of a very negative experience.'

Naomi Pfeffer's plea is explicitly inspired by personal experience: she is herself infertile and underwent various reproductive therapies. Other feminists, who argue against an exclusive political assessment of IVF, wonder why personal experiences with the new technologies cannot be viewed as political. Marge Berer, for example, considers the unilateral rejection of reproductive technologies by 'radical' feminists, and their ignoring of experiential feminist perceptions, downright dangerous from a political point of view.[14] Reviewing *Test-Tube Women* and other books written by FINNRAGE-members, she attacks the authors on three counts: they deploy conspicuous rhetorical tactics to sell their argument, they construct women as helpless victims, and they play into the hands of religious anti-abortionists.

The articles in *Test-Tube Women*, Berer argues, are short on factual information; the book is essentially a polemical collection of articles in which facts yield to speculation. Berer reproaches Renate Klein that she jumps from surveys into predictions, using historical precedents of genocide to 'prove' future femicide. She also observes that Klein's rhetorical strategies are even more suspect than those used in most popular sensationalist media. Therefore, Berer urges feminists to look for alternative modes of representation and to avoid the discursive pitfalls laid out by dominant discourse.

One of these compelling conventions in mainstream journalism is, for instance, the depiction of issues in terms of winners and losers. Berer argues that Gena Corea falls into this trap when she describes all infertile women as 'totally passive and brainwashed victims of a male conspiracy.' In Corea's sweeping indictment of scientists, she indeed presents women as lacking a mind of their own, which Berer contends to be a very dangerous assumption: 'It is not just doctors twisting our arms; if we accept as feminists that women have to define their own needs and interests, then even other feminists should not presume to do it for us' (35).

Most importantly, Berer points out that FINNRAGE's arguments against reproductive technologies are dangerously similar to those of foetal rights and anti-abortion supporters. The motive to protect foetuses overlaps with the motive to resist IVF: both interfere with the 'natural' reproductive process. Anti-abortion supporters also depict women as helpless victims of abortionists – a depiction barely distinguishable from Corea's concept. No wonder, Berer argues, that mainstream and conservative press are so eager to take on FINNRAGE's arguments: they are perfectly compatible with the conservative agenda of reproductive politics. In 1985, Renate Klein spoke at a press conference organized by anti-abortion lobbyists in favour of the 'Unborn Children Protection Bill' which obviously sought to outlaw more than just IVF clinics. As Berer shows, 'radical' feminist opposition to IVF is perfectly consistent with the religious argument against artificial reproduction, assuming the same terms of debate. Both Berer and Pfeffer warn against a monolithic formulation of power which can easily be turned against women; allowing for individual differences among feminist interpretations of reproductive technologies will strengthen, not weaken a feminist standpoint.

Marge Berer and Naomi Pfeffer criticize the FINNRAGE group for being blind to difference, and for favouring a political over a personal, experiential definition of IVF and infertility. Few feminist point out that these two views of reproductive technologies need not necessarily be mutually exclusive. In her 1986 article for *Ms* magazine, Ann Snitow seems to waver between Pfeffer's experiential definition and Berer's indignant rejection of a radical political definition.[15] Snitow evaluates the issue of IVF not in polarized pros and cons, but in terms of possible benefits and disadvantages in relation to woman's power to control her reproductive capacity. In her opening paragraph, she admits that though she wants to propose a clear argument, it is difficult for her to decide in what terms she is going to discuss these technologies, which have triggered such opposite responses among feminists:

As a feminist, I expected that – in this area at least – I would always be unambivalent, would always know my own best interests and true desires. But no . . . The new technologies have the potential to take control and autonomy away from women in newfangled ways. But, at the same time, I'm attracted by the possibilities, which I see as part of a long line of social developments – like easily available contraception and assisted childbirth – that have changed women's lives fundamentally, and for the better. (42)

Snitow never tries to solve her ambivalence; she tries to locate herself between her 'typically American faith in a fatherly doctor and his devices,' and an 'equally deep impulse to spurn the sexist pig for the arrogant impostor.'

Exposing readers to an array of arguments and counter-arguments, Snitow particularly focuses on the 'evolution' of feminist responses to reproductive technologies. First Firestone's and then Corea's assessments are viewed in their historical contexts; Snitow considers Corea's response compelling, but points out that it lacks an analysis of infertility as a social construct. Sketching the different feminist positions, Snitow urges to think of this issue not exclusively in terms of gender, but to consider other social factors such as race and class in the assessment of possible ramifications of reproductive technologies. Citing statistics that show a significant correlation between socioeconomic background of women and infertility, she backs up her claim that whenever a new therapy or test is introduced, 'gender, race, and class set the stage, determining its use and users.'

At the same time, albeit hesitantly, Snitow starts questioning the discursive arrangements that structure the journalistic format of her own publication. Presenting her argument as a dialogue of different voices and alternating positions, she takes the reader on a circular mental journey. Taking a 'dialectical position,' making 'mental loops' and listening to 'internal voices whispering' she suggests at the end of her essay that the issue of reproductive technologies should invite women to speculate and organize, philosophize and take action. In order to really change the perception of IVF, they need to go beyond the set boundaries of available discursive modes. Snitow herself sets an example by deviating from conventional rules of journalistic discourse that require her to quote experts – doctors, scientists, specialists – to convey information on specific technological aspects. Rather than invoking experts, she relies on her own authority to interpret the issue and extrapolate meaning from her own analysis. In addition, she does not simply balance off two sides on the issue, but painstakingly reveals the interests and drawbacks of every position, including feminist views. The awareness that power is always coextensive with discursive structures funnels her attention to discourse and language. In other words, feminist assessments of new reproductive technologies do not only lead to the investigation of gender constructions, but also of genre constructions: a reconsideration of conventional ways of knowing and representing the reproductive body.

This critical awareness, expressed by Snitow, resonates in several academic collections of articles, which bring together a variety of feminist perspectives on legal, medical, social, and cultural implications of reproductive technologies.[16] Like Snitow, Michelle Stanworth (1987) acknowledges the inherent tensions involved in individual reproductive choices that are embedded in controversial sociopolitical contexts. She states that it is useless and hypocritical to be against all technology; women have a communal interest in safe abortion, they profit from technology that makes pregnancy and childbirth safer, and most women favour the reproductive freedom brought about by chemical or intra-uterine devices. Women are not collective 'victims' of technology, as Corea and others want us to believe, or individual 'beneficiaries,' as Pfeffer seems to propose. Instead, Stanworth argues for a feminist understanding of how science and technology *work*, rather than a univocal position of feminists for or against the technologies.[17] Acknowledging the fact that women or feminists do not represent one and the same perspective, she includes feminist views from various conventional and interdisciplinary academic fields.

Besides expressing their concern in feminist magazines and academic writing, feminists have also addressed the issue of reproductive control in science fiction novels. Science fiction as a genre appears to offer more opportunities than other discourses to draft alternative visions of reproductive arrangements in society. In the past decades, feminist novelists have increasingly exploited the margins of popular fiction to discuss the issue of reproductive rights. Yet along with a growing interest in this genre, there was also a growing awareness that the genre itself is encoded by dominant ideology. Just as Ann Snitow questions the conventions of journalism, feminist science fiction authors have subjected the genre to scrutiny – gender struggles reflected in genre struggles.

IMAGINING REPRODUCTION: FEMINIST FICTIONS OF SCIENCE

In the years between 1984 and 1987, two popular feminist science fiction novels were published that had new reproductive technologies as their topic: Margaret Atwood's *The Handmaid's Tale* (1985) and Octavia Butler's *Dawn* (1987).[18] In their novels, Atwood and Butler imagine a world where reproductive technologies are essentially part of everyday life. Atwood pictures a society in which women are oppressed by a group of male rulers who use reproductive technologies to exert their power to control women's lives. In contrast, Butler's speculative narrative incorporates a vision of reproductive technologies as potentially benign instruments, whose beneficence depends on the way society deploys them. Both authors address issues of gender and power in relation to reproductive arrangements in a society, using the science fiction format; but in order to voice their feminist concern, they deploy the genre in significantly different fashions. While Atwood's depiction emanates from the construction of a feminist countermyth, Butler's novel seems more in line with later differentiated feminist assessments of new reproductive technologies.

Atwood's *The Handmaid's Tale* consists of two parts: the story of Offred, and an appendix titled 'Historical Notes to the Handmaid's Tale.' The story of Offred is set in the 'near future' in the Republic of Gilead, formerly the United States; time and place are indicative of a society that is not too far away, since Offred can still vividly remember the present-day USA. In Gilead, a group of religious military men has seized power, and women have become mere instruments in the hands of men. Disease, nuclear radiation and other disasters have caused a dramatic decline in birth rates, and the few white women who are still fertile are turned into 'handmaids' – birth machines to the ruling elite. Handmaids are basically reduced to the functioning of their reproductive organs; as 'two-legged wombs' they are policed by a battery of state institutions, such as the military, the media, the church, health-clinics, the legal system, and educational centres. Handmaids are not allowed to smoke, drink alcohol or coffee, and they are forced to undergo frequent medical examinations at the health clinic to control their reproductive cycles. Poor, infertile women and women of colour are sent to the colonies to clear up nuclear waste and die; this fact we learn from Offred, the protagonist who is selected as a handmaid by the Commander and his wife; the entire story is told from the point of view of Offred, as she relates her experience of oppression and victimization.

The Handmaid's Tale can be characterized as a dystopian novel; Atwood herself has called her story a 'what-if-tale,' emphasizing the close relation between the imagined future and contemporary reality. In an interview with *The New York Times*, Atwood explains that she simply took trends existing in the 1980s, and stretched them to their logical conclusions: 'I did not include anything that had not already happened, was not under way, or that we don't have the technology to do.'[19] Referring to the rising popularity of religious anti-abortion groups that accompanied the push of new reproductive technologies, Atwood concludes that the combination of these two developments led her to imagine the ultimate ramifications. The acknowledgment that her novel is 'merely stretching' contemporary social reality, indicates that Atwood considers her dystopian map to be a critique of what she perceives as the world surrounding her. *The Handmaid's Tale* thus reveals the author's interpretation of new reproductive technologies in relation to her understanding of arrangements of power, gender and language.

In Atwood's imaginary Gilead, reproductive technologies are used as instruments of oppression; in the hands of men, they help monitor women's reproductive cycles and regulate their reproductive capacities. In this ideological arrangement, women are exploited as resources who lack the power to exert any control over their reproductive organs. Atwood's dystopian critique represents power as a property that can be possessed and exercised by one group of people to repress another group in society. Gilead's fictional reality is therefore reminiscent of Klein and Corea's speculative projections: (reproductive) power in the hands of a group of evil men will be used to exploit women. Yet this depiction at once attacks and reinforces contemporary arrangements of power. In *The Handmaid's Tale*, power is embodied in clearly identifiable social institutions, which in fact masks the complicated operation of power and the way it is exercised through multiple discourses; rather than being imposed through institutional mandates, power circulates through norms. Coercion through state apparatuses is a mode of oppression very unlikely to occur, since distribution of power through norms is far more pervasive and effective. Like Corea's speculations of scientists conspiring in their ivory tower against women, Atwood's explanation of reproductive repression may be equally dismissable as exaggerated fear projected in fantasy.

Atwood perceives reproductive power principally along gender lines; paradoxically, her imaginative society turns out to be both poignant criticism and affirmation of contemporary reproductive arrangements. In Gilead, poor white women serve as 'breeders' to the upper class of white rulers, whose wives are virtually all infertile. In the 'doublespeak' ideology of Gilead, infertility is officially defined as a woman's disease, a plague which has disproportionably affected white, upper class women. Yet everyone in Gilead knows that environmental pollution and radiation have seriously diminished the quality of sperm. Doctors thus 'help' fertilize handmaids who are supposed to be impregnated by sterile men, such as the Commander in Offred's case. While this depiction critiques the 'infertility plague,' as constructed in medical research and extended in magazines like *Time*, it also endorses that very myth.

A similar ambiguous appraisal can be detected in Atwood's representation of race and class. Minority and poor women are apparently sent away to the colonies, a practice symbolizing the racist agenda of the ruling elite. Yet by having coloured women relegated to the 'outskirts' of the novel, race and class seem to disappear as significant factors in the construction of a fictional society. While this depiction is clearly meant as a critique, it also reinforces the dominant perception which highlights gender as the foremost locus of oppression. Perhaps inadvertently, the intended revelation of what is wrong with contemporary society seems to confirm the very pillars this oppressive ideology is built on. Despite her avid criticism, Atwood remains within the gendered categories of defining infertility and reproductive power, and thus reinscribes women as a category of powerless victims contained by their sex-roles.

Atwood's ambivalent perception of power and gender is parallelled by an equally ambivalent critique of feminism as a way to oppose the ruling elite. The reader is confronted with feminism as it is personified in two characters: Offred's mother and Moira, a fellow handmaid. When Offred is forced to watch an 'unwoman documentary' at the Red Center, the institute for the ideological indoctrination of handmaids, she suddenly detects her mother, a staunch feminist who joined the radical women's movement in the pre-Gileadean era, to be among the protestors in the film. Offred's rejection of organized feminism appears from her refusal to be the 'incarnation of her [mother's] ideas,' implying she does not want her own ideals to be dictated by yet another ideology.[20] When Moira succeeds in escaping the Red Center by attacking several Aunts, Offred is critical of her fellow handmaid's violent method of opposition. Offred's obvious rejection of both Moira's and her mother's tactics suggests that she perceives of organized feminism as an inherently militant, aggressive kind of resistance, thereby reducing all feminists to radicals. Offred's own method of opposition seems to be a form of inner resistance – the development of a 'refined mode of perception.'[21] Offred's preference for an individual rather than a collective form of resistance seems to endorse the binary opposition between 'radical' and 'experiential' feminist critics, as exemplified by the dispute between Corea c.s. and Pfeffer. Consequently, Atwood accentuates the binary opposition between 'anti' and 'pro' technology women – a framework that is also enhanced by most mainstream news media.

The ambiguous effect of Atwood's dystopian critique is perhaps most noticeable in her representation of academia, at the end of her novel. The story of Offred's unsuccessful struggle to resist her ordeal is followed by an 'Appendix,' the aforementioned 'Historical Notes.' This appendix largely consists of a transcript of the Twelfth Symposium on Gileadean Studies, which is set in the year 2196. Historians from all over the world have gathered to share the latest findings on the Gileadean period. Professor Pieixoto, director of the '20th and 21st Century Archives' and keynote speaker of this conference, reports his finding of the 'Handmaid's Tale,' a text found recorded on thirty cassette tapes. By virtue of his position, Pieixoto is supposed to make sense of Offred's narrative, but he actually does the opposite: he discounts the 'Handmaid's Tale' as a valid object of study. Offred's tape-recorded story, he argues, cannot be true or authentic since no further documents have been found to prove her existence. Historians value scriptural proof over oral items of evidence; following the 'scientific' method of verification and deduction, Pieixoto concludes that Offred never existed.

The professor literally dismisses Offred's tale to the realm of fiction, because it is not true and thus useless as an object of academic research. As an academic expert, Pieixoto favours the question 'Is it true?' at the expense of the question 'What does it say?' His view on history reverberates the still dominant paradigm that historians are objective translators of the past, whose only task is to 'tell as it was,' without acknowledging any ideological bearings on the present. The scholar Pieixoto situates himself outside history, invoking the paradigm of objective science to justify his abstinence from interpretation. This stance relieves him from the obligation to assume social or moral responsibility towards the past and the present.

The character Pieixoto is obviously the personification of the male-dominated academic institution. Not the story of Offred, but the dismissal of her narrative by producers of 'official' knowledge, accounts for the real dystopia; Atwood frames current academia as an institution approving of, and enhancing discriminatory practices. On the one hand, the Appendix clearly shifts the accent of Atwood's concern from oppression through state institutions to oppression through its discourses; academia is apparently a powerful agent in perpetuating the status quo. On the other hand, the depiction of Pieixoto as a caricature of male dominated academia may also suggest that academia itself is useless as an institutional site of resistance. Just as Corea and Klein rejected science discourse as a mode of discourse hostile to feminist concerns, Atwood seems to regard academic discourse as an area infected by 'malestream' ideology, which is impenetrable by criticism.

While implicitly rejecting the discourse of academia as a possible venue to voice feminist criticism, the appendix to *The Handmaid's Tale* also argues for a revalidation of (science) fiction as a serious mode of discourse; Atwood proposes a re-evaluation of discursive boundaries as hierarchical markers of what counts as valid knowledge and what does not. The author seems to adopt the conventional genre of the dystopian novel to construct a countermyth without reconsidering the ideological encoding of this genre. In line with Corea, Klein, Mies and others, Atwood remains within the parameters set by dominant discourses; while intending to sharply criticize current arrangements of reproductive power, she simultaneously adheres to them by using the same binary frameworks as deployed in mainstream discourse.

This may be the reason why her novel appears vulnerable to co-optation by mainstream forms of popular culture. The Hollywood-movie based on *The Handmaid's Tale*, released in 1990, turns Offred into a heroine who succeeds to escape Gilead and deliver a child in 'freedom' outside this police state.[22] The movie, and particularly its ending, suggests that oppressive reproductive practices may happen in a fantasized, dystopian world, but that there is another reality out there – offering a true relief from the bleak prospect of Gilead. The movie script actually remains very close to the text of the novel, except for the appendix: Pieixoto's lecture – which in the book at least draws attention to discursive forms of oppression and erasure of women's experience from history – is replaced by the happy ending. Apparently, Atwood's feminist dystopia can be smoothly appropriated to fit the comforting Hollywood view of present political arrangements. The mode of appropriation by mainstream discourse is not unlike the *Wall Street Journal*'s incorporation of radical feminist critique of new reproductive technologies.

Two years after the publication of Margaret Atwood's successful novel, Octavia Butler publishes *Dawn*. Like Atwood, Butler imagines a world in which reproductive technologies are part of everyday life; she relates perceptions of power, gender and discourse to reproductive arrangements. Yet Butler's novel offers not so much a distinct critique of current practices, but an exploration of alternative visions of community organization and validation of reproductive tasks. At the beginning of *Dawn*, the protagonist Lilith awakes from a centuries-long sleep to find herself aboard a vast living spaceship. Lilith learns she is saved from the Earth which is destroyed by human-caused nuclear war; her saviours are the Oankali, creatures covered in writhing tentacles. As she gradually becomes acquainted with the Oankali, particularly with her 'guardian' Ooloi Nikanj, she finds out that they are attempting to heal planet Earth; they saved its few survivors by curing them from cancer and genetic disorders, and they will now prepare them to return to Earth. Lilith has to lead her people back to this planet, on the condition that the humans will in turn interbreed with the Oankali. The gene-trade is mutually beneficial: while the humans can use Oankali features to gain strength and get rid of physical disabilities, the Oankalis need gene-diversity to survive as a species – they live by virtue of continuous change and gene-variation. Both Lilith and her fellow humans have problems adjusting to this concept of 'trading,' which raises important questions concerning reproduction and the tolerance of difference.

Butler depicts new reproductive technologies not as instruments of control, but as tools which can be used to the benefit or detriment of people -depending on the ideological intention of their users. The Oankali use genetic engineering as a means to cure Lilith's cancer, and to increase physical strength enabling her to resist illnesses. Before the war, however, genetic engineering and reproductive medicine were deployed for entirely different purposes, as Lilith can still remember:

> Human biologists had done that before the war – used a few captive members of an endangered animal species to breed more for the wild population. Was that what she was headed for? Forced artificial insemination, surrogate motherhood? Fertility drugs and forced 'donation' of eggs? Implantation of unrelated fertilized eggs. Removal of children from mothers at birth . . . Humans had done these things to captive breeders – all for a higher good, of course. (58)

Lilith's only frame of reference is a concept of reproductive technologies as instruments of oppression. As the Oankali teach her otherwise, she develops a more balanced idea of technology; not technology itself, but the way it is used and validated gets most emphasis in this novel. For the Oankali, genetic engineering generates whole new concepts of 'parenthood' and 'family.' By mixing the genes and cells of five adults – a human male and female, an Oankali male and female, and a sexless Ooloi – a child has at least five parents, and can therefore be cared for by an extensive family of relatives. Even though the female human or Oankali gives birth to a baby, all relatives are intensively engaged in the delivery process.

Butler's fictional concept reminds one of Marge Piercy's imaginative rearrangement of reproductive tasks in *Women on the Edge of Time*, as quoted at the beginning of this chapter. In Piercy's utopia, babies were also not 'owned' by two parents, but manufactured with the help of reproductive technology, and conceived and raised by different parents. However, the essential distinction between Butler's and Piercy's world is that while Piercy wants to abolish the difference between male and female reproductive roles, Butler's vision is geared towards a revalidation of the tasks of pregnancy and childbirth. In *Women on the Edge of Time*, technology completely replaces conception and childbearing, so that there are no more biological bonds between offspring and parents. In *Dawn*, women still carry children, and the process of pregnancy, birth and the first years of childhood are an important time for children to 'bond' with their relatives. Butler's depiction of pregnancy and nurturing increases rather than diminishes the importance of bonds between baby and relatives. Unlike Piercy, who views pregnancy as a physical 'hindrance' to equality, Butler locates the source of inequality not in physiological difference, but in the unequal validation of reproductive tasks.

Dawn is thus replete with images of possible social and cultural arrangements, induced by the new technologies. On the other hand, Butler makes clear that these new structures will never evolve if humans are unwilling to change their conventional norms and values. According to the Oankali, the biggest obstacle to humans in developing an alternative social structure is their tendency to be 'hierarchical' (37). Ingrained in the world view of humans is the assumption that social reality is made up of oppositional categories that are hierarchically organized. Human bipolar concepts, such as male/female, human/alien, human/machine, human/environment, prohibit a full understanding of the Oankali world, where there are no easy distinctions between these categories. For instance, when Lilith asks Ooloi Nikanj whether it is a male or a female creature, it answers: 'It's wrong to assume that I must be a sex you're familiar with' (11). While exploring the spaceship, Lilith also discovers there is no distinction between the Oankali and their environment: the spaceship is a living creature, and by mishandling their environment the Oankalis would hurt themselves. Human binary frameworks evidently do not apply to the world of Oankali, and therefore, humans are forced to reconsider their conventional ways of making sense. Lilith is obviously more open to developing new frames of reference than some of her fellow humans, who fiercely defend and justify their traditional world views, privileging distinctive hierarchical categories. They refuse to accept Oankali as 'different,' instead looking upon them as 'alien' and 'inferior.'

Butler does not define reproduction exclusively along gender lines; the category of gender is intricately interwoven with categories of race and class. Lilith, as a black female, is not as much looked down upon by the Oankali as she is by some of the other humans. She experiences her inferiority as a woman when she is nearly raped by a human male, Paul Titus, and she feels a deep racial hatred against her when she is almost killed by Curt.[23] Lilith's 'difference' as a black female turn her, in the eyes of the humans, into an ally of the 'aliens'; her tolerance of the Oankali renders her an enemy of her 'own' people. Race, gender, class and appearance are all implicated in the human construction of power, which the Oankali refer to as 'hierarchy': not difference itself, but the validation of difference in terms of good and bad is problematic. The gene-trade proposed by the Oankali will change the genetic make-up of humans and Oankali alike, so that 'your young will be more like us, and ours more like you,' as Nikanj explains to Lilith.(40) Everyone will become an amalgamation of differences; binary and hierarchical categories will no longer apply. The aim of the trade is not to create a sort of *Übermensch*, or to privilege one race, type, gender or class over another. By absorbing the 'other's' features, easily identifiable categories will disappear. However, erasure of difference in itself will not change humans' inclination to discriminate; they need to make a conscious, voluntary effort to ban hierarchy out of their system, which is something the Oankali cannot impose on them.

In her creation of a hierarchy-free society, Butler also considers the role that language plays in the construction of reality; it is instructive to compare her configuration of language to that in Atwood's imaginative Gilead. As a handmaid, Offred was supposed to converse in a kind of formulaic language which had a preinscribed, uniform meaning in Gilead. Since she was not allowed to read or write, Offred's strategy to escape ideological indoctrination could be labelled as 'linguistic anarchy': playing around with words, she forces herself to always recognize ambiguities, and her most subversive acts are the games of Scrabble she plays with the Commander. In Atwood's novel, language – much like reproductive technologies – seems to be either an instrument of oppression or of liberation. While the ruling elite imposes a new language, aimed at prohibiting all critical thinking, Offred uses the old language to subvert this form of control.

In Butler's *Dawn*, language and writing are not in themselves liberating or oppressive tools. As the Oankali make clear to Lilith, language is often used by humans to enhance their hierarchical tendencies; more precisely, hierarchy is inscribed in discourse, so it is almost impossible to come to a democratic consensus using language as a means for negotiation. The Oankali themselves have far more effective and democratic means to communicate and learn: they use a kind of body-language, plug into each other's sensitory organs, and send waves through living material like trees in order to find out the opinion of the community at large: 'They could give each other whole experiences, then discuss the experience in nonverbal conversation. They had a whole language of sensory images and accepted signals that took the place of words' (237). The Oankali consider it important to learn a number of human languages, in order to be able to communicate with humans on their own terms. Like the trading of genes, the Oankali want to mix their different communicative skills with those of humans, so that language will no longer be an instrument of power. The construction of consensus thus gets a different meaning in the Oankali world: everyone is involved in the debate, and no one is excluded, due to the very nature of communication channels.

The new world (re)created by Octavia Butler in *Dawn* is not a perfect world, nor are the Oankali a perfect 'people.' Despite their ability to manipulate genes, to communicate easily and democratically, and to intensify family bonds, the world they create and its inhabitants remain vulnerable to destruction; after all, the Oankali cannot ban evil from society or coerce humans into consenting to their system from the top down. As a result, Earth is still inhabited by groups of people who hold on to a destructive and exploitative mentality. While Piercy's imagined reality was obviously utopian, and the world created by Atwood thoroughly dystopian, Butler's concept seems to be in between:

there is not one 'good' society existing distinctively from a 'bad' society. Utopian and dystopian communities live on the same earth, still struggling to coexist peacefully and nonintrusively. Butler engages in a reconsideration of the conventional concept of science fiction as either utopia or dystopia; rather than presenting a possible critique or re-vision of contemporary social reality, she profoundly questions the very frames according to which it can be imagined.

This strategy clearly foregrounds the questioning of conventional genres as reinscription devices; as Ormiston and Sassower (1989) poignantly argue, the utopian/dystopian dichotomy 'presents the perimeters of its discourse: each side of the demarcation specifies an alignment with or against science/technology' (24). To comply with this dichotomy means that one is confined to the assessment of technology as an instrument in itself, which can be used either to the benefit or to the detriment of people. In order to escape the constraints that existing discursive modes impose on the construction of alternative models of reality, some feminist critics feel they have to reconsider conventional forms of representation that shape reality. Using the immense popularity of the science fiction genre, feminist authors try to reach a large audience; Octavia Butler's trilogy, like Atwood's novel, was distributed by a 'mainstream' publisher and thus marketed among a general readership, not a specific feminist one.[24] In that respect, Butler's science fiction novel reflects the more recent awareness of feminist critics to reconsider both gender and genre arrangements, and look for alternative publication strategies to express feminist dissent.

FEMINISM BETWEEN MARGIN AND MAINSTREAM

Reviewing feminist responses to the new technologies in a historical perspective, we can see how these reactions suit the changing spirit of the decades. Firestone's and Piercy's celebration of the new technologies reflects their involvement with the women's liberation movement of the 1970s: they aimed at removing all social and political hurdles that prevented women's emancipation. The new technologies, like the contraceptive pill and legalized abortion, represented instruments of freedom. In the 1980s, this positive perception of the new technologies radically changed. FINNRAGE members vehemently opposed all new reproductive technologies, considering them to be instruments of patriarchal and capitalist oppression. In retrospect, the strong reaction against these technologies is understandable if we take into account how, in the course of this decade, conservative government leaders dealt severe blows to the status and reproductive autonomy of women. Reagan's conservative agenda included strong support for anti-abortion politics and Margaret Thatcher continuously called for revaluation of traditional family values. It is against this political background, that Margaret Atwood created her speculative dystopia of a society where women have lost all political influence and thus the power to make their own reproductive choices.

The establishment of FINNRAGE and other radical feminist groups to the new technologies had an important function: they alerted many women to possible implications of the new technologies. Consciousness raising was an important goal of these groups; from that perspective it is understandable that radical feminists almost exclusively addressed a sympathetic audience. Rejecting science and technology altogether, they also rejected the discourses in which scientific knowledge is commonly produced, and the publication channels through which it is disseminated. Most feminist responses of this kind appeared in specific (radical) feminist journals or at best in publications which were geared towards a more general leftist audience. They presumed a clear distinction between the discourses that promote these technologies and the (feminist) counterdiscourses that are used to combat them. Yet in doing so, they have often imitated the very genres, verbal coatings and publication formats of the discourses they so vehemently opposed. Consequently, these voices were easily prone to incorporation by dominant voices and mainstream discourses, as exemplified by the article in the *Wall Street Journal* and the filmed version of *The Handmaid's Tale*.

In reaction to the countermyth constructed by radical feminists, another group of women started to oppose a unilateral political assessment of the new technologies, and advocated a moderate feminist approach. They warned for a simplified evaluation of technologies; women, they argued, have gained reproductive freedom through the availability of technology such as the contraceptive pill and intra-uterine devices. Feminist critics like Ann Snitow and Rosalind Petchesky considered the use of new reproductive technology to be both an individual matter and a sociopolitical issue; the new technologies should be assessed as a complex phenomenon which requires multiple feminist views from very different personal and disciplinary perspectives. This group of feminists also called for an increased awareness of the very discursive frameworks and publication strategies through which feminists voice their criticism. Petchesky, for instance, assembles cross-disciplinary perspectives on the new technologies, whereas Snitow explores the margins of journalism discourse, and Octavia Butler reinterprets the conventions of the science fiction genre.

These two groups, representing the numerous diverging feminist positions on new reproductive technologies, approach the issue from distinctively different assumptions. Radical feminists presume there is a dominant 'pro-technology' standpoint, expressed in mainstream science and journalism discourse, and a feminist 'anti-technology' standpoint, expressed in special interest journals. This presupposed separation between science and technology and their discourses on the one hand, and feminism on the other, facilitates the view that science discourse is a privileged, contained domain in which public consent is constituted, and which is impermeable by criticism. In this perception, feminist voices are inherently ostracized from the mainstream, and are destined to remain within the periphery of the public debate. The second group of feminists seem to realize that while they feel excluded from established discourse, they are necessarily imprisoned within it.[25] Since there is no 'escape' from technology or discourse, feminists may as well attempt to change the parameters of discussion. Some detractors of new reproductive technologies start to call for a deliberate infusion of feminist perspectives in mainstream discussions and discourses; feminists, they argue, should not take for granted a position on the outskirts of the public debate, but should manoeuvre their views to the centre.[26]

In the mid-eighties, radical feminists assumed a unified, collective feminist stance on the issue of new reproductive technologies. Since then, feminist opposition has diverged and splintered. In 1987, 'feminism' clearly defies its categorization as a counterdiscourse; in fact, what made feminist criticism dismissable or vulnerable for co-optation was precisely its own construction as a unified category of women who are 'anti-technology' or 'victims of technology.' By acknowledging a variety of feminist responses one not only prevents exclusion from the general public debate, but also expands the possibilities for subverting common sense definitions. To speak of feminism, then, is to recognize more than one legacy; to speak of feminism is to recognize the interlacing of feminisms, and the multi-layeredness of its origins. The discord among feminists on the issue of reproductive technology, is thus a paradoxical correlative to its critical strength. Evidently, all feminists are concerned with the erosion of their reproductive rights. Solidarity, however, does not necessarily have to result in a uniform standpoint or opposition strategy.

As the public debate continues after 1987, the confrontation of dominant and feminist meanings sometimes even result in the entanglement of two previously irreconcilable discourses. It becomes increasingly difficult to distinguish between dominant and oppositional meanings, as feminist voices strategically attempt to enter the mainstream arenas of debating, and concurrently, dominant voices try to recapture the voices of dissent and incorporate them in common sense definitions. Such an entanglement requires an even more astute awareness from the critic of the forces of underlying discursive arrangements and rhetorical strategies.

5 From Cure to Commodity: The Naturalization of IVF

The pool of patients who might benefit from in vitro fertilization is believed to exceed 1 million, and this population is growing.

(*New England Journal of Medicine*, 31 March 1988)

It [IVF] used to be an option of last resort . . . Today a couple in their 30s with undiagnosed infertility is likely to be told to skip invasive tests and exploratory surgeries and go straight to in vitro or related technologies.

(*Time*, 30 September 1991)

Marissa stood up and went to a small blackboard . . . Picking up a piece of chalk, she wrote down 600 000. 'This is the number of couples in the U.S. that fertility specialists estimate need IVF if they want to have a child that is genetically theirs. If we multiply that by fifty thousand dollars we get thirty billion dollars. That's billion. Not thirty million, thirty billion. And that's just in the United States. IVF could rival the world's illegal drug industry as a money-maker.'

(Robin Cook, *Vital Signs*, 1991)

INTRODUCTION

The year 1987 marks a key moment in the public debate on new reproductive technologies. On March 31, 1987, the Superior Court of Bergen County, New Jersey, handed down the verdict in the now famous 'Baby M' trial. This case was the first major court case concerning surrogate motherhood and the brokering of surrogate agreements, that attracted widespread attention from the national news media. Mary Beth Whitehead, who had signed a contract with Bill Stern to be artificially inseminated and to carry the foetus to term for the Sterns, opted instead to keep the baby girl. In the lawsuit that followed, Judge Sorkow of Bergen County decided to give sole custody to the father, denying Mary Beth Whitehead her 'natural' maternal rights, and thus upholding the surrogate contract. The verdict was later reversed by a higher court.[1] Even though there was not much reproductive high-tech involved in the conception of 'Baby M' – artificial insemination being the simplest form of so-called assisted reproduction – the trial and verdict had a substantial impact on the legal definition of reproductive roles.

The landmark decision signifies how the emphasis in the debate has shifted: nine years after the birth of the first test-tube baby, reproductive technologies regularly result in new social practices, which in turn require legal regulation. In the 'Baby M' case, reproductive arrangements are discussed in terms of commercial transactions: can surrogate pregnancy be regulated by legal contracts? The court case also reveals the shift in focus from the 'need for' to the 'right to' infertility treatment; calls for consumer protection and regulation of the market frequently surface at this stage of the debate.

The widespread application and 'success' of IVF and similar techniques seems almost beyond dispute; the need for them appears to be a premise, rather than a contestable assumption. As we learn from the opening quotes of this chapter, previous arguments of technical contrivance are replaced by arguments of economic feasibility. The availability of IVF is debated in terms of supply and demand, and recipients of IVF treatment are referred to as consumers rather than patients. According to the *New England Journal of Medicine*, the 'pool of patients exceeds one million.' *Time* magazine adds to the already diagnosed patients an infinite number of undiagnosed potential users of IVF. And in the third quote, the protagonist of *Vital Signs* states that the infertility business has become a profitable industry.

Between 1987 and 1991, IVF becomes a common product, the need of which is now beyond dispute. As a consequence, opposition to the new technologies revolves less around questions of need, and the debate becomes less polarized in terms of ethical, religious or feminist opposition. Oppositional voices seem to vanish, but in fact they are just harder to identify.

Feminist critics strategically move towards the mainstream public debate, and dominant voices move to absorb criticism previously launched by feminists. At the same time, the boundaries between medical discourse, mainstream journalism and popular fiction diffuse, and this convolution of discourses actually becomes an important part of the 'naturalization' process. Medical discourse incorporating narrative, and journalism deploying medical language, make IVF appear as an unequivocal fact. Traces of previous controversy and discussion disappear as soon as feminist and other oppositional voices are encapsulated in the 'logic' of dominant discourses. The institutional languages of medicine and journalism appear to construct and endorse each other in their medical definition of IVF. Yet feminist voices are not rendered mute: both feminist writers and readers may deploy the very conventions of genre and discourse to promote an alternative interpretation of reproduction.

At this stage of the debate, it is essential to bare the interwovenness between the production of technology and the construction of public knowledge. Narrative appears literally instrumental in the process of 'manufacturing' public consent. Technological instruments do not just affect the terms of debating; they actually change the very perspective from which reproduction can be argued. The clinical gaze, which displays a view from the inside of (female) body through laparoscopic cameras and microscopic lenses, visualizes reproductive body parts as autonomous actors. New optical instruments and photographic techniques profoundly shape the narratives that constitute the public debate on new reproductive technologies, both in medical discourse, journalism and fiction. A combination of visuals and narrative appears to be a powerful agent in the construction of common sense – the appearance of IVF as a 'natural' commodity.

PLAYING THE ODDS: THE NUMBERS GAME

In Chapter 3, I have outlined how the 'need' for IVF and related technologies was gradually established; in the late 1980s, previously argued 'real need' for IVF is definitely replaced by 'real demand.' References to long waiting lists of desperate couples awaiting infertility treatment provide the implicit justification for expanding research and treatment facilities. The marketability or mercantilization of technology has thus become the rationale for its development, and has simultaneously created the imperative to use it. But increased demand does not obviously result in the perfection of IVF technology. 'Success rates' are quite often the focus of medical reviews reporting on IVF or variations thereof. Optimizing success rates is the explicit or implicit aim of virtually any research project in reproductive medicine. Infertility programmes claim success rates anywhere between fifteen and thirty-five per cent. The problem with these percentages is that it remains utterly unclear what they actually mean. Some articles quote the outcome of treatment programmes in terms of pregnancy rates per patient, others in terms of pregnancy rates per reproductive cycle. Moreover, 'success' appears to be a highly ambiguous term, as it includes IVF-administered pregnancies, as well as live births.[2]

Regardless of their interpretation, success rates of clinics remain invariably low. A 1987 review in the *British Medical Journal* rejects as a myth the claim that 'great technical advances in the past twenty years in treating infertility have led to high success rates in treatment.'[3] After a detailed review of various IVF programmes, the authors conclude that 'less than eighteen per cent of the infertile population may conceive as a result of medical intervention.' Surprisingly, this conclusion does not lead to a critical reassessment of the technologies involved, but instead serves as an argument to support further government funding of IVF: 'We could increase the overall success of infertility services to about thirty-four per cent if IVF and GIFT were widely available on the National Health Service – a doubling of the success rate for medical intervention' (155).

Rather than evaluating medical data, the rhetoric of medicine is deployed to authorize a political demand; government should help increase the effectiveness and efficiency of medical technology, and alleviate the financial burden of infertile couples. A *New York Times* article echoes this request for government funding, stressing that 'infertile couples in the USA are paying for the lack of federally funded research in the extremely high financial costs and emotional stresses of a treatment that works only eight per cent of the time.'[4] Low success rates are thus invoked to prove the need for government sponsoring, and consequently, the lack of federal involvement is held responsible for the financial and emotional suffering of infertile couples.

At this stage of the debate, there is a clear shift in the articulation of a demand. The 'infertility myth' seems to have become obsolete as an argument in defense of IVF; growing numbers of people seeking treatment provide the essential numerical support to justify the need for IVF research and treatment. A report in *Nature* claims that IVF and GIFT treatment programmes are gaining acceptance 'witnessed by the growing numbers of clinics providing these services.'[5] Indeed, consumer demand has replaced patient need, a shift reflected in the many references to patients as 'consumers' and clinics as providers of 'services.' Like the reports in the *British Medical Journal* and *The New York Times*, the journal *Nature* argues that increasing demand justifies government regulation on the grounds that consumers of IVF are easily prone to commercial exploitation. The National Institute of Health is called upon to break the legal limbo on the status of IVF: if recognized as a proven medical therapy, IVF treatment could be regulated by the state. Emphasizing the need for 'some protection to consumers of IVF services,' the article urges government intervention as a means of regulating IVF businesses.

Growing numbers of IVF consumers not only increase success rates – as the *British Medical Journal* wants us to believe – but naturally benefit the economic efficiency of treatment programmes. Profitability, however, is an illegitimate basis for argumentation in medical discourse. The very admittance of economic interest would threaten the alleged neutrality and objectivity of the institution as inscribed in medical discourse. Efficiency is thus always argued in terms of 'cost awareness' or it is argued in comparison to other treatment programs. A report in *Ob.Gyn.News*, for instance, states that IVF performed on an outpatient basis is more 'effective and economical' than inpatient programmes.[6] Clinics are also reported to constantly look for cost-efficient alternatives for IVF, in order to keep the expenses for clients down.[7] However, efficiency is never discussed in terms of profit for IVF clinics.

More importantly, the very admittance of economic interest distinguishes 'good' from 'bad' science. An article in *Fertility and Sterility* warns against 'bad' clinics whose 'motive [for] establishing IVF programs may not be a strong interest in such programs or the desire to fill a void in the community, but an attempt by a hospital corporation to increase its market share.'[8] This qualitative distinction, however, is a rhetorical fallacy, since all infertility treatment programmes in the USA are privately and corporately funded, and are hence interested in turning a profit. Claiming that 'bad clinics' are out to profit financially from the innocent consumer, the article implies that (reproductive) medicine as such is an altruistic and disinterested pursuit. Despite the acknowledgment that IVF centres are part of a 'consumer-driven medical care system,' the authors deny economic profit as a valid motive. They disqualify treatment centres which lure patients by advertising unverifiable or inflated success rates, and which present these rates as the official outcome of clinical-scientific research. In their drive for new markets, the authors argue, bad clinics have exploited medical discourse by misquoting research results to advertise their services. Honourable specialists should resist consumer pressure, and not quote inflated pregnancy rates that may lead to false expectations. Like other professional publications, the journal *Fertility and Sterility* calls upon the government to regulate the IVF business, and offer consumer protection.

Typically, medical reports insist that while demand for IVF is extremely high, and overall success rates of clinics are 'promising,' individual chances for success through IVF treatment are very low. In addition, success only comes at a high price and a great deal of emotional and financial investment from the patient. Seeking treatment through medical intervention is likened to an 'expensive gamble' (*Nature*), a metaphor which persistently recurs in journalistic accounts. Engaging in IVF treatment is compared to 'playing the lottery' and a 'gambling addiction' (*Time*); phrases like 'risk analysis,' 'hitting the jackpot' and 'playing the odds' frequently surface in newspapers and magazines. The gambling metaphor suggests that though failure is the norm, you cannot win unless you play. 'Success rates' thus become the equivalent of calculating statistical chances to win a game, turning successful treatment into a scarce commodity. An article in *Time* contains a description of a waiting room in an IVF clinic in Boston, where a small picture of a bird on the wall is accompanied by the message: 'You never fail until you stop trying.'[9] The game-playing metaphor implicitly shifts the responsibility for successful IVF treatment from doctors to patients. Just like low success rates were used to back up a call for more funding, here they are used to stimulate more trials. 'Chances increase if patients keep trying' is a common argument in medical journals to account for the low success rates per patient.

Playing the game thus becomes the norm, even if the odds weigh against you. Like most lottery advertisements, mainstream journalistic accounts of IVF treatment highlight the ultimate luck of the persistent player, rather than the much more common fate of the loser. An article in *Nursing Times*, a British journal for health care professionals, is representative of these kinds of stories.[10] Consisting of two parts, the first half of the article describes IVF treatment in medical terms; the second half is a case story, relating the conception and birth of Michael. The story of Michael serves as a personal narrative which instantiates the previously depicted medical problem. As becomes apparent from the factual description, infertility treatment is 'unpredictable and its success rate does not yet approach that of nature' (27). Readers are warned four times that the actual success rates of clinics can be put no higher than fifteen to twenty per cent. Nevertheless, the 'typical' case story is the conception of Michael, a 'charming, lively toddler with a mass of curls and clear grey eyes' (30). In the case of Michael's parents, IVF was administered because of the husband's infertility. Instead of opting for donor sperm, they chose IVF because they wanted a child 'of their own.' Confirming the unique status of genetic offspring, the story evolves like a fairy tale: Ann gets pregnant on the first try, and thanks to the 'camaraderie, general support and reassurance' from the hospital staff, she delivers a healthy baby boy. A dream come true, as the article concludes: 'Their story was one of courage and conviction. The odds weighed heavily against them, and there is little doubt that without the assistance of IVF/ET Michael would never have been born' (30).

Low success rates and rare chances all become part of the IVF gamble, an expensive speculation which can naturally have few winners. By highlighting success rather than failure – the lucky winners rather than the many unfortunate participants – the exception becomes the norm. Just as the profitability motive is never a part of medical discourse, in this journalistic report the surest winner of all is remarkably absent: the IVF industry. To stick to the gambling metaphor, infertility clinics, like casinos, make a profit on every attempt at in vitro fertilization, whether successful or not. But as the story of Michael shows, the metaphor turns poor clinical results into acceptable terms of chances, allotting responsibility for failure to undefined forces rather than medical capacities. More importantly, the gambling metaphor allows multiple repetition of clinical trials to become a normal part of medical treatment. It even adds notions of suspense to what is actually a physically and emotionally charged procedure. In addition, implicit and explicit comparisons of IVF treatment to a gambling addiction infer the connotation that a woman's strong craving for pregnancy is responsible for the many trials involved.

The impact of this structuring metaphor does not escape the attention of feminist journalists. Sue Halpern, in a 1989 cover story for *Ms* magazine picks up the gambling metaphor in order to subvert this pervasive image.[11] The headline of her article, 'Infertility: Playing the Odds,' suggests another account of a happy mother winning the IVF lottery after playing just a few cycles. From the beginning of the article, however, Halpern makes clear the title is an ironic twist to the image she wants to contradict. Like the article in *Nursing Times*, this one also consists of two parts: a medical explanation of this particular kind of treatment, and a few case-stories. Borrowing the conventional journalistic format, the *Ms* magazine reporter depicts the failures of IVF rather than successes, the losers rather than the winners. Instead of interviewing doctors as experts, Halpern quotes women who have undergone treatment, suffered lots of pain, and who have actually experienced the many side effects of the extensive drug therapy involved in treatment. In doing so, she establishes women as authoritative agents instead of stages on which the infertility drama unfolds. By attributing the authority to define to women rather than doctors, the *Ms* magazine reporter reverses the journalistic routine of 'quoting the expert' to prove the ineffectiveness of IVF.

Halpern gets most of her information simply by reading specialized articles on this issue, but reading them in a different way. Emphasizing the tricky rhetorical loopholes involved in medical discourse, Halpern analyses journal articles as if they were advertisements, 'stressing the one out of ten potential for success, rather than the ninety per cent chance of failure' (151).

Objective, scientific research results published in prestigious journals appear nothing but a mess of numbers, Halpern concludes. She further notices that the confusing collection of 'success rates' statistics paradoxically lack a uniform measuring standard which would warrant the very notion of assumed objectivity. Reversing reading conventions, the *Ms* magazine reporter reads medical discourse as advertising discourse, and uses her own positionality to unmask the 'disinterested' position of medical science. As her analysis of information flyers for prospective candidates reveals, the omission of drug therapy as part of the procedure signals the interest of the medical industry to promote IVF as a clean, nonintrusive and mechanical intervention. Advertising and medical discourse appear to have blended in these flyers, as well as in many medical journal accounts, according to Halpern.

The *Ms* magazine journalist also exploits the convention of the personalized side-story to illustrate her factual account. Unlike the 'happy-mother-loves-happy-toddler story' in *Nursing Times*, *Ms* magazine features two cases of IVF treatment: one of a happy couple who decided to adopt an infant, after finding out about their infertility; and another story of a woman who stopped treatment after undergoing several unsuccessful cycles, and started to work on accepting her childlessness. Even though the article in *Ms* magazine uses the same story frame as mainstream articles on the same subject, the filling-in of this structure is almost diametrically opposite: whereas mainstream magazines emphasize the rare, lucky winner, *Ms* magazine instantiates the alternatives to IVF.

Sue Halpern excavates the conventions and routines of mainstream journalism to present a particular feminist point of view on the effect of IVF treatment. Reversing the hierarchical positions of professional experts and female patients, she allots the authority to define to women undergoing treatment. In addition, Halpern rejects the inscribed reading conditions that prescribe how to interpret medical discourse, and foregrounds her own authority as a journalist to present interpretations. Halpern's subversive deployment of journalistic conventions is part of what Bybee (1990) labels the 'microphysics of power.'[12] By this she means that feminist journalists can give authority to themselves or women quoted in the story. In order to prevent 'symbolic annihilation' – the marginalization of feminist viewpoints to the special interest sphere in public discourse – Halpern recreates the journalistic framework to produce a common sense account.[13] Peculiarly, Halpern's mode of perceiving and representing the issue of reproductive technologies is explicitly feminist, without ever mentioning feminism as an 'interested' positionality. Her perspective seems implicated in her method of perceiving, analysing and writing.

Even though Halpern deploys mainstream journalistic conventions, she publishes her account in a magazine which mainly addresses middle class, progressive women. It is hence arguable whether she succeeds in moving her feminist viewpoint into the mainstream arenas of discourse. At any rate, her use of conventional journalistic discourse to articulate feminist opposition leads to a reconsideration of marginality as a position. This blending of conventional discursive frames and feminist oppositional voices is significant; Halpern's account signals the increasing mingling of medical and feminist arguments, as well as the fusion of conventional forms of discourse with counter-discursive narratives. On the one hand, exploiting and subverting conventional modes of discourse allows feminists to reach a broad audience, and popularize an oppositional, marginalized point of view. On the other hand, this mingling of medical and feminist meanings increases the danger of the latter being silenced by the former. In the marketplace of public meanings, medical definitions of IVF appear more powerful than feminist meanings, and it is exactly in the amalgamation of these discourses that domination becomes more subtle, and therefore more effective.

THE NATURAL CONSTRUCTION OF MEDICAL FACTS

At this most recent stage of the public debate on new reproductive technologies, feminist voices seem to be gradually absorbed by and transformed into mainstream discourses. The incorporation of feminist arguments does not mean they are fully wiped out; rather than being dismissed from the discussion, feminist interpretations are realigned to fit medical definitions of IVF and related technologies. It is important to analyse this process of domination and signification, because it reveals how 'naturalized' concepts come to be constructed. The teleological construction of medical facts is manifest in both medical journal articles, mainstream journalism accounts, and popular novels. Three examples, one of each discourse, may illustrate how the blurring of discourses actually reinforces medical authority; they also exemplify how feminist arguments come to be included in 'naturalized' definitions of IVF.

A 1988 review article on the current state of reproductive medicine, published in the *New England Journal of Medicine*, leads off with the premise that IVF is advantageous, successful and desirable as a cure to infertility.[14] The opening paragraph of the *NEJM* article rivals advertisements and magazine descriptions in their efforts to promote the endless potentials of new reproductive technologies. The ever growing number of centres performing treatment, the more than 3000 live births registered as a result of IVF treatment, and the still growing 'pool of patients' all serve to confirm the indispensable need for new reproductive technologies. The concept of IVF treatment is literally and metaphorically aligned with nature; the author repeatedly compares IVF to the 'natural' process of reproduction, and claims that it is at least as efficient – if not more so – than nature itself. The low success rates of most infertility centres, estimated by the *NEJM* at ten to fifteen per cent per cycle, are relativized by referring to the low chances for success in natural reproductive cycles:

> To place this apparently low success rate in perspective, one must recognize that the human reproductive system is very inefficient. Of 100 eggs exposed to potential fertilization among fertile couples, only 31 will actually produce a viable offspring. The other 69 will be lost, usually within the first two or three weeks of pregnancy. Therefore, if we could do as well as nature, we would anticipate only a 31 percent success rate. (831)

The comparison is structured by a seemingly unproblematic opposition between 'natural' and 'assisted' reproduction. However, the distinction is far from self-evident, since most reproductive decisions are, one way or another, affected by medical or chemical expedients. The comparison of reproductive technology to so-called natural reproduction seems a paradoxical attempt at upgrading technology to an equal, yet higher, level of efficiency. Even though the author argues we cannot expect technology to do better than nature, medicine actually claims to be more efficient, hence better. This argument is frequently echoed in news media reports on IVF research and treatment.[15]

The comparison to nature yields the idea that scientists have control over the impalpable reproductive process, and that they simultaneously have an instrument to measure and manage quality. Elsewhere in the article, the reader is confronted with the inefficiency of nature: phrases like 'the natural cycle has two disadvantages' imply that reproductive medicine is able to correct 'natural' mishaps and irregularities. Obviously implied in this assumption is the myth that men can do better than God: the vocation of scientists being not to imitate but to emulate the master of nature.

The naturalization of IVF is also apparent on a semantic level. Previously launched metaphors and analogies, used to illustrate and imagine the IVF process, now function as non-figurative, denotative terms. Whereas IVF procedures, in accounts predating 1987, were likened to kidney transfers and heart bypasses, the latter image resurfaces in this *NEJM* article not as an analogy but as a verb: 'The process of in vitro fertilization *bypasses* the Fallopian tubes' (829, emphasis added). Alongside blocked Fallopian tubes, IVF becomes the perfect 'bypass' for male infertility and unexplained infertility. Even the gambling metaphor, which is frequently used in journalistic accounts, almost unnoticeably becomes part of the web of facticity in medical discourse:

> Although relatively few patients go through the procedure repeatedly, a recent study suggests that those who do so have an *increasing chance* of success. After six *attempts*, the *rate* of ongoing pregnancies *may* approximate 60 per cent. (831, emphases added)

Medical discourse erases all traces of gambling as an image, instead incorporating it as factual language.

Along with the transformation of verbal coatings, the very notion of argument or controversy disappears from the medical account. Whereas at the initial stage of the debate the discussion section of a medical journal article was frequently exploited to rebut religious or moral objections to IVF, this 1988 *NEJM* review contains only marginal traces of previous argument. Religious objections to IVF resonate in the casual statement that the Catholic Church has approved of the GIFT procedure because it occurs 'in vivo.' As for feminist opposition, this article briefly touches upon emotional reactions to IVF procedures, suggesting that intensive psychological counselling will help alleviate the 'inconveniences' for women undergoing treatment. These inconveniences appear to be emotional rather than physical, once again trivializing the effects of drug therapy which is an essential component of IVF treatment. Objections which were extensively discussed in earlier medical journal articles are now casually referred to not as remnants of an argument, but as agreed upon facts – statements with no modalities and no traces of contest.

One objection to IVF technology is prominently dealt with in this *NEJM* article: the complaint that IVF is too expensive and therefore inaccessible to all infertile couples. Financial considerations are extensively weighed, and subsequently translated into a request for public funding:

> The cost in most centers approaches 6000 dollars from the start of the menstrual cycle to the outcome of the pregnancy test two or three weeks after the transfer of the embryo . . . Therefore, many couples for whom advances in reproductive technology offer the only chance to achieve biologic parenthood still continue to be denied reimbursement for these procedures. (832)

Having erased all traces of feminist or religious objections, the author simultaneously digresses into what is clearly a political statement. Medical discourse appears able to transform arguments into facts, and subsequently turn these 'facts' into political demands. These medical 'facts' seem to constitute the implicit warrant that women have a right to biological parenthood, and thus have a right to get reimbursed for the innate desire for a genetically linked child. In this teleological construction of medical facts, cause and effect appear only natural in the arrangement of described events.

Even though the *NEJM* review article is structured by medical discourse – a discourse which supposedly privileges 'facts' – an extensive narrative highlights the process of in vitro fertilization. It is instructive to recall the first medical report on IVF, published by Steptoe and Edwards in *The Lancet* of 1978. As described in Chapter 3, this account hardly contained any descriptive details on the IVF procedure, merely providing data to reinsure the apparent normality of the patient: Lesley Brown, the mother of the first test-tube baby. In the 1988 *NEJM*, a narrative of the IVF procedure dominates the first half of the article, successively describing induced ovulation, oocyte retrieval, fertilization, and embryo transfer. Every step in the process is described minutely from the point of view of a doctor using technology to perceive the process:

> Looking through the laparoscope, the surgeon pushes the needle tip into the follicle, and the oocyte and the surrounding fluid are aspirated by gentle suction. The follicle is then filled to its former volume with culture medium and reaspirated at least once. The collecting tube is taken to the laboratory, which should be ideally adjacent to the operating room. The contents are poured in a petri dish, and the oocyte is identified with a dissecting microscope. (829)

The extensive narrative in this medical account seems to make the process of IVF appear more 'natural,' since it turns factual data into events, and impersonal techniques into agents. As can be inferred from this description, technologically advanced instruments figure as agents in the process of reproduction. Laparoscopy, microscopes and ultrasound technology enable the visualization of the insides of the body, and turn the smallest units of human life into visible entities.

The discourse of medicine directs readers to take the place of the (medical) researcher, and look to these processes through the eyes of the clinician. The perception of the reader is led by the perception of the doctor who handles the equipment. This kind of 'clinical gaze' is also transmitted to more popular accounts of reproductive technology, either printed or broadcasted on television. Sarah Franklin (1993) for instance, analyses the BBC television series 'The World of the Unborn,' aired in 1988, shortly before the Human Fertilisation and Embryology Act was introduced in British Parliament. She shows that the spectator's position is established through the clinical gaze as the camera moves down with the laparoscope. 'The viewpoint is thus not only that of the clinicians, it is through their technology' (537). It is exactly the same visualizing technique as is used in the *New England Journal of Medicine*: the perspective or point of view goes unnoticed, so it seems as if there is no subject position from which the 'facts' are argued. An almost imperceptible focus 'naturalizes' the clinician's perspectives and turns it into an 'objective' one.

But it is not just the subject which renders itself invisible; these optical instruments also turn the object imperceptible. The woman undergoing IVF treatment – previously the prime object of the doctor's concern – disappears from the scene, textually and visually barely leaving a trace of her presence. In the *NEJM* review, the female body is defined in terms of reproductive parts and functions, a view which is enabled and enhanced by ultrasound pictures of fertilized oocytes and 'a needle traversing the bladder into a follicle.' A woman appears as a collection of body parts, either serving as a vessel for receiving fertilized eggs, or as a machine to donate eggs. In semantic terms, the very word 'woman' appears only twice in this long *NEJM* article; instead, the female body is referred to as a 'patient,' a 'recipient,' a 'donor,' a 'volunteer,' a 'candidate,' a 'prospective mother,' or a 'couple.' Noticeably, each term connotes a commercial or clinical function of the female body. 'Recipient' and 'donor' labels all people involved as 'givers' and 'takers,' as if donating sperm is equal to the procedure of removing or inserting (un)fertilized eggs. By the same token, the smooth replacement of 'woman' by 'couple,' equates male and female contributions to the reproductive process, ignoring the fact that it is the woman who undergoes painful and intrusive IVF treatment.[16]

Technology itself thus becomes the focus and fetish of medical discourse, turning the woman's body into an environment and erasing her social function.[17] The clinical gaze magnifies the moment of conception, the union of eggs and cells; the optical instruments turn eggs and sperm cells into autonomous actors, who with the help of technology, are drawn together to create a human being. The word 'pre-embryo,' which has rapidly become an accepted term in medical discourse, signals that tiny cells and organs have become the focus of medicine.[18]

The naturalization of IVF, through the visualization of the instruments and agents of reproduction, also reverberates outside medicine. A 1991 *Time* cover story imitates medical discourse to the extent that journalism and medicine are barely distinguishable.[19] The full colour picture on the cover consists of an ultrasound picture of a foetus in a womb. Since a considerable number of *Time* issues, both in the United States and in Europe, have to be sold at the newsstand, the picture is obviously retouched to make it appear as a thumb-sucking baby hanging in space. The cover story, which is eight pages long, is extensively illustrated by several enlarged photos. Two very large pictures immediately catch the eye of the reader: one of a sperm entering an egg, and one of a two-day old embryo 'heading for the uterus' as its caption explains. Similar to the article in the *NEJM*, the moment of conception is the central focus in this news narrative, evidenced by the prominent role that eggs and sperm play both in the text and in the pictures.

Textual evidence in *Time* is clearly subordinate to the visual evidence presented, yet the textual narrative is crucial to the whole story. Adding a mythical dimension to the pictures, the story draws the readers into the 'inner sanctity' of human life to witness the moment of conception. The opening paragraph of this article is illustrative in this respect:

> Couched in a halo of nutrient cells, an egg smaller than the dot on an i drifts slowly down a Fallopian tube, one of a pair of narrow passages that lead from a woman's ovaries to her womb. Like a beacon guiding ships at night, the egg sends forth a calling signal. A convoy of sperm – remnants of an armada that was once a couple of hundred million strong – sails into view, their long tails trashing vigorously. Lured by the chemical signal, several hundred of the most energetic swimmers close in on the egg, their narrow tips unleashing a carefully timed sequence of biochemical salvos . . . One and only one succeeds. The successful seed then releases its tightly coiled package of DNA, which fuses with the egg's own DNA and sets in motion a series of genetic events that culminate, nine months later, in the birth of a new human being. (56)

The narrative functions in the same fashion as the photographs: it blows up tiny eggs and cells to life-size objects – images of ships, hundreds of brave men fighting to conquer new land, and a luring Siren. The process of conception is equated to the invasion of an army, an extended metaphor which turns the womb into a mere site of struggle, and the egg into a trophy of an all-male military contest. Superimposing the narrative of the Siren – luring innocent men adrift at sea – onto the narrative of reproduction, the author turns this story into a classical myth. Body parts are now featured as autonomous actors; eggs are identified in terms of appearance and sperm is closely scrutinized as it 'swims up' to the egg. The autonomy of cells is enhanced by several illustrations – prints of ultrasound photographs. Finishing the extensive description, the sentence 'This is how it is supposed to work,' marks the normative definition of the reproductive process.

The enlarged photograph of the sperm penetrating the egg does not speak for itself, and neither do the other pictures of embryos and cells. The laparoscopic image needs 'expert' interpretation, a narrative explaining the picture for a lay audience. Medical photography does not render nice, clear snapshots of easily identifiable body parts or fluids; for a non-medical reader, the pictures may mean anything from ink stains to coloured clouds. In the 1978 article in *Time*, discussed in Chapter 3, images (mostly drawings) still functioned as mere illustrations to the text; in this 1991 issue of *Time*, the narrative serves to explain the pictures.[20] Micro-photography creates its own story, enlarging the invisible and positioning the reader as a witness to the moment of conception. The accompanying narrative enhances the focus on the genesis of life, and sets the stage for a heroic presence of IVF engineers and doctors who 'help when nature fails.' Reproductive technology thus becomes incorporated in the myth of natural reproduction – the artificial smoothly aligned with the 'natural.' The combination of text and pictures appears a pivotal inscription device – establishing the 'facts' of (assisted) reproduction as visible slices of reality.

The virtues of reproductive medicine, like in any of the previous *Time* articles on IVF, are uncritically endorsed. Doctors are heralded as celebrities who push the scientific envelope further, and who are now in charge of every aspect of the reproductive process: 'The beauty and power of IVF are that it allows doctors to take many key events in reproduction out of the body, where they are subject to the vagaries of human biology, and perform them in vitro' (60). The implicit victorious conclusion in the *NEJM* article is rendered explicit in *Time*:

IVF is not equal to, but better than nature. It is actually so successful that conventional infertility therapies and routine testing 'might as well be skipped to go straight to IVF technologies.' Quotes are overwhelmingly elicited from medical experts; women undergoing IVF treatment are literally muted in this article. The only woman quoted in this article is described as 'a couple' that has 'finally hit the jackpot' and became pregnant through IVF.[21] As evidenced by the gigantic photos of eggs and cells, women are textually and pictorially dissipated into tiny components. The narrative, which privileges the personification of sperm and eggs, leaves no room for identification for women who might be subject to treatment; women as social subjects seem to have disappeared from this journalistic account.

As became clear from the *NEJM* review article, IVF is no longer presented in medical discourse as a controversy; religious and feminist objections were smoothly incorporated as facts. In *Time* magazine religious or moral considerations have vanished altogether. Feminist objections, however, are not erased but reframed to support the medical definition of IVF, and rendered invisible as arguments. A significant example of this rhetorical strategy can be noticed in the following paragraph, in which the causes of the 'infertility epidemic' are summed up:[22]

> The advent of the Pill, the woman's movement and an economy that pushes women into the workplace during their most fertile years have led many members of the baby-boom generation to wait so long to have children that they are in danger of waiting forever. This same generation was also party to the sexual revolution, and that too has taken a toll. With the exposure to more sex partners came a sharp rise in sexually transmitted diseases and other infections that can impair fertility. In addition, tens of thousands of women now in their 30s and 40s were born with malformed reproductive systems as a result of their mothers' use of DES, which was widely prescribed in the 1940s and 50s to prevent miscarriage. (56)

As can be inferred from this quote, feminists are not only held responsible for the infertility epidemic, due to their behaviour, but they are responsible by analogy for the widespread use of DES, a dangerous drug which was actually prescribed to women to promote fertility. By equating 'sexually transmitted diseases' and 'the use of DES' the *Time* journalist blames women for taking DES, rather than blaming the pharmaceutical industry and the medical establishment for administering and pushing the drug. Clearly resonating Direcks's and Holmes's comparison of IVF and DES – as described in Chapter 4 – the feminist argument against new reproductive technologies is thus twisted to fit the public relations campaign for IVF.

While some arguments are distorted or erased from the debate, others are sharpened to endorse the feasibility of IVF. Economic arguments to support the efficiency of IVF abound. Echoing the political demand stated in the *NEJM*, *Time* laments the absence of government regulation and funding of infertility treatment. State funding becomes an issue of national pride, as 'Britain and Australia are surpassing us in research because of the restraints we face in this country' (62).[23] The government's ban on IVF funding causes great financial stress for infertile patients, and moreover, it is responsible for the morbid growth of ill performing obstetricians. Several horror stories of poorly trained physicians who offer substandard treatment are used to illustrate the need for government involvement. These horror stories of immoral financial exploitation of infertile couples seem to have replaced earlier science fiction speculations.[24]

The *Time* article firmly endorses the hierarchy of discursive authority: medical definitions of IVF are supported by arguments of economic feasibility and efficiency; legal and socioeconomic considerations occasionally enter the debate, but only to explain the difficulties encountered by medical practitioners. Feminist arguments are marginalized and reappropriated, and religious objections have simply disappeared from the discussion. The accumulation of facts, quotes, and images appears as a heterogeneous collage of voices; yet the narrative conventions of framing, ordering, inclusion and exclusion are used to affirm the authority of medical definitions. Whereas science and journalism initially, in 1978, rivalled for the power to define, the conventions of journalism are here fully deployed to absorb medical discourse, which in turn lends its authoritative power to journalism itself. Promotional enthusiasm coincides with the full adoption of scientific discourse; not just its model of argumentation, but also its use of 'evidence' becomes part and parcel in the struggle for defining the meaning of reproductive technologies. Science journalists appear to be 'brokers' in the construction of common sense, as science and journalism discourse practically converge.[25]

Another example of the merger of discourses concerning IVF can be traced in *Vital Signs* (1991), a novel by Robin Cook – acclaimed 'master of the medical thriller.'[26] This popular novel blends medical, journalistic and fictive discourses to construct a highly ambiguous image of IVF technology. Like the articles from the *NEJM* and *Time*, the novel incorporates dominant medical as well as oppositional feminist meanings of IVF; yet unlike these previously analysed articles, *Vital Signs* seems to foreground feminist assessments of new reproductive technologies. The protagonist of *Vital Signs*, Marissa Blumenthal, is a celebrated paediatrician and research scholar. When she enters the Boston Women's Clinic for a routine check-up, she is unknowingly injected with a mysterious virus which causes infertility. After years of trying to become pregnant, Marissa returns to the clinic to start IVF treatment, but she becomes suspicious when several women who are treated at the clinic turn out to have similar symptoms of blocked Fallopian tubes, caused by a very rare bacterium.

In her subsequent journey to discover the truth behind this medical mystery, she has to face all the hurdles of a tough detective: a failed effort to gather patients' data from the Boston clinic, an assault on her life after detecting fraudulent claims of success rates in medical journals; the loss of her best friend and her husband as both get killed by the Hong Kong maffia, who appears to be involved in what turns out to be a worldwide network of IVF clinics. American, Australian and Asian doctors are implicated in a conspiracy aimed at expanding the IVF market. In a concerted effort to promote the use of infertility services, they first cause infertility – injecting upper class women with a virus – and subsequently persuade them to undergo at least eight cycles of IVF. Not babies, but a billion dollar business is the objective of this capitalist enterprise.

The narrative plotting of *Vital Signs* reflects another negotiation of the meaning of IVF from the mass of discourses that have proliferated over the last decade. The plotting or sequencing occurs within the textual framework of the detective thriller; the struggle between different meanings of IVF takes place within the conventional space of the genre. The form of the detective novel is in fact used to encode conflicting discourses on IVF: the dominant view of institutionalized medicine and oppositional feminist voices. *Vital Signs* incorporates many of the same discourses, arguments and narrative strategies as previously analysed articles in the *NEJM* and *Time* magazine. Since the novel contains a remarkable number of scientific details, this fictive account provides a rather complete view of the many aspects involved in IVF treatment.

Yet medical discourse serves to simultaneously question and undermine the authority of medicine. Medical 'facts' are ordered and interpreted through narrative, like in the *NEJM* and *Time*. The opening scene of the book, which describes the virus being injected in Marissa Blumenthal's Fallopian tubes, resembles the earlier quoted descriptive paragraph in *Time*:

> The infected bacteria came in a swift gush as if flushed from a sewer. In an instant, several million slender, rod-shaped microorganisms filled the lumen of the Fallopian tubes. They settled against the velvety convolutions of the mucosa, nestling in warm, fertile valleys, absorbing the abundant nutrients and expelling their own foul excretions. The delicate cells lining the interior of the oviducts were helpless in the face of a sudden invading horde. The putrid waste of the bacteria . . . burned like acid, resulting in instant destruction of the fine cilia whose normal function was to move an egg toward the uterus. The tubular cells released their defensive and messenger chemicals, signalling the body for help. (11)

Whereas in *Time* magazine the inside of the female body was described in terms of a 'luring Siren' attracting a strong army of male sperm, in *Vital Signs* female reproductive organs are described in terms of a fertile landscape, which is being invaded by a destructive army of chemicals. Yet the fictional scene is characterized by the same clinical gaze that structured the medical and journalistic accounts of IVF, and which has become pervasive in popular culture.[27] In this opening paragraph, nature is not assisted by human technological invention, but deliberately disrupted by doctors who inject a malicious virus into a perfectly healthy body. The personification of technology in *Vital Signs* points at doctors as the cause of the infertility epidemic, as they unlawfully penetrate the inside territory of a woman's body.

Contrary to what might appear from this scene, medicine is not the unequivocal culprit of the epidemic, and neither are women the ultimate helpless victims. Rather than reinforcing the binary opposition between the male doctor and female victim, *Vital Signs* breaks it down. The reversal of traditional positions of power is embodied in the protagonist: Marissa Blumenthal is both a doctor and a woman undergoing IVF treatment. As a medical expert, she is authorized to speak for the medical establishment; as a patient, she represents the voice of countless women who 'have suffered the emotional and physical trials and tribulations of infertility and its modern treatments.'[28] Her dual ideological inscription as acting subject and medical expert allows the reader several possibilities for identification.

Since the subject position is the discursive equivalent of the reading position, the reader is confronted with several discourses through the protagonist. Because of her scientific training, the female detective is capable of understanding and explaining specialized medical journals. While studying the data of IVF research, Marissa turns them into graphs – the sketches of which are included in the book – and detects that the curves suddenly change from pregnancy rates per cycle to pregnancy rates per patient.[29] Explaining to a friend how the statistics are tampered with, Marissa lucidly unravels complex scientific argumentation to a lay audience of readers. She swiftly relates statistical analyses to results of lab tests, to arrive at the conclusion that the infertility 'epidemic' must have been induced by humans. Her expert command of scientific logic enables her to undermine the very authority of medical discourse.

Through the same eyes of the protagonist, the reader is confronted with the experience of IVF treatment – causing physical stress and emotional imbalance, and frustrating her professional career and marriage. The experiential feminist definition of IVF gets as much weight in the novel as the clinical descriptions, since her authority as a physician is transposed to her authority as a patient. Marissa Blumenthal's capability to judge scientific procedures is occasionally questioned by her husband and distrustful colleagues, who view her personal involvement as an impediment to her scientific objectivity. However, Marissa insists that she is more, not less capable of evaluating infertility problems and IVF treatment precisely because of her personal experience and involvement. Medical discourse, in this novel, cannot 'mute' or discredit the physical experience of the scientific object, because she is authorized to speak for herself as an expert.

The variety of voices present in this novel – patient's, doctor's, expert's, feminist's and others – is also reflected in the bibliography included at the end of *Vital Signs*. An unusual attribute to a popular novel, the bibliography includes everything from 'how-to guides' for infertile couples to Renate Klein's 'fiery feminist' account of IVF, as well as Spallone's *Beyond Conception*. The list seems to reflect the multiple discourses and voices involved in the debate and included in the novel. In fact, *Vital Signs* often appears as an amalgamation of discourses, incorporating paragraphs from medical journals, quotes from journal articles or images from popular news magazines.[30] All ingredients and arguments of the public debate on IVF and related technologies seem to be reshuffled and reframed in this novel, which is truly dialogic in the Bakhtinian sense: voices struggle with the inscribed authority of discourses, and therefore question their immanent hierarchy.[31]

Even though a feminist perspective is strongly represented by the protagonist, a definite 'feminist' reading of this novel seems contradicted by the plotting of the story. When Marissa Blumenthal has unravelled the global conspiracy, she explains to some of her colleagues how the complex network of IVF clinics could render huge profits. In one of the last scenes of the book, she states that the IVF industry rivals the illegal drug industry as a money-maker, echoing the argument of Marxist-feminists that women's bodies are exploited by medical technology. However, her subsequent explanation could come straight out of a journal of the American Medical Association: 'The whole infertility industry is totally unregulated and unsupervised. It's grown up in a no-man's land between medicine and business. And the government has just looked the other way' (387).

Implying that the IVF industry could be acceptable if greed, exploitation and abuse would be ruled out or restricted through government regulation, the author telescopes the radical feminist viewpoint of IVF with the medical definition. As in the analyses of Klein, Corea and other FINNRAGE supporters, *Vital Signs* seems to argue for a personified image of institutional power: men concocting a conspiracy against women. Locating the culprit in the specific personae of a few men, the novel affirms the idea that power can be pinpointed in one (part of the) political system or in one (exceptionally bad) medical enterprise. The linear narrative arranges several discourses to appear as a natural pattern: it identifies evil doctors as the exception to an otherwise noble profession. The narrative thus obscures the fact that the exercise of power is multiple, and is not located in one institution or person.

Although *Vital Signs* gives room to feminist considerations, the ultimate discounting of a feminist voice may be attributed to the deployment of the conventional genre. The plotting seems inscribed in the nature of the detective novel: the crime must finally be solved. Despite the breakdown of traditional male/ female roles, the female detective is not engaged in an attempt to redefine infertility, or the social practices that arise as a result of the implementation of reproductive technology. Marissa Blumenthal's quest results in the dismantling of an unlikely male clan, which is out to mercilessly exploit women's desire for a genetically linked child. After the mystery has been solved, the reader may be absolved by locating the construction of an infertility epidemic in a particular group of villains, whose conspiracy can easily be dismissed to the realm of fantasy. The inclusion of a radical feminist viewpoint does not change the assessment of new reproductive technologies, but instead leads to a reinscription of dominant (counter)myths, collective assumptions and distorting images. This reshaping of feminist arguments into the dominant medical definition may eventually be more harmful than the much more blatant colonization of feminist voices in the *NEJM* and *Time*. Through this bestseller, the 'naturalized' meaning of reproduction becomes part of the cultural (un)consciousness, and is thus a vital component in the framing of common sense.

Robin Cook's deployment of the detective novel to reinscribe normative patterns and social structures may give rise to the impression that conventional popular fiction is wholly unsuitable to frame feminist criticism. Yet, as far as genre fiction is concerned, feminist authors such as Amanda Cross and Sara Paretsky have proved that it can be an appropriate means to package feminist critique.[32] Like Sue Halpern demonstrated in her article in *Ms* Magazine, and Octavia Butler in *Dawn*, dominant modes of discourse – whether journalism, (science) fiction, or others – do not have to be skewed in the search for feminist modes of representation. A critical reappropriation of conventional modes of discourse may yield fruitful ways to address feminist issues, and redirect feminist contributions to the centre of public discourse.

RECONSIDERING OPPOSITIONAL STRATEGIES

Tracing the various stages of the public debate on new reproductive technologies, it becomes evident that IVF gets promoted as the 'natural' solution to a common problem. Arguments of efficiency and effectivity abound in medical discourse, and optimizing success rates appears to be the only sensible answer to alleviate the long waiting lists for IVF clinics. Advanced technology also directly shapes arguments concerning IVF: the instruments to monitor the IVF process – laparoscopy, ultrasound, micro-photography – become vital rhetorical strategies in the public relations campaign for the new technologies. The omnipresence of technology, that magnifies the components of the reproductive process, results in the erasure of differences between the sexes; the medical focus disembodies reproductive organs and functions, turns cells and genes into agents, and privileges the moment of conception. From the depictions in the *NEJM* and *Time*, we can infer that male and female contributions to reproduction are presented as equivalents: sperm and egg play equally important roles in the moment of conception. Pregnancy and childbirth – subsequent stages in the reproductive process – can thus be transformed into mere 'services.' It is not the instruments themselves that lead to a devaluation of female contributions; rather, the way the instruments are framed and presented reinforces the ideologically ingrained validation of conception over gestation, the product over the process, and the father over the mother.

Rendering themselves invisible as a shaping force, these optical instruments significantly contribute to the popular public image of the foetus (even the pre-embryo) as an autonomous object, while the pregnant woman loses this status. Instruments of medical technology merge with their discourses, resulting in a pervasive clinical gaze that starts to dominate much of popular culture. In addition, the institutional discourses of medicine and journalism merge to mutually reinforce the authority inscribed in the respective discourses. Apparently, they can only prolong their claims to truth by exploiting the resources of narrative. The narrative mode of discourse included in medical journal articles and news magazines, accounts for the self-evident arrangements of facts, and is pivotal in the establishment of a normative definition. Like the technological instruments, this discursive mechanism renders itself invisible, hiding itself in the appearance of a 'natural' hierarchy between discourses.

The changing definition of new reproductive technologies, from magical procedures to products that can be purchased and traded, prompts feminist critics to reconsider their strategies. As the use of reproductive technology becomes naturalized, they can no longer be viewed as mere instruments, but have to be regarded as practices that are fundamentally reshaping forms of life. The implications for women, while less easily identifiable, appear even more urgent. Technological developments affect the very function, status, and identity of women in terms of reproduction, on the one hand erasing sex/gender as a physical and social category, on the other hand setting women on a pedestal as consumers. Deploying the authority of 'factual' discourses, dominant meanings of IVF also effectively absorb feminist and other oppositional voices in the process. Only by resisting the inscribed reading conventions, we can still notice traces of previous contestation and argument; otherwise, feminist voices have been 'adjusted' to fit medical definitions.

How do feminists in turn respond to these refined tactics, these subtle discursive alignments? How can the opposition ring through a sophisticated mechanism of 'consensus-building?' As the debate progresses, radical feminist voices are further encapsulated in the mainstream debate; they are effectively appropriated almost beyond recognition to enhance dominant meanings of IVF and reproduction. Ironically, the kind of opposition that resisted mainstream arguments most vocally, has itself become an integral part of the web of facticity construction. Yet there have also been attempts to subvert and resist dominant meanings from within mainstream discourses. Like Sue Halpern, who excavated the conventions of journalism, numerous feminists have tried to take on scientific discourse. Between 1987 and 1991, the stream of books and articles written by feminist academics from various disciplinary angles, focusing on the implications of the new technologies for women, is impressive. Many of these feminist accounts have dealt with the way in which the clinical gaze perverts medical discourse, and how this gaze is accepted outside medical discourse as a valid and 'objective' method of evidence construction.

As described in the previous chapter, initial feminist assessments of new reproductive technologies mostly appeared in (radical) feminist pamphlets, in publications distributed among a small group of sympathetic subscribers, or at best in a general feminist magazine. In 1988, we witness a particular strategic move towards the centre of the debate: the journal *Issues in Reproductive and Genetic Engineering (IRGE)*, published by Pergamon Press, offers an academic platform to reflect on the new technologies in a 'mainstream' discursive format. In contrast to journals which address a grass-roots feminist audience (such as *Women's Studies International Forum*) or a specific academic feminist audience (such as *Feminist Studies*), *IRGE* apparently caters to an audience of (academic) readers interested in the new technologies, yet these technologies are consistently approached from a feminist perspective.

The journal is interesting in more than one respect. The format of articles published in *IRGE* perfectly fits the academic mode of discourse which conventionally requires solid research, well argued hypothesis, abundantly footnoted evidence. Yet besides scholarly articles, *IRGE* also contains fictional pieces, varying from a surreal comedy to a novel on genetic engineering; an editor's note explains that the 'women's movement has long recognized the power of fiction as feminist criticism,' which warrants the inclusion of fiction in an otherwise academic context.[33] The merger of science and journalism discourse deployed by dominant forces in the debate is thus parallelled by feminists through a juxtaposition of science and fiction in an academic journal. Equal appreciation of expansive formats reflects the awareness that science needs not necessarily be criticized within its 'proper' discursive domain. This awareness also speaks from most contributions to *IRGE*; favouring approaches to reproductive medicine from a variety of disciplinary angles, the new technologies are evaluated as a social and cultural construct, rather than a scientific one.

IRGE departs from previous publication strategies in yet another way: the journal solicits views from a variety of feminists, including radical, moderate and experiential stances. In addition to Renate Klein's well-known political argument, we can also find articles in which reproductive issues are analysed in relation to a postmodern cultural context.[34] Most illustrative of the strategy to include a wide range of feminist perspectives is Lisa Woll's case study of FINNRAGE's activities in Australia, published in a 1992 issue of *IRGE*.[35] Woll evaluates the effect of this group's struggle to oppose the new technologies. Interviewing a number of active members, sympathizing supporters and critical detractors, she finds that most people believe that FINNRAGE had a noticeable impact on policy making and that it profoundly changed public opinion concerning assisted reproduction. However, while acknowledging their impact, they also criticize the unyielding position and strategies preferred by FINNRAGE members. As Woll concludes:

> While some [of the FINNRAGE volunteers] fully agree with FINNRAGE's position, others feel that the position is overdrawn and lacks political sophistication. Others accept portions of their position, such as opposition to surrogacy, while rejecting others, such as opposition to IVF. (33)

As illustrated by this and other articles in *IRGE*, the call for a 'unified feminist response' to the new technologies has now definitely given way to an array of feminist voices, arguing from a number of different perspectives and (disciplinary or discursive) angles. Each of these feminist voices positions itself strategically in the spotlight or back in the wings, deploying various rhetorical strategies to resist, subvert or shape dominant definitions of reproduction and the female body.

It is important to untangle this process of contestation, domination and reappropriation, not just to bare how a specific medical definition of the foetus and the reproductive body is established, or to show how this meaning is (in)effectively counteracted by feminists. As the debate continues after 1991, it becomes imperative to analyse how the struggle for public knowledge is also reproduced outside the discourses of science, journalism and fiction. The technological-discursive instruments which enable a disembodied view of the reproductive process are reinscribed in other discourses, noticeably law and politics. Ever since the 'Baby M' trial moved reproductive technologies into court, the voices constituting the public debate are increasingly manifest in legal arenas. Higher and lower courts are confronted with the results of the newest IVF applications, and lawyers and judges are called upon to explore legal interpretations of reproductive arrangements in the wake of rapidly changing technologies and practices.

Arguments voiced in previous stages of the public debate, as analysed so far, play an important role in the construction of a legal definition; the impact of naturalized meanings on legal rulings is evident. As I will show in the next chapter, public consensus informs legal rulings, since legal interpretations are firmly rooted in dominant social and cultural values. Conversely, legal decisions also shape the public debate and actually affect the process of signification.

6   From Need to Right: The Legalization of Genetic Motherhood

> Within the space of a single dazzling week this fall, this hoary old noun [mother] was redefined so thoroughly, in such mutually exclusive ways, that what it means now depends on which edition of the newspaper you read.
>
>   (Katha Pollitt, *The Nation*)

> It [the definition of legal motherhood] is so uncharted. Depending on what court you happen to walk into, you get a different outcome.
>
>   (Dr James Goldfarb, quoted in the *Los Angeles Times*)

INTRODUCTION

In the early 1990s, the new technologies have turned conception, pregnancy and childbirth – formerly an indivisible process – into separable reproductive 'services'; this fragmentation of the reproductive process appears to be a prerogative for the commercialization of motherhood. Commodification of reproductive services, body parts, and fluids moves to the centre of the debate. The possibility of buying or selling sperm or eggs, or renting out the womb as a gestating space is no longer a science fiction scenario: frequent advertisements for surrogate mothers, sperm and egg donors indicate the emergence of a market inhabited by sellers, buyers and brokers. A 'reproductive marketplace' is both welcomed and fiercely rejected. *Time* magazine, for instance, lauds the number of reproductive 'options' that doctors are now able to offer to their clients; women should appreciate the many 'choices' that offer them 'reproductive autonomy.' By contrast, radical feminists consider

149

the fragmentation and commercialization of the reproductive process the ultimate exploitation of women. Not coincidentally, both groups frame their arguments in terms of 'rights': the right to choose from a number of reproductive options versus the right of women to retain their reproductive integrity.

After the Baby M case in 1987, the American debate on reproductive technologies moves to the courtroom, the arena where 'rights' are commonly disputed, and where new legal definitions of parenthood take shape. The newest applications of IVF and GIFT provide the option of splitting genetic, gestational and social motherhood; a couple providing the sperm and egg, subsequently fertilized in vitro, may hire another woman to carry the zygote to term. Technically, a child may thus have several parents: the provider of the egg, the provider of the sperm, the woman who carried and/or delivered the baby, and those who raise the child. When fragmentation of parenthood surpasses the stage of mere technical feasibility and becomes reality, notions of ownership enter the debate and are brought before the court. In the USA, legal rulings are not being viewed as moral or ethical guidelines, but as official definitions which mark reproduction in terms of property. In other words, the court is not consulted to regulate the consequences of new reproductive technologies, but to decide who 'owns' the consequences of these technologies. In the 1990s, the legal system is increasingly called upon to chart the changing landscape of reproductive arrangements.

As the public debate is taken up by the American courts, the question of what constitutes 'motherhood' becomes paramount in the discussion. The Baby M case, in which the surrogate mother both provided the egg and carried the foetus to term, is in 1990 already dubbed 'traditional surrogacy,' implying the occurrence of much more complicated forms of contract pregnancy. Indeed, a legal ruling involving a 'normal' surrogate mother would not cause headlines any longer. A complex case that did make the headlines of American newspapers in 1990 happened in California, where the Superior Court Judge of Orange County was asked to decide whether a child 'belonged' to his genetic or gestational mother. The Orange County case turned out to change the legal definition of motherhood from the woman who carries and delivers the child to the woman who provides the genetic material.

Briefly outlined, the facts of the case are as follows: Crispina and Mark Calvert, an affluent white couple, hired Anna Johnson, a black vocational nurse and co-worker in the hospital where Crispina Calvert worked, to carry to term the foetus that was created in vitro out of the Calverts' egg and sperm. A hysterectomy performed on Crispina Calvert had made it impossible for the couple to conceive a child. They signed a contract with Anna Johnson to pay her 10 000 dollars plus medical costs for carrying and delivering the baby. Johnson, who was implanted with the fertilized egg in January 1990, announced seven months into her pregnancy that she intended to keep the baby due in October, and she filed a lawsuit to get custody over the child. The Court hearings took place in October, and on the 23rd of that month Judge Parslow ruled that the Calverts were the 'legal' parents of the child.

The Orange County case was extensively covered by the news media, in particular the *Los Angeles Times (LAT)*. Since the Court's ruling was expected to have a substantial impact on future federal legislation, the *LAT* assigned a special reporter to the case. Just as Louise Brown, the first test-tube baby, was heralded by the press as a scientific 'milestone,' the Orange County case was coined a 'legal landmark' by the news media. But the press played a significantly different role in 1990 than it did in 1978. Rather than contesting science's power to define, like the news media did in the case of Louise Brown, in this case the Judge's radical reversal of previous legal definitions of motherhood was hardly questioned. On the contrary, the *LAT* even became a decisive actor in the normative definition of genetic motherhood. The *LAT* 's coverage of the Orange County case reveals three important shifts in emphases in the public debate since 1978: the institutional discourses of science and journalism merge to reinforce normative – and in this instance legal – definitions of motherhood and pregnancy; feminist arguments are twisted to fit dominant discourse on reproduction; and scientific methods and instruments which were previously used to prove the 'need' for IVF, are now indispensable in proving the 'right' of owners of genetic material to the end product.

When a legal issue is reported in the news media, a common frame of representation is that of a contest: two parties claiming their rights to something. Implied in the use of this frame is the assumption that there are only two sides to an issue, and only one of the two parties can be right. News discourse actively shapes legal cases in yet another way; covering a court hearing or legal event, a journalist never merely reports legal discourse, but interprets a case by adding narratives: for instance, journalists may interpret the case by putting it in a certain context, they can add descriptions and quotes of persons involved, and include observations of events inside and outside the courtroom. By selecting, ordering and framing events, journalists actually reinscribe a legal decision, while pretending to merely 'cover' it.

A rhetorical analysis of the *LAT*'s coverage of the Orange County case will illustrate how the legal definition of 'mother' as 'genetic mother' emanates from, and is supported by, the merger of scientific and journalistic discourse. While trying to define the implications of IVF in legal terms, the court heavily relies on scientific-medical evidence. Medical definitions, which have come to dominate public consensus, inform a 'naturalized' meaning of reproductive technologies; in turn, this common sense meaning – and the parameters within which it is argued – informs legal discourse. The law both mirrors and constructs public consensus; like science and journalism, legal discourse does not merely reflect but also shape actual social practices.

The *LAT* 's reinscription of a legal definition is evidently rooted in 'naturalized' meanings of reproduction and motherhood. The California newspaper published at least twenty-four articles on the court case between July 1990 and April 1992.[1] Even though the articles appeared scattered in different sections of the newspaper, ranging from the health page to the front page, I will not regard them as a collection of isolated incidences of reporting, but as a 'continuing story' of the courtroom drama. As the drama unfolds, the powerful role of the discourses of journalism and science become evident in the articulation of a legal decision.

ANNA JOHNSON VERSUS THE *LOS ANGELES TIMES*

In the Calverts versus Johnson case, the issue is clearly framed as a dispute between two oppositional parties of which only one can be right. Two months before the actual case is debated in court,

Anna Johnson is already tried by the *LAT*. Three days after filing her lawsuit, on 13 August 1990, the newspaper features a news article, whose headline 'Surrogate Mother in Custody Fight Accused of Welfare Fraud' sets the tone for the *LAT*'s further depiction of Johnson.[2] The article reports that Anna Johnson is charged with two felony counts of welfare fraud, for allegedly failing to report income, while receiving food stamps and Aid to Families with Dependent Children (AFDC). An extensive quote from the Calverts' lawyer contends that because of these charges, Johnson 'cannot be trusted in everything she has said so far.' Implied in the choice of words are several important characterizations of Johnson: she is defined as a 'mother' but only with very negative attributions attached to this word. First she is identified as a 'single mother,' which in relation to her blackness connotes poverty and welfare dependency. Second, the word 'surrogate' in the headline suggests she is not a real mother, but serves as a substitute to the real thing. Third, the combination of these terms with charges of welfare fraud imply that she is also an 'unfit mother,' incapable of raising children.

Before she is even tried on these charges, Anna Johnson is framed in the *LAT* as a liar and a thief, the subtext of which is that she cannot be a good mother. Even if she had stolen money in order to feed her three-year-old daughter, the very fact that she is an alleged thief make her a bad mother. The charges are indeed dismissed after it becomes clear that the 5000 dollar surplus in food stamps were administered to Johnson partly because of a mistake of the AFDC agency. The allegations of welfare fraud, however, do not only shape Johnson's image before she is tried; in the ensuing court hearings, they will consistently be brought up as relevant facts in the characterization of Johnson as an unfit mother. This contention is underscored by a picture that shows Johnson in an unfavourable light: her dark, unhappy face seems to 'prove' everything that she is accused of in this article. Even without these accusations, Johnson's status as a black, welfare dependent single mother has already rendered her suspect; as Valerie Hartouni (1994) argues in her analysis of the case, popular portrayals of black women as welfare queens – defrauding the community while imperturbably breeding children – precede Anna Johnson's portrayal in the news media.[3] Reminding ourselves of the way in which black 'breeders' were previously pitched against 'desperate infertile white women' in the construction of the infertility 'plague,' we can see how these stereotypes inadvertently structure the depiction of single cases.

The *LAT*'s stance in the 'stand-off' between two opposing parties becomes evident when the description of Johnson is compared to that of the Calverts. Referring to them as 'the couple *whose* baby Johnson is due to deliver in October,' the legal definition seems anticipated in the newspaper's use of the possessive pronoun. As if to prove that the Calverts show conventional signs of parental feelings, the *LAT* reports how they are in a 'rush to finish decorating the baby's room,' which they have wallpapered with bright Disney characters. The Calverts are consistently depicted as the all-American nuclear family, in contrast to Anna Johnson, the single welfare mother.

In the article that announces the birth of the baby, the 'genetic parents' are further pitched against the 'surrogate who was implanted with an infertile couple's embryo.'[4] Johnson is now even stripped off the epithet 'mother,' while the Calverts are consequently designated as the 'owners' who have planted their seed on fertile soil to let it grow. The prevalence of the contribution of seed over the contribution of a fertile environment appears from the description of the infant's court-appointed lawyer, who races to the Court to obtain 'an order forcing immediate DNA-testing of the baby to confirm its parentage.' The superiority of genes is already implied in the crucial function of DNA testing: scientific, medically obtained evidence is the only legitimate proof of motherhood. The fact that Johnson actually delivered the child is never mentioned in this respect.

The first intervention of the Santa Ana Superior Court is reported in the *LAT* on September 22, 1990.[5] Judge Richard N. Parslow is asked to grant temporary custody of the baby to either Johnson or the Calverts. A tale from the Old Testament structures this news story, as Judge Parslow is likened in the first sentence to King Solomon. In the biblical tale, King Solomon offers to solve a dispute between two women, both claiming to be the mother of a baby, by cutting the child in two. Whereupon the true mother of the child comes forward and proposes to surrender the child to her contender, rather than see it harmed. King Solomon then appoints the child to her, since he interprets the woman's offer as a sign of real motherly feelings. The likening of King Solomon to Judge Parslow, however, is deceptive. In the dispute between the two 'mothers' of Baby Boy Johnson, the Judge threatens to put the child in a foster home; whereupon Anna Johnson comes forward and proposes to surrender the child to the Calverts, rather than having it put in a foster home. But unlike King Solomon, the Judge accepts Johnson's proposal and gives temporary custody to the Calverts. The *LAT*'s reporter cites the biblical metaphor to imply that the judge made a 'wise' decision, but never recounts the significant ending of the story, which would prove King Solomon's decision to be the opposite of Parslow's.

Even though Anna Johnson's generous offer to let the baby go home with the Calverts adds to her credibility as a 'mother,' the *LAT*'s reporter is quick to balance off a praising quote from her lawyer, Gilbert, by a less favourable quote from the infant's court-appointed lawyer, LaFlamme. Harold LaFlamme paints 'a less heroic portrait of the surrogate mother' saying that Johnson just 'caved in' when she realized the Judge would not give her the baby. Subsequently, LaFlamme is quoted as saying: 'If Saddam Hussein decides to withdraw from Kuwait, should he be considered a hero?' The analogy reinforces the idea that Anna Johnson's body is merely a piece of land which can be owned and exploited. Paradoxically, in this quote she is not only being likened to occupied land, but also to the (unlawful) occupier of the land. Implying that she is not the 'owner' of the resources exploited in her own body, the analogy simply turns Johnson's body into an area that is not hers. It is significant to add that, while Gilbert's praising comment was made in court, LaFlamme launched his analogy outside the courtroom; the report in the *LAT* thus deploys the narrative strategy of inclusion to arrange these comments in such a way that it turns Anna Johnson into a non-mother. Both the analogy of King Solomon and of Saddam Hussein are twisted to fit the interpretation of the Judge's 'wise' decision in favour of the Calverts.

An editorial on the Court's decision, in the same edition of the *LAT*, barely adds any 'opinion' to the so-called objective news article.[6] The editorial explicitly endorses the Judge's decision to appoint the baby to the Calverts, because the baby needs a 'good home in which to grow and mature.' Johnson's claims should not be taken seriously, because she has made many false statements in the past; the editorial advises the Judge to take her claim that she has bonded with the foetus, and her 'sacrifice' to let the baby go home with the Calverts, with a grain of salt. Referring to accusations of welfare fraud and her breach of contract, the editorial goes to great lengths to disqualify Johnson as a mother. Significantly, the author argues that her claims to motherhood are grounded 'outside the realm of science,' while the Calverts' claim to the child's parentage can be scientifically proven. Insisting that lab tests of DNA tissue are the only valid evidence in this case, the editorial concludes that permanent custody should be given to the *'true* genetic parents.' Science is thus invoked not only to 'prove' the prevalence of genetics in defining motherhood, but also to dismiss Johnson's interpretation of that term, as well as her nine months of pregnancy, to the realm of fiction or 'non-science.'

On the day Baby Boy Johnson is taken home by the Calverts, a large picture of Mark Calvert carrying the infant to his car dominates the front page of the *LAT.* [7] Apparently, the reporter accompanies the Calverts on their trip, since she extensively describes how the baby is welcomed into his new home:

> The 34-year-old insurance underwriter ran to the front door and onto the steps, smiling and extending his arms so Steiner [the Court-appointed guardian] could hand him the still-sleeping baby. After he crossed the threshold of the Calverts' home, the infant's life began to look a little more traditional. A houseful of relatives leaned over him, talking baby talk and watching rapturously as his diaper was changed.

The description of the welcoming home of the baby by the extended family adds to the notion of the Calverts as the 'real parents,' who can offer all the amenities of a 'true home.' This home is clearly an affluent home: the reporter describes how Crispina Calvert went on a shopping spree and bought a 'white changing table, a baby monitor, an infant bathing tub and a few tiny T-shirts' for the baby.

Implying that the Calverts are 'true parents' because they can afford to raise a child, their framing sharply contrasts the framing of Anna Johnson, who appears later that day to visit the boy. The visit, according to the only comment drawn from Johnson, went 'fine,' but the reporter adds other details to clarify Johnson's part in the childbearing. Quoting her lawyer, the journalist reports that Johnson 'probably has to stop breast-feeding the baby, because arrangements would be difficult and she feels that the Calverts do not want her to bring breast milk for the baby.' The description evokes a far from innocent stereotype: that of a black slave woman who was used to (breast)feed white babies. Like a female slave, the contracted birth giver is legally alienated from her child; her body lies open for use by white men of social standing and power.[8] Reinforcing Johnson's image as a 'breeder' – an image already invoked by the depiction of her as a black welfare mother – she is also coded as a black servant, who should put her natural fertility to the service of white 'owners.'

Most notably, race is *never* mentioned as a factor which could possibly play a role in this court case; the *LAT* not once mentions the fact that Johnson is black and the Calverts are of Caucasian-Filipino background. But the pictures provide the visual subtext for the conspicuous absence of racial identification: they underscore the common sense assumption that a white baby can never 'belong' to a black woman. Photographic evidence thus serves to support the genetic definition of parenthood, evidently denying any visible link between the (black) woman who was pregnant and the (white) baby she delivered.

When the court hearings for awarding permanent custody get under way, the *LAT*'s staff writer, Catherine Gewertz, almost daily reports the arguments made by the lawyers of the opposing parties. The reporter's choice of framing this legal argument immediately reveals her stance on the issue. In an October 10 article, the expert witness called in to testify for Johnson is already disqualified in the headline: 'Consultant says surrogate is child's mother.'[9] Michelle Harrison, a psychiatrist at the University of Pittsburgh, testifies that any woman who gives birth to a child and gestates it is a mother. But Harrison is immediately identified as a 'consultant to the National Coalition Against Surrogacy,' which turns her into an 'interested' party, and therefore renders her unqualified as an expert. In other words, her academic expertise is discredited because she has an ideological stake in the case and can thus not be an expert witness. Harrison's remarks are further discounted by a quote from the Calverts' lawyers contending that she is 'illogical.' The 'logic' is subsequently provided by LaFlamme, who cleverly asks Harrison why it is 'acceptable to define a father by his genetic contribution but not the mother?' Harrison's reply to this invocation of the 'equality' argument is that a definition which works for a father need not necessarily apply to a mother, which is subsequently dismissed as a 'belief'; while Harrison apparently has a belief or conviction, the opposing lawyers – who have an outright stake in the battle – use 'logic' in stating their claim and invoke 'scientific evidence' to back it up.

Besides giving evidently more space to the lawyer's dismissal of Harrison's claim, the journalist adds to the negative framing of Johnson in yet another way. When recounting several attempts by Van Deusen, the Calverts' lawyer, to question Johnson's credibility, she includes in her report the sentence: 'Van Deusen also tried to question the reliability of Johnson's claims by bringing up her guilty plea to two counts of welfare fraud, but Parslow barred that.' An argument not allowed in the court room is deliberately included in the media report, where it reinscribes dismissed allegations as truth. The journalist thus deploys her narrative power to adjust the admission of arguments in court.

The influence of the *LAT*'s reporter, Catherine Gewertz, on the course of the case becomes even more apparent as the court hearings continue. An October 11 article, headlined 'Surrogate Says She Secretly Aimed to Keep the Baby,' signals a curious stage in the testimony.[10] After her previous attempts to discredit Johnson in the *LAT*, the journalist herself is called to the witness stand to testify that Johnson is a liar. The Calvert's lawyer, Van Deusen, has questioned Johnson extensively to decide if, and if so at what point during her pregnancy, she had bonded with the baby. In order to prove that she has not bonded at all, he calls upon Catherine Gewertz, who has interviewed Anna Johnson in early August, to testify. During that interview, Johnson had allegedly told Gewertz that she did not feel attached to the baby. In the October 11 report, Catherine Gewertz describes her own role in the court drama in the following manner:

> During more than two hours of intense examination by Van Deusen, Johnson denied telling *The Times* in an interview in early August that she felt no connection to the baby because she knew it did not belong to her. Johnson told a reporter that she did not feel bonded to the child in her womb because it was not made from her genetic material.

Interestingly, there are several layers of facticity construction at work in this scene: the *Los Angeles Times* is called upon in Court to testify that Johnson is not telling the truth. The *LAT* is apparently regarded as an institutional authority that can act as an expert witness to verify 'facts.' Moreover, Gewertz then authorizes her own role in the court room by reporting herself as an institution: Catherine Gewertz does not say 'I testified that...' but writes instead 'Johnson told a reporter' and refers to herself as '*The Times*.' The journalist's objectification of her own testimony obviously serves to obscure her 'special' or subjective interest. An apparent conflict of interest is perfectly covered up by the professional routine of distancing. Gewertz's report of her own testimony basically allows her to verify that her article published in August was 'true' and 'factual,' and that Johnson must be lying.

Despite her direct involvement in the case and her explicit stance in the court hearings, Gewertz continues to report the case for the *LAT*. In her October 18 article, the closing statements of both sides' lawyers are extensively weighed.[11] As in previous articles, the Calverts' lawyer gets more space and the significant last word in the matter. In his final statement, Van Deusen is reported as saying that Johnson is 'trying to steal the Calverts' child,' the baby that is 'genetically theirs.' To support this contention, two of Van Deusen's arguments are fully quoted in the newspaper article. Both quotes resonate arguments launched in previous stages of the public debate: first, the lawyer argues that endorsing Anna Johnson's conduct and deception would open the door to 'exploitation of every infertile couple' that wants to have a baby by means of IVF. His second argument is that 'a woman must have a right to choose to let another couple's child grow in her uterus.'

The first point clearly echoes the argument launched previously in *Fertility and Sterility*: that IVF could lead to undesirable exploitation of infertile couples by evil and unqualified medical specialists. It also invokes objections to commercial IVF treatment voiced by feminists, that doctors may exploit woman's desperate yearning for a child to make huge profits. However, in this *LAT* article, these arguments are sharply turned around to fit the lawyer's claim that infertile couples are vulnerable to exploitation by 'surrogate' mothers, implying that poor, black welfare mothers are out to rip off innocent white couples. Indeed, the social hierarchy constituting the basis for exploitation is simply reversed, as black fertile women are pitched against white infertile women. Anna Johnson embodies the cultural stereotype of the black welfare dependent who is out to defraud the state and to undermine the traditional family concept.[12]

The second argument, that a woman must have the right to 'choose' to gestate another couple's zygote, is an even more remarkable twisting of a feminist argument. Presenting Johnson's claim to motherhood in relation to her 'right to choose,' the lawyer – and by extension the *LAT* – tries to deploy feminist rhetoric to support the definition of genetic motherhood. Obviously, the invocation of 'choice' appeals to the rhetoric used by the women's movement in defense of legal abortion. The right to reproductive freedom and autonomy is simply extended from a legal right to obtain medical help to terminate pregnancy, to the legal right to dispose of one's own reproductive organs to foster pregnancy. The use of 'choice' in this context is particularly tricky, since the purported expansion of freedoms may in fact be a disguise for an expansion of domination. Johnson obviously needed the 10 000 dollars offered to her in exchange for her reproductive 'services'; apparently, none of the Calverts' friends 'chose' to offer their reproductive capacities to the couple out of friendship. Moreover, a woman's right to choose for any kind of reproductive arrangement is not at stake in this case; at stake here is the question who owns the fruits of reproductive labour. The rhetoric of choice perfectly accommodates the perception of reproductive technologies as commodities, and simultaneously subverts the feminist argument that a woman has a right to make her own reproductive decisions.

There is another tricky tenet implicit in this argument: by stating that everyone has a right to dispose of his or her own reproductive organs, body parts, or fluids, the lawyer asserts an equal validation of male and female contributions to the reproductive process. For a woman to offer her womb as a gestating space, according to the lawyer, is the equivalent of a men donating sperm or a woman donating eggs. This legal argument, which explicitly erases sex-specific contributions to the reproductive process, finds its roots in previous stages of the public debate: as we have observed in medical journals and news media accounts, the 'un-gendering' of reproduction is articulated in an exclusive focus on the moment of conception, in which eggs and semen play equal parts. The specific female role, her gestating function, disappears almost completely. In this legal argument, gestation becomes a reproductive service literally subordinated to semen and eggs; yet the legal argument is merely an extension of *Time*'s visual annihilation of pregnancy as part of the reproductive process. The 'logic' that everyone must have the right to sell their blood, semen, and thus (the use of) their uteruses, is underscored by the closing statement of LaFlamme, the infant's court-appointed lawyer. He invokes the California law which requires bloodtests to determine parental rights. Whereas the law is called upon to back up scientific logic, science is invoked to certify the law.[13] And this circular argument is in turn enhanced by the newspaper, which frames as perfectly logical the assumption that the donation of sperm or blood equals the use of a uterus as a gestating space.

Now that *LAT* reporter Catherine Gewertz has become personally involved in the court case, the credibility and objectivity of the newspaper is at stake. In an October 22 news analysis, staff writer Sonni Efron scrutinizes the role of the news media in the Orange County case. He primarily deals with the public's complaint that the news media is 'playing out the courtroom drama to sell newspapers.'[14] Recounting the scene of scores of journalists trying to get a glimpse of the baby, the media-circus peculiarly resembles the siege of the hospital when Louise Brown was born.[15] Following a court order from Judge Parslow barring the two parties to distribute pictures of the baby, most newspapers featured a front page picture of the court-appointed custodian or the father carrying the baby wrapped in clothes. According to Efron, the news media, while scrambling to get the first photo of the baby, may indeed have intruded upon the privacy of the persons involved.

Yet while criticizing the role of the news media in general, Efron defends the *LAT*'s influential role in the courtroom drama. To justify the involvement of the *LAT*'s reporter in the court case, Efron argues that she has unwillingly been drawn into the case, since 'the Calverts' lawyers forced the *Times*' reporter covering the case to testify.' Gewertz's participation in the Court hearings is described as 'involuntary,' even though she has clearly been welcomed into the Calverts' house and has been awarded frequent quotes from the couple and their lawyer. Johnson's lawyer's request to have Catherine Gewertz barred from the courtroom, following her testimony which would no longer allow her to maintain her objectivity and credibility as a journalist, was reportedly rejected by the Judge. The author subsequently calls upon journalism experts to confirm the rightness of that decision. Efron's 'news analysis' somehow cleanses Gewertz from her involvement in the case, arguing that the *LAT* should be involved because of its duty to inform the audience.

The role of the press as a reluctant witness is confirmed by Efron's general depiction of the newspaper as a 'victim' of publicity-eager parties; both lawyers allegedly use the news media to get publicity. Yet whereas the Calverts' meddling with the media is described as an attempt to counteract the 'outrageous accusations' made by Johnson, Johnson's invocation of the media works to her disadvantage. 'Her willingness to use the media to publicize her case demonstrates that she is an unfit mother' the Calvert's attorney is quoted as saying. Johnson's comment that she turned to the media 'in desperation' to have her point of view heard, also works against her: according to her ex-roommate, who has been called to the witness stand, Johnson was motivated to keep the baby by 'a desire for money and publicity.' By playing the legal contestants off against one another, the journalist tries to uphold the newspapers 'disinterested' or impartial position.

When the final verdict in the case comes out on October 22, the *LAT* reporter's testimony appears to have played a substantial role in the Judge's decision. In a front page article 'Genetic Parents Given Sole Custody of Child,' Catherine Gewertz reports extensively on the decision, stating that 'the judge agreed with Mark and Crispina Calvert ... that the couple's genetic relationship to the baby makes them the only true parents.'[16] In his address to the courtroom, Judge Parslow likened Anna Johnson's role to that of a foster parent who voluntarily cared for the child because the real mother was unable to do so. Extensive parts of the Judge's address are literally quoted, specifically the part in which Parslow states that his decision is 'pro-child.' The use of this term hooks into the public debate on abortion, and is reminiscent of the term 'pro-life', coined by anti-abortion protestors to identify themselves.

Parslow's refusal to 'split the child emotionally between two mothers' is underwritten by a quote from the infant's court-appointed guardian, who contends that 'this child needs a consistent figure in his life.' Implying that Anna Johnson is an unstable and unreliable figure, Catherine Gewertz brings up her own part in the testimony; in his decision, Judge Parslow agreed there was 'substantial evidence' that Johnson had never bonded with the child. Johnson's claim of bonding is discredited because claims registered by an institutional authority – the *Los Angeles Times* – are validated over her own experience.

The legal ruling is of course welcomed by the Calverts' lawyer, who once again gets the opportunity to repeat his argument that 'women are entitled to do what they choose with their reproductive powers.' The only comment to balance off the positive assessment of the verdict comes from the ACLU, who favoured a three-parent ruling in the case. The larger part of the article is dedicated to prove the 'rightness' of the Judge's decision. The *LAT*'s editorial that same day therefore becomes almost obsolete, since the newspaper's stance on the issue is already abundantly clear from the framing of the news article.[17] The editorial statement that the 'surrogate was a genetic and hereditary stranger to the baby' who is 'not to be mistaken for the real mother' merely confirms what had already been implied in Gewertz's report.

Judge Parslow's decision on October 22, 1990, to name the Calverts the official parents is not the end of the *LAT*'s coverage of this story. Three months later, the *Los Angeles Times Magazine* features a ten page article by Martin Kasindorf on the Johnson versus Calvert case.[18] The report recounts the story in retrospect, recasting all major actors and defining their roles in this landmark case that will now make its way to the higher courts. In contrast to previous articles in the *LAT*, this one is not a news story, but a background report. Rather than an overview of events, a background report can be considered a 'historical reconstruction' or reinscription. Unlike daily news reports, a background story purports to explain particular events in a wider (historical, legal, social) context. It is particularly the provision of context that discloses the ideological imprint of the story.

The *LAT*'s stance on the issue can be inferred by just looking at the photographs of the actors involved in the court case. Even though the pictures speak for themselves, the captions are very explicit about the role each person plays. A picture of Anna Johnson is captioned: 'The Surrogate: Anna Johnson's legal revolt is certain to transform the all's fair status of surrogacy in California.' A picture of the Calverts embracing each other on the next page is subtitled: 'The Parents: Mark and Crispina Calvert's experience is a cautionary primer for infertile couples desperate to have children.' The pictures set the visual stage for the interpretation of past events. Johnson's history of welfare-dependency and fraud, her social status as a single mother, and her habit of lying and cheating, all serve to explain her 'legal revolt.' In his attempt to regard these characters and this case in a wider social context, the author points out that Anna Johnson is an exception when it comes to surrogate mothers: surrogates are typically white and working class, most of whom want to 'make amends for loss of an earlier pregnancy, such as an abortion' (14). Johnson's minority and lower class background thus does not fit the profile of the 'common' gestational surrogate. The Calverts, on the other hand, represent the typical desperate infertile couples who are usually white and of middle class or upper class background. Their desire for a genetically linked child is justified by a scientific study that shows how 'heredity is even more influential than researchers believed, accounting for seventy per cent of intelligence.'

General data and research reports are thus invoked to explain that the Calverts' desire for a child of their own is normal, whereas Johnson's 'revolt' is rather uncommon.[19] Johnson, if she would have reacted 'normally' would never have bonded with a child that is not genetically hers. To prove her deviancy, the author quotes two other 'surrogate mothers – one from Massachusetts, another from Ohio – who deny they have ever bonded with the child they were carrying. Johnson's experience is thus defined as abnormal, untrue, and by implication illegal. The contribution of her pregnancy is not merely discounted, but even depicted as a possible liability to the well-being of a foetus: 'The physiological contributions of a gestational surrogate – who can hurt a fetus by using tobacco, alcohol, or crack cocaine – could be accorded a legal perch alongside biological contributions' (14). Defining Johnson's interpretation of motherhood as deviant from the norm is a very powerful way to discount her personal experience as invalid.

Whereas Catherine Gewertz in her reports of the court hearings never even mentioned race as a factor in this case, Kasindorf brings up the issue in a peculiar way. He contends that race – 'which was no factor originally' – was exploited by Johnson to push her legal claim. Rather than providing statistics and background information on the poor financial situation of black single mothers, the author shows how Johnson's lawyer 'creatively used' her minority status in the hearings. Because of Johnson's partial Native-American descent, her lawyer essayed a claim under the federal Indian Child Welfare Act, which requires tribes to be notified when a member puts up a baby for adoption. Dismissing this claim as trivial, the *LAT* author also ridicules a letter Johnson wrote to popular talkshow host Geraldo Rivera, explaining why she refused to appear on his show by stating 'I am not a slave. Semper Fi.' Like Johnson's experience of pregnancy, her experience of race and racism is also systematically discounted and erased from the *LAT*'s account. Just like the Judge's denial of a different (gendered) definition of reproduction, the journalist does not allow a different (racial) assessment of the event. Actually, allowing an interpretation of this case in the context of race and class would change the parameters of the dispute; it would bring in social arguments, whereas the Court and the newspaper have restricted the range of admissible arguments to genetics and physiology. The background report in the *LAT*, a genre which could be deployed to view this issue in a different light, reinforces the Court's definition.

As we learn from the byline, the author of this piece, Martin Kasindorf, a correspondent for the New York based newspaper *Newsday*, is also a lawyer by training. The journalistic report has quite a few features that would qualify it as legal discourse. By evaluating the ruling in the context of research data, quotes from experts, and other court cases, he brings together a host of scientific, anecdotal and statistical evidence to 'prove' the Judge's decision. The author never questions the primacy of genetics as the determining factor in defining motherhood. Even though the Court has turned around the California legal definition of 'mother,' from the woman who gives birth to the child to the woman who provides the egg, the journalist/lawyer merely registers that the 15-year-old version of the Uniform Parenting Act no longer applies; he calls this law, which recognizes the birth mother as the only parent, a 'technologically outmoded legal presumption.' Now that the Judge is called upon to map uncharted legal terrain, the lawyer/journalist does everything in his discursive power to explain why the Judge simply *had* to make this decision: his journalistic narrative makes it seem as if the Judge had no other option than ruling the way he did. The journalist thus assumes the role of 'public lawyer' who concurrently informs the audience and constructs a journalistic extension of legal evidence presented in court.

THE NATURALIZATION OF A LEGAL DEFINITION

What the discourses of journalism and law have in common, is that each is assumed to reflect 'facts' or common sense, even as both busily construct it. Analysing the *LAT*'s coverage of the Orange County case, we can see how the discourses of journalism and law tend to authorize one another. Both the Court and the newspaper act out their interpretative skills in the name of the public: the Judge is asked to 'read' the law in order to inform the people about what is right, whereas the journalist is supposed to 'read' the court case to inform the audience about what has happened. In the court's as well as the newspaper's interpretation, science is invoked to justify the definition of genetic motherhood. In addition, both the Judge and the journalists of the *LAT* make it appear as if their readings are the only possible interpretations of this case. Relying on each other's institutional independence, their mutual invocation of authority enhances the illusion of objectivity. Obviously, neither law nor news are as neutral or disinterested as they would like to appear; judges and journalists are actively involved in the production of cultural meanings.

As we can infer from the coverage of the court hearings, the Judge purportedly saw himself drawn into a legal area that had not been explored before. In the absence of legislative guidance or political decisions, Parslow implies that technology forced him to set new legal standards, yet he does not use this opportunity to adjust outdated definitions of parenthood. By denying even visitation rights to Anna Johnson, he reinforces the conventional definition of 'family' as consisting of one mother and one father, despite the fact that there are various provisions in American law to grant custody or visitation rights to persons other than the 'natural' or 'legal' parents. Grandparents or siblings, for example, can get visitation rights, which at least recognize their social bond with a child. The Judge chose not to use these legal provisions, instead claiming that a 'three-parent, two-natural-moms plan is a situation ripe for crazy-making.'[20] Rather than 're-mapping' the borderlands of reproduction, the Judge uses this occasion to reinscribe an even more traditional definition of parenthood than was already provided for in the law. Other readings of the definition of motherhood are outlawed, so the norm becomes the law.

In a similar vein, the *LAT* deployed journalistic conventions to validate the traditional interpretation of motherhood offered by the Court. The newspaper thoroughly relied on conventional routines of balancing and distancing to frame two supposedly 'opposite' parties. From the very beginning of the coverage, Anna Johnson was pitched against the Calverts in a way that almost prohibited a view of Johnson as a mother, or even a co-mother. Terms used in headlines, like 'stand-off,' 'court battle,' and 'custody fight,' suggest that only one of the parties can finally be 'right.' The depiction of Anna Johnson as a single black welfare mother made it difficult for a newspaper reader to possibly perceive her as the rightful parent of a white, healthy baby boy. In contrast to the depiction of the Calverts as the happy, loving, affluent white couple, the Judge's decision to name them the 'natural' parents becomes almost self-evident. Rather than exploring how this court case could open up possibilities of redefining motherhood and reproduction, the journalists consistently interpreted legal discourse in the wake of traditional family norms, using familiar frames.

The *LAT*'s outspoken support for the Judge's decision, and its disqualification of Anna Johnson, may be even hardly noticeable to a casual reader. Ideological preference only shows when the newspaper stories are read in connection to one another; moreover, journalism and legal discourse have to be analysed conjuncturally, in order to recognize their interdependency and mutual inclusion. The mechanism of allotting discursive authority is rendered invisible by institutional routines: the Court affirms the authority of the journalist by allowing her to testify in court; by the same token, the newspaper enhances the authority of the Court by providing 'factual' evidence to support its legal interpretation. But the institutional discourses of law and journalism can only uphold their inscribed authority by insisting on independence and autonomy: their appearance as separate, institutional discourses serves to guarantee claims to objectivity and neutrality.

The verdict and the journalistic account of it seem only 'natural' in the wake of a public consensus on reproductive technologies. Obviously, the Judge and the *LAT* reporter consider their interpretations to be a reflection of common sense, as they present their definition as the only logical one. Both the newspaper and the Court assume that DNA-testing and blood samples provide the essential evidence to prove parenthood; the conclusion that genetic contribution is the prime factor in determining motherhood thus becomes mere deduction – the logical aligned with the natural. The text, the narrative that is constructed, conditions its own authority: in fact, there is no appeal to any source of authority outside the text itself. Hence, the laws of nature to which the text turns for support, are textual laws. The logic of nature seems beyond interpretation, as it appears to be a truth that can be understood by everyone, regardless of ideological orientation.[21]

In the *LAT*'s coverage of the Court hearings, we can also witness how traces of contestation and argument are erased, and how opposing voices are reshaped to suit the legal definition of genetic motherhood. Feminist arguments – arguing against exploitation, for the right to choose, and for 'equality' – frequently surface in dominant discourse. Public consensus, in fact, does not imply that divergent interpretations of reproduction have been reconciled, but that opposing views have been absorbed by dominant meanings. A (legal) definition, as Treichler (1990) has pointed out, is indeed less democratic than a meaning. In this particular court case, alternative definitions of motherhood – meanings unwarranted by 'scientific evidence' – are excluded; arguments of gender, race and class are dismissed from legal discourse, and expelled from the newspaper. All attempts by Johnson and her lawyer to bring in these factors as relevant, are rejected on the grounds that they do not belong to the realm of logic.

The *LAT*'s reporting of the Calverts vs. Johnson case cannot simply be dismissed as bad coverage. As compared to some other (local and national) papers, the *LAT* seems rather reticent in sensationalizing the issue; the *San Diego Tribune*, for instance, is exclusively focused on the discreditation of Anna Johnson.[22] Neither of these California papers gave any space to interpretations deviating from Judge Parslow's verdict. Few national newspapers, such as the *Wall Street Journal*, actually did publish dissenting voices on the Court's ruling, but only as Op-Ed pieces; other papers, notably the *Christian Science Monitor*, framed the Orange County case in the perspective of similar claims to legal parenthood and custody.[23] If viewed in isolation, the outcome of this particular court case may seem insignificant; the *LAT*'s coverage of these hearings may be looked upon as an unfortunate incidence of biased reporting. Yet in the perspective of the previously analysed public debate on new reproductive technologies, we can see how the arguments and facts brought up in the court and the newspaper emanate from a normative 'consensus' that has been constructed over the past years. The legalization of genetic motherhood is firmly rooted in the normalization of procreative technologies, and the naturalization of IVF as a means to obtain a child of one's own.

After the legal ruling by the Orange County Judge, Johnson's lawyer Gilbert takes his case to the California Supreme Court. On 20 May 1993, the State's Supreme Court decides to uphold Parslow's decision that Johnson has no maternal rights to the boy, who is by now two-and-a-half years old. In a six to one vote, the Justices state that the decisive factor in determining maternity is the 'intent of the two women who together fulfil the biological role of mother.'[24] While acknowledging both women as 'biological mothers' only one of them can intend to procreate a child, and according to the Justice who wrote the majority opinion, this one is 'she who intended to bring about the birth of a child that she intended to raise as her own.' The only woman on the state's Supreme Court, Justice Joyce L. Kennard, writes the dissenting opinion. She warns that the role of pregnancy should not be devalued: 'A pregnant woman intending to bring a child into the world is more than a mere container or a breeding animal.'

In addition to granting exclusive maternal rights to the genetic mother, the Court also validates the rather controversial and up to then illegal surrogate contract between Johnson and the Calverts. According to the majority opinion, parts of which are quoted in the *LAT*, 'the woman who enters into gestational surrogacy arrangements is not exercising her own right to make procreative choices; she is agreeing to provide a necessary and profoundly important service without (by definition) any expectation that she will raise the resulting child as her own.' The words written by the Justice and highlighted in the *LAT* resound two arguments that have been brought up previously in the debate: the 'right to choose' and the idea of offering a 'gestating space' as a reproductive service. The *LAT*'s front page article is finished by two quotes, providing opposite views on the Court's decision: one by a representative of the national Center Against Surrogacy in Washington, who states that this decision turns 'childbearing into a business, a commodity'; and one quote from the Calverts' lawyer, who states that 'everyone should be celebrating because Christopher [the baby] is the real winner.' An editorial in the *LAT* of that same day underscores this conclusion, while also calling for more legislative guidance in surrogacy matters.[25]

An attempt by Johnson's lawyer to have the US Supreme Court challenge the state Court's verdict strands five months later. The Supreme Court declines to review the precedent setting California case. In the *LAT* report, Johnson's lawyer Gilbert is quoted as saying that the Court 'missed the opportunity of the century' to create clarity in future gestational surrogacy cases.[26] A large picture accompanying the article, the Calverts proudly show off their final prize: after three years of fighting in court, they can call this smiling, all-American boy 'their own.' A disappointed Anna Johnson, according to the California newspaper, plans to pursue a new venue: Congress. Echoing earlier calls for politicians to set standards in surrogacy matters, single legal rulings set the stage for legislative definitions of what may count as motherhood.

Between 1978 and 1993, the widespread use of IVF and related technology has become accepted as a normal procedure in reproductive medicine; subsequently, the 'naturalized' meaning of assisted reproduction informs the legal definition of genetic motherhood. Legalization of this definition serves to protect the interests of producers of technology: without legal confirmation of the supremacy of genes over gestation, the technical devices would be less valuable. If both genetic and gestational mothers could claim the right to 'own' a baby, IVF would lose much of its market value. In the rhetoric of the marketplace, the issue revolves around questions of ownership; the highest Court affirms that only one father and one mother can claim the right to parenthood. To complete the circularity of argument, the very technology which caused the split between genetic and gestational motherhood, is also called upon to prove the superiority of offspring over its 'gestational environment.' Single cases and court decisions, finally, prompt politicians to create legislative rules, which will in turn be informed by the very 'public consensus' that underlies the outcome of court cases.

THE DIVIDED FEMINIST BODY

The call for legislative guidance can be heard from both proponents and opponents of contract pregnancy. Medical specialists involved in IVF treatment urge for legislation that would protect the customer against exploitation by commercial 'surrogacy brokers'; feminists opposing surrogacy demand legislation that would outlaw any commercial activity with regard to assisted reproduction. However, there is no such thing as 'the feminist stance' just as it is hard to identify a clearcut 'mainstream view' on this particular issue. The question of paid surrogacy triggers a flood of diverse reactions. After the Baby M controversy, but particularly following the Calvert vs. Johnson case, hundreds of books, articles, position papers and reports appear, in which feminists argue the pros and cons of contract pregnancy.[27]

These feminist publications range from fierce rejections of the reproductive marketplace to a firm embracement of it. Christine Overall (1987), for instance, compares contract pregnancy to prostitution, and considers the exploitation resulting from surrogacy arrangements inevitable; on the other end of the spectrum, Lori B. Andrews (1989) defends the position that opposing surrogacy would seriously undermine a feminist agenda, because the desire for a biological child is morally appropriate.[28] Experiential definitions of surrogacy are equally divided: some feminists describe the positive attributes of 'shared reproduction' between women or sisters, while others relate their own negative experiences as surrogate mothers.[29] There are also a number of books published in which feminist arguments for and against surrogacy are juxtaposed.[30] In all these accounts, the question of gender is paramount to the question whether surrogacy arrangements should be supported.

In addition to gender, the Calvert vs. Johnson case brings the issue of race to the spotlight. Various scholars criticize Judge Parslow's decision and sketch the legal implications resulting from upholding the contract that validates genetic over gestational motherhood. Alexander Capron (1991), for instance, worries that the outcome of the Orange County case could make gestational surrogacy legally attractive; Rita Arditti (1990) warns that the verdict in fact endorses the profit motive in surrogacy, which may particularly lead to the exploitation of black women.[31] In response to Anna Johnson's defeat in court, Katha Pollitt, writing for *The Nation*, argues that paid surrogacy is bound to degrade black women, since racism is a decisive factor in the determination of legal custody.[32] Laura Purdy disagrees with Pollitt; she argues that 'would not always be racist for a white couple to use their own egg' just as it would not be racist for a black couple to desire an egg from a black woman.[33] If regulated to avoid exploitation of the lower classes, Purdy argues that contract pregnancy might help black or poor women to better their circumstances.

Yet another view is provided by Valerie Hartouni (1994) who, after a careful analysis of the racist prerogatives involved in this case, surprisingly concludes that the outcome would not have been different had Johnson been white. Even though the court – and the news media, for that matter – played out Johnson's racial disposition, the court's primary aim was to restabilize conventional understandings of parent and family. According to Hartouni, all legal rulings are out to contain potential radical effects of new reproductive practices. While reproductive practices are determined by racial, gender and class hierarchy, the aim of the struggle is to underscore the concept of the nuclear family; even more socially disturbing than assigning a white child to a black mother would be for the Court to recognize that a family may consist of more than two legal parents. The social norms with regard to motherhood certainly lag behind technological feasibilities.

By 1993, feminist positions on contract pregnancy, as exemplified by these instances, have become as divided as the female reproductive body itself. How many feminist positions can be identified with regard to this issue? On the one hand, there is the ultimate liberalist argument of feminists who advocate surrogacy on the premise that women are free to make any reproductive choice. Another group of feminists calls for a ban on all forms of IVF treatment, including surrogacy, because it exploits and degrades women. Some feminists argue in favour of surrogacy, but only if it is tightly controlled and regulated by state laws. A fourth group states that contract pregnancy should be outlawed, while surrogate pregnancy among relatives or friends should be allowed. By the same token, some feminists are against the division of gestational and genetic motherhood: they object to gestational surrogacy, but accept 'traditional' surrogacy. A sixth type of feminist position wants to foreclose international or interracial surrogacy arrangements, in order to prevent potential exploitation of Third World or poor women of colour. Finally, there are feminists who want to allow contract pregnancy, on the condition that the surrogate mother may change her mind during the pregnancy, while some want to allow it providing that the 'intending mother' has a dysfunctional womb and cannot carry her foetus to term.

As soon as the debate on new reproductive technologies enters the realm of rights, it appears impossible to speak of a 'feminist' position. Feminism and mainstream arguments are tightly interlocked, and can be found in both mainstream and oppositional publications. Yet what strikes me in many feminist accounts is that most arguments follow the traditional format of debating: you are either for or against contract pregnancy, like in earlier stages of the debate you were either for or against IVF, or you were either favouring or rejecting science. The discourse of 'rights' seems particularly tricky because rights may be understood both as a woman's private liberty to use her own body and as a woman's power to defend her bodily integrity; both sides invoke the court or legislators to protect this right. For feminists to adopt the binary frameworks of argument means to stay within the parameters set by dominant discourse. Rather than arguing for or against the 'issue' – whether technology itself or an application thereof – few feminists plead to take a different venue: 'reproductive rights' must always be linked to a broad range of social, economic and cultural conditions.

The (feminist) focus on specific applications of IVF or individual, precedent setting cases, however significant and important, often distract from the wider implications involved in the application of new technologies. Controversies and court cases, as we have seen, easily fit the preferred debating conditions set by institutional discourses, e.g. medicine and journalism. Indeed, the division between gestational and genetic motherhood results in even more complicated issues and cases, as we will see when we move on to the most recent stage of the debate. Gender, race and class are not the only factors that have to be taken into account when it comes to defining motherhood; the age of women is also a case in point. Yet the more factors are involved in questions of motherhood and reproduction, the more pointless it becomes to approach these matters using reductive binary frameworks.

7 From Legalization to Legislation: Race and Age as Determining Factors

The problem is not one of runaway science or technology. It is the artificial way our society grades people according to colour. If we lived in a non-racist society, it would be as immaterial whether a child was black or white as whether it had big or small feet. The logical consequence of the argument for a ban on transracial implementation is a ban on transracial relationships. That used to be called apartheid.

(Kenan Malik in the *Independent*)

If age is now a criterion by which central government decides whom science may assist at birth, what other criteria are on the agenda? There must be a case for banning teenage pregnancy, on the statistical evidence that the children may experience a broken home. Certain genetic features may also be unwelcome: for instance, a history of mental illness or disability. Perhaps HIV or addicted parents should be impeded from conceiving.

(Simon Jenkins in *The Times*)

INTRODUCTION

While in the USA, judges and lawyers are increasingly calling for politicians to tackle the thorny business of reproductive technologies, in Britain and other European countries the application of IVF and related techniques has already led to government regulation. Traditionally, in American society the courts are designated to settle disputes concerning ownership

175

and control of human tissues or services; the use of reproductive technologies is subject to no other than general medical regulations. Beginning in 1987, American politicians are urged to pass laws which would protect citizens from commercial exploitation by infertility clinics; judges ask for appropriate political guidance because they lack jurisdiction in these new fields. Contrastingly, in Britain the new technologies have been discussed mostly in terms of moral and ethical restrictions rather than in terms of ownership or contract law. In response to the government's inclination to control reproductive practices, we can witness a strong current arguing for deregulation. There is a constant anxiety that the state might interfere with the individual's right to privacy, and objections against state regulation can frequently be heard.

In the wake of British tradition, it is not surprising that the first attempt to regulate IVF centres dates back to 1985. The Warnock report – named after baroness Warnock who chaired the committee – was the first written code intending to curb the rapid proliferation of IVF centres. The report resulted in the installation of a Voluntary Licensing Authority, which issued licenses to IVF centres subjecting themselves on a voluntary basis to its formal ethical code. When in 1990 the Human Fertilisation and Embryology Act was passed, the statutory body responsible for its enactment formulated an official Code of Practice. Fertility centres wanting to obtain a licence were now required to follow the rules set by the Human Fertilisation and Embryology Authority (HFEA). Since 1990, the HFEA has developed the Code of Practice, and has licensed over one hundred IVF clinics in Britain; furthermore, the HFEA has kept a confidential register of donors to IVF programmes, and has made regular recommendations to Parliament. Britain was the first country to regulate infertility treatment and practices, and the Authority is under close scrutiny throughout Europe.

The HFEA consists of twenty-one people, varying from lawyers and scientists to church leaders and actresses; they guard the central tenet of the Act, which says that the welfare of the child born by IVF or related techniques must always be considered before the desires of the parents. Since the year of its inception, the HFEA has addressed divergent questions raised by doctors and patients alike: Should success rates of different clinics be published? Should donors of genetic material remain anonymous? How many 'pre-embryos' should be implanted in a woman's womb in one single treatment cycle? Should lesbian couples get access to infertility services? Should sex preselection of embryos be allowed?[1] Because of changes in public perceptions and attitudes, as well as scientific advances, the HFEA constantly faces new challenges.

During the turn of the year 1993-1994, the HFEA and the public were confronted with three new ethical dilemmas in the area of reproductive medicine. On Christmas day, a 59-year-old British woman gave birth to healthy twins; after having been denied infertility treatment in a British clinic, the woman had sought the help of an Italian doctor, who fertilized an egg from a younger donor with her husband's sperm, and implanted the zygote into the British woman's womb. A few days after Christmas, another peculiar case prominently figured on the front pages: a black woman in Italy had been implanted with an egg donated by a white woman, which was fertilized by her white husband's sperm. That very same day, it became known that British doctors were contemplating a similar case of transracial impregnation. And on top of this, a new type of infertility treatment involving the use of eggs from aborted foetuses was proposed to the HFEA on 3 January, 1994. This method was desperately needed, according to specialists, to alleviate the serious shortage of donor eggs.

All three incidences are 'natural' consequences of the new technologies, resulting from the feasibility of separating gestational and genetic motherhood. By 1993, the method to fertilize eggs in vitro and implant them in another body had been used for quite a number of years. What caused public outcry was not so much the technology itself, but its new beneficiaries – women past menopause and black women – and new sources from which to draw genetic material. It was probably the realization that the technologies will indeed change traditional social and cultural relationships that triggered debates all over Europe. Headlines introducing terms like 'granny mums' and 'custom designed babies' reflected the fear of traditional boundaries of motherhood being desecrated. Not just in Britain, but all over Europe, people called for tighter legislation and bans on reproductive 'excesses'.

The debate in the British newspapers quickly evolved into a reductive argument on whether to allow postmenopausal pregnancy and transracial implantation. Parallel to this 'pro-con' discussion runs the argument for or against government regulation. More people, among them the HFEA board, start to realize that a real public debate is needed to discuss the underlying rationale of the new technologies rather than solve isolated incidences on an ad hoc basis; legislation only works if it is supported by a public consensus. But how can a debate be transformed from a narrow discussion on specific cases into a broad platform where these issues are discussed in their wider social and cultural contexts?

POSTMENOPAUSAL PREGNANCIES

The relation between age and fecundity has been pivotal to the debate on new reproductive technologies from the very onset. As we may recall from Chapter 3, the infertility myth was partly based on the assumption that (liberated) women postponed childbearing, instead opting for a career. In the rhetoric of the 'plague,' women called infertility upon them, because by waiting too long to get pregnant they run the risk of loosing their most fertile eggs. A 1982 article in the *New England Journal of Medicine* reflects this anxiety. French researchers found that fecundity in females begins to reduce at age thirty, and significantly decreases after thirty-five.[2] The ramifications of these results are crystal clear, according to an editorial in that same issue: 'The age of women should now be considered in deciding when to start an infertility workup or stop treatment for infertility, and in selecting appropriate candidates for tubal surgery and IVF' (425).[3] After the publication of this and similar research reports, women over forty were effectively barred from IVF programmes on the pretext that their physiological conditions were too poor to guarantee success. Indeed, success rates was what this was all about: women over forty, and certainly women past menopausal age, kept valuable success rates of clinics down, so doctors were simply not interested in these patients. Moreover, allowing older women to IVF treatment would contravene the ideology prevailing at that time, that women should spend their most fertile years on pregnancy and childbirth. Or, as the *NEJM* editorializes: 'Perhaps the third decade should be devoted to childbearing and the fourth to career development, rather than the converse, which is true for many women today' (425).

Eight years later, in 1990, the decrease of female fecundity with age is viewed from a quite different perspective, due to recently developed methods of egg donation and oocyte transplantation. The problem with reduced fertility after the age of forty becomes itemized: chances for producing viable eggs are considerably reduced if women are over forty, but older women have equal capacity to gestate and deliver babies than younger women. An article in the *NEJM* reports successful treatment of seven women with ovarian failure between forty and forty-four years of age.[4] The method of egg donation and oocyte transplantation had already been frequently applied to younger women who suffered from 'early menopause.' We learn from this *NEJM* article that almost ten per cent of the female population stops ovulating before they reach the age of forty. As compared to this group of younger women with ovarian failure, postmenopausal women are doing just as well in gestating and delivering babies, which leads the researchers to conclude: 'Since women in this age group with functioning ovaries are considered appropriate candidates for infertility treatment, it seems appropriate that those without ovarian function [postmeno-pausal women] should also be allowed a chance to experience pregnancy if they desire it' (1160).

That very same day, *The New York Times* promises in its headlines that 'menopause is no bar to pregnancy'.[5] This new method – retrieving eggs from younger donors who are paid 1500 dollar to have their ovaries stimulated with hormones – will advance infertile women over forty who previously failed 'traditional' IVF treatment. It simultaneously opens up the possibility for all postmenopausal women to become pregnant. The limits of childbearing years 'are now anyone's guess' as *The New York Times* quotes the editorial statement from the prestigious medical journal. The editorials in the 1982 and 1990 issue of the *NEJM* reflect a remarkable shift: in 1982, women were summoned to devote their most fertile years to childbearing and clinics were advised to bar older women from IVF treatment; in 1990, doctors argue that older women should be allowed a fair chance to experience pregnancy. Does this signify a shift in ideology? I am afraid the shift is the result of changed economic prospects rather than changed ideological motives. With the advent of egg donation and oocyte transplantation, success rates for treatment of older women may considerably increase. In other words, postmenopausal women are discovered as a new segment of the consumer market; after all, they tend to be wealthier than younger women and their numbers are considerable.

Tapping a new outlet of the IVF business was exactly what doctor Severino Antinori did. The Italian gynaecologist started his Rome-based clinic in 1988, 'specializing' in IVF treatment to postmenopausal women. In most European countries, women over forty or forty-five are barred from IVF treatment in regular, government licensed clinics. A 59-year-old British woman – in most newspapers described as a 'millionaire business woman' – had unsuccessfully tried to receive treatment at an IVF clinic in Britain. Even though the law does not set an upper age limit for treatment, doctors are required to assess the welfare of the child and health risks for the mother under the rules set by the HFEA. After being rejected for those reasons by British clinics, the woman travelled to Italy, where doctor Antinori helped her to get pregnant. Even though she was not the oldest woman in the world to become pregnant – Antinori had also helped a 62-year-old Italian woman – the birth of her twin babies on Christmas Day 1993 caused a newspaper storm which lasted for almost two weeks. Old and new questions were raised by several interested parties and individuals. The event elicited two types of reactions in the British newspapers: those in favour of postmenopausal treatment and those rejecting any extension of a natural childbearing age.

Both *The Times* and the *Guardian* concentrate their reports of the twin babies' birth on reactions from officials who are appalled by this incidence, and who call for tighter regulation.[6] Virginia Bottomley, British Secretary of Health, is extensively quoted in both newspapers; she wants to draw up an international ethical code to govern infertility and prevent future 'reproductive tourism.' Mrs Bottomley is supported by Dr John Marks, former chair of the British Medical Association Council, who said that the latest case 'bordered on the Frankenstein syndrome.' According to the *Guardian*, Marks found it quite horrifying that the woman would be sixty-nine when the twins were ten years old. Professor Robert Winston is added to the choir of alarmed citizens, saying that it is outright dangerous for a woman of her age to give birth, and it is certainly detrimental to the welfare of the children. The only counter-argument in the *Guardian* comes by means of a quote from Dr Sandy MacAra, current chairman of the British Medical Association, who argues that older women have as much a right to a baby as older men, and that grandmothers have traditionally played an important role in childrearing.

A similar depreciating tone prevails in *The Times*; the newspaper casts a serious shadow of doubt and mistrust on doctors who perform infertility treatment on older women. In a special article, Dr Antinori is labelled 'no stranger to controversy' and 'someone who is well accustomed to media attention.'[7] Like in the case of Anna Johnson, the villain is always conspicuously eager to pull off publicity coups, even if he or she explicitly undertakes action to keep journalists away. It was actually the British press that invaded Dr Antinori's office, to the point where the gynaecologist had to call in the police to remove journalists and camera crews from his premises. According to *The Times*, Antinori learnt the rudiments of reproductive medicine as a veterinarian, and he is now 'applying to humans fertility techniques that were developed for cattle and pigs.' What the newspaper does not say, is that all fertility treatment is first developed and tested on animals. The news article is replete with dubious imputations: Antinori was under investigation for alleged tax fraud, and for defrauding four of his disappointed patients by failing to produce the desired child. His work is purportedly condemned by the Vatican.

The *Guardian* also adds a special column on the work of the Italian 'pioneer with God's gift.' According to this newspaper, the doctor is a 'devout Catholic despite the Vatican's hostility towards his work.'[8] Yet he considers his work a gift of God, and 'a crusade for the freedom and rights of women.' The *Daily Telegraph* describes Antinori as 'the man who defied nature' and depicts him as someone who is only interested in extending the borders of natural motherhood. Besides a special article on the Italian doctor, the *Daily Telegraph* also devotes a special column to Dr John Marks, who is a fervent opponent of older mothers. He is quoted as saying that the 59-year-old woman 'had forty years in which she could have become a mother yet she had chosen to complete a career first.'[9] These arguments clearly resound echoes of earlier stages of the debate, like the argument that women should let childbearing prevail over a career. The fusion of religious and feminist arguments – a doctor who considers his work simultaneously a gift of God and a crusade for the rights of women – seems rather peculiar. Yet as we have witnessed numerous times, feminist arguments for 'choice' and 'equality' are easily twisted to fit the rhetoric of sometimes opposite political agendas.

Most mainstream British newspapers, as illustrated by the articles in *The Times*, the *Guardian* and the *Daily Telegraph* declare that doctors and officials are 'equally split' on the issue of postmenopausal pregnancy. All three newspapers give ample space to proponents of IVF treatment for older women, yet positive assessments do not receive the same weight. While the headlines and news articles heighten anxiety about 'retirement pregnancies' acquired abroad, the Op-Ed pages and commentaries provide the 'other view.' Simon Jenkins, in an Op-Ed piece for *The Times*, calls the controversy that has arisen sheer hypocrisy: 'Such women are no more defying nature than is abortion or IVF or hormone replacement therapy.'[10] He points at the danger lurking behind government's intrusion of women's private domains – restricting older women's 'choice' by excluding them from infertility treatment. The argument of choice is consistently brought up in Op-Ed pieces written by those in favour of postmenopausal pregnancy. Even though both sides appear to get equal space, the spatial disposition of arguments is clearly indicative of the newspapers' stance: opponents of older mothers dominate the 'objective' news columns, while proponents are relegated to the 'subjective' opinion pages.

Not all newspapers try to uphold an appearance of impartiality on this matter. The *Daily Mirror* devotes six pages to the 59-year-old British mother of twins, celebrating this new form of motherhood in every inch of the paper.[11] A page wide headline 'Look Who's Talking' covers the front page; this headline explicitly refers to the movie featuring a foetus/baby who coaxes his (single) mother into traditional family life. This reference to popular culture is quite significant: postmenopausal pregnancy is viewed by the conservative news media as an instrument that strengthens the traditional family concept. Yet the *Daily Mirror* pays abundant lip service to the liberalist goals of the feminist movement: terms like 'choice' and 'equality'

appear in almost every paragraph. In six pages, all arguments in
favour of postmenopausal pregnancy pass in review: women
have a right to choose and to determine their own reproductive
future; men can have babies until they are very old, so why can't
women; older women have more time and money for babies;
older women have more self-assurance and are more confident
than younger women, and so on and so forth. In a special article,
female rock stars who became pregnant after forty comment on
the 'joy of leaving it late.'

The *Daily Mirror* takes the opposite stance from the
mainstream press. The newspaper expresses its horror at the
Health Secretary's plan to press a European ban on the
treatment of infertile women past natural child bearing age. In
an article headlined 'Don't Deny the Granny Mums this Joy,
Europe Tells Virginia' the *Daily Mirror* emphasizes the
conservative stance Britain takes in these issues: 'In Italy,
Holland, Spain, and the Scandinavian countries it is up to the
woman to decide.' The tabloid paper argues not so much for
postmenopausal pregnancy as for the deregulation of medicine;
in the ultimate liberal marketplace, health services are available
to anyone who can afford them, and no one should be impeded
by moral or ethical restrictions. Not surprisingly, doctor
Antinori is celebrated in the *Daily Mirror* as a successful business
man; his wealth turns him trustworthy rather than suspicious,
like *The Times* insinuated. According to the tabloid, doctor
Antinori is a genius 'who was trained as a vet but went to
Vatican medical school to study gynaecology and obstetrics,'
simultaneously confirming his credentials and his devout
character.

Depicting the doctor as either a devil or a genius is a narrative
technique used by the news media at all stages of the debate: as
we may recall from previous chapters, doctors often became the
personification of good or evil, depending on the news media's
stance on a specific reproductive issue. It seems that with every
new incidence involving reproductive technologies, whether it is
a new technique or a new application, the debate is reduced to a
specific single question: Should we be for or against IVF? Should
we prefer genetic or gestational motherhood? Should we allow or
not allow older women infertility treatment? In fact, the *Daily
Mirror* aptly sums up the nature of the public debate on new
reproductive technologies in a small column on page 7: 'What do

you think? Should she have been allowed fertility treatment at her age? If yes, phone 0891 318111. If no, phone 0891 318112.' This way of framing reproductive issues is typical of most news articles and other publications. Every single incidence is evaluated in isolation, and shaped into a pro-con kind of discussion. Even if several incidences of remarkable IVF-induced births happen in one week, these events are rarely viewed in their broader context.

TRANSRACIAL IMPREGNATION

Just a couple of months after Judge Parslow's decision had been confirmed by the California Supreme Court, a black woman in Italy gave birth to a white baby; she had been implanted with an egg from a white donor, which was fertilized in vitro by her white husband. The woman – who is in most newspapers consistently referred to as a 'Third World citizen' – opted for a Caucasian child because it would have better chances in life and suffer less racial discrimination than if it were a half-caste. She also wanted the baby to look like its father, as we learn from the newspapers. Oddly enough, the news hit the front pages in Britain on 31 December 1993: six months after the baby was actually born, and a few days after the 59-year-old British woman had reportedly given birth to twins. According to *The Times*, an Italian doctor made the case of the black woman public because he was stunned and outraged by the couple's request.[12] It may not be a coincidence that the black woman's case became news right after Dr Antinori made the headlines, even though the two Rome-based clinics were not connected.

On the same day that the news of the black woman baring a white child breaks, the *Daily Telegraph* reports that a British IVF team is facing a similar case.[13] Doctors of Bourn Hall Clinic in Cambridge want to implant a black woman with an egg from a white donor, but for a very different reason: there is no egg from a black donor available. For four years, this woman has been waiting in vain for a black donor, and she finally opts for a white one. The British woman, quoted in *The Times*, had said right at the beginning of the procedure: 'Because my husband is of mixed race, I do not mind if the egg is from a white or black donor. We want a child we love.'[14] Doctor Peter Brinsden, from Bourn Hall Clinic, emphasizes in the *Observer* that although the British case is very different, he supports the Italian doctors who helped a woman to conceive a child of different racial origin: 'It could be right, in exceptional circumstances, to help a black woman have a white child if the alternative is a mixed race or half-caste child, because they tend to have more problems.'[15] In the *Independent*, doctor Brinsden adds to this comment that he would be against providing a white egg to an all-black couple or vice versa.[16]

Most headlines suggest that couples should be barred from 'choosing' the race of their babies, and news articles provide ample quotes to illustrate typical consumerist behaviour. The spokesman for Bourn Clinic reassuredly states that they would never have complied with the black woman's request if there had not been a shortage of (black) donor eggs. In *The Times*, doctor Brinsden notices that their team had turned down a request from a Pakistani man who wanted a 'blonde, blue-eyed, fair-skinned daughter' because it would be easier to find her a husband.[17] Couples who want to 'design' their own babies are explicitly condemned in the newspapers; the idea of the clinic as a supermarket for physiological features appears horrifying. Yet *The Times* editorializes that even worse than this prospect would be the prospect of a government ban:

> But the having and raising of children is too intimate a part of life to be regulated by the blunt instrument of law. No legislation could be framed to deal with the nuances and complexities of parental desire in a way which did not travesty them. This is a fit matter for public debate but it can be resolved only by private conscience.[18]

The call for moral and ethical guidelines concerning transracial impregnation is met by a call for individual choice and a warning against state regulation.

It is interesting to compare the British woman's predicament to that of Anna Johnson, as described in the previous chapter. On the face of it, the casting in the British case appears similar: a black woman is implanted with the egg of a white donor. Yet the circumstances are significantly different. In the Calverts vs. Johnson case, the black woman was hired to render gestational services; the genetic contribution to the reproductive process turned out to be the determinant factor in the decision over motherhood. The British black woman is the 'intending' mother, requesting donor eggs; as a consequence, pregnancy is not turned into a mere 'service,' but it constitutes the essence of motherhood – essential to producing a 'child of her own.' The pregnant woman from Britain is not coded as a black breeder: she is the one paying for donated tissue. Consequently, gestational motherhood is not by definition subordinate to genetic or biological ties; the roles of buyer and seller of reproductive services appear to be determined by more factors than just race.

In the previous chapter, I cited Hartouni's suggestion that the outcome of the Calverts versus Johnson case would not have been different had Anna Johnson been white; the Judge preferred the unity of a traditional nuclear family over alternative arrangements, such as a three-parent ruling. But would the outcome have been different if Anna Johnson had been the egg donor and Crispina Calvert had gestated the child? The point of raising this question is that it makes one realize such role reversal could have never taken place: the white Calverts would never have accepted a black donor because they wanted their child to look like them. In the Italian case, the black woman wanted her child to look like her white husband; the donated genetic material obviously helps 'upgrading' the child's status. The argument of racial matching also plays an important role in the British case. Dr Brinsden from Bourn Hall Clinic denies in the newspaper any 'accusations of deliberate racial mismatching' by stating he would meet the black woman's wish to have a white child if its father were white; being of mixed race is apparently considered a social handicap.

Assisted reproduction is doubly used to fortify traditional social and cultural classifications. Not only do the new technologies enhance the nuclear family, but they are also used to reinforce racial and ethnic predispositions. In the case of Anna Johnson, we have seen how the court and the newspaper jointly erased Johnson's experience of racism and supported a new definition of motherhood to prevent a black single mother from becoming a parent of a white baby. In the British case, the slightest appearance of 'racial mismatching' or 'colour design' leads to agitated headlines and calls for government regulation. Transracial impregnation, as reflected in both the American and the British press, feeds dubious concepts of 'racial contamination.'

Most newspapers blame technology for confronting the people with moral dilemmas and ethical hurdles. Yet, neither of these controversies are the result of 'runaway technology' but of social and cultural hierarchy. In a poignantly argued Op-Ed piece in the *Independent*, Kenan Malik states that transracial impregnation is not a problem caused by technology but by 'the artificial way our society grades people according to colour.'[19] The very term 'racial mismatching' would not exist if society did not obviously value whites over blacks, and if it did not prefer people to remain within their 'natural' categories. In other words, 'racial mismatching' or manufacturing a child of mixed race would not be considered a problem if we lived in a non-racist society. By the same token, if older women were considered equally valued members of society, they would not be barred from getting pregnant. And if the burden of childrearing would be equally divided among men and women, the need for postmenopausal IVF treatment might even disappear.

Yet postmenopausal pregnancy and transracial impregnation are regarded as moral dilemmas brought upon us by technology; the technical possibility to divide genetic and gestational motherhood purportedly caused a third ethical problem during that same week. On January 3, 1994, *The Times* reports that doctors want to use eggs from aborted foetuses – a technique likely to be banned in Britain.[20] Research has proven that immature eggs from aborted foetuses may be retrieved and cultivated in vitro until they are ready for fertilization. This technique might help alleviate the serious shortage of eggs donated by fertile young women to use for infertility treatment. Not just eggs from black donors, but eggs in general are in short supply, so they are very expensive for infertile women to obtain. In the second paragraph of the news article, *The Times* already drops the terms 'womb robbing' and 'creating babies from the dead' – words used by opponents of this new fertility treatment. 'How can the medical profession consider producing children from a mother that never existed?' a member of Parliament is quoted as asking. Specialists, church leaders, and politicians queue up to express their horror at this proposed treatment, stating that it defies 'natural' limits of life and death in reproductive medicine.

Proponents agree that there is 'an unquantifiable yuk factor' involved in this technique which cannot be ignored, yet they argue that views in society change over time, and people will get used to it. Dr Peter Brinsden of Bourn Hall Clinic, who previously defended the donation of white eggs to a black woman if this woman had a white husband, welcomes this development, and tells *The Times* that the use of ovarian tissue from foetuses is 'inevitable.' Society already condones the use of foetal material, such as foetal nerve, liver, and pancreatic tissue in the treatment of certain conditions; consequently, eggs from aborted foetuses should be extracted and used to help infertile women become pregnant. And if abortion is legal, is it not logical that foetal tissue may be used to help women getting pregnant? Or, in the words of James Fenton writing for the *Independent*, 'are we moving into a society where a woman has a right to an abortion but not to a child?'[21]

The three incidences combined lead to complicated questions of rights and entitlement. Which groups are entitled to treatment? What kind of treatment is allowed and to whom should it be applied? Reproductive techniques are now so advanced that the list of possible beneficiaries is endless. However, what seems accepted for one group of women is not necessarily viewed as acceptable for other women. A newspaper article in the *Guardian* reflects the incongruencies in the public's perception of postmenopausal treatment, transracial impregnation and the use of foetal eggs.[22] Five women, who have themselves benefitted from some kind of reproductive technology, are asked in an interview to respond to these three types of infertility treatment. An Italian woman who became pregnant at age 62 favours postmenopausal treatment and transracial impregnation, but is hesitant to approve of using ovarian tissue from aborted foetuses. The Lawrences, a couple of Caucasian-Asian descent who wanted to adopt a child of mixed race, but whose request was turned down on the grounds that they 'had not suffered enough racial abuse,' were baffled by the furore over the black British woman. As far as postmenopausal pregnancy is concerned, this couple thinks doctors 'are pushing the boundaries too far.' Ms Hetherington, a lesbian mother who got pregnant through artificial donor insemination, neither approves of older mothers, nor of the use of foetal tissue. Kathy Shaw bore two sets of twins with the help of IVF, and fervently argues in favour of using ovarian foetal tissue, yet she is very apprehensive about postmenopausal pregnancy. Apparently, women who have themselves benefitted from assisted reproduction do not agree on which types of treatment should be allowed.

Most British newspapers frame the issues in arguments for or against technology and its applications. Whereas the *Daily Mirror* reduced the discussion to two phone numbers, requesting a clear yes or no, the *Guardian* applies a more sophisticated variant of the binary model: pro-con arguments are specified according to various types of beneficiaries. While the combination of three related events in the course of one week might have spurred contemplative background reports, the public debate in the press proceeds along traditional lines. Arguments are invariably phrased in terms of entitlements, reflecting the British fixation on legislation and regulation. If we were to believe the news media, there would only be two views on reproductive technologies, each of which is supported by a distinctive set of arguments.

NATURE, LOGIC AND THE PUBLIC DEBATE

The three incidences that occurred during the first week of 1994, shook the British public because it made them realize that 'technology had defied nature.' As a result of technology, a child may now have two mothers, a 'retired' mother, a differently coloured mother, or no mother at all – someone who has never even existed. Journalists and concerned citizens invoke the laws of nature to argue that these techniques need to be banned or restricted. Yet historically, despicable and atrocious practices have been defended in the name of nature. Lesbians and gays have been prosecuted due to their 'unnatural' sexual preference; ethnic groups have been victimized because some people claim to be 'naturally superior' to people of a different race or ethnic background; and for centuries, women have been regarded intellectually inferior than men, an argument often supported by referring to the sexes' 'natural' dispositions.

The problem with the new technologies is not that they are defying nature, but that they are defying culture. They profoundly challenge our preconceptions of a society that seems 'naturally' divided along axes of gender, race, class, age and physical or psychological condition. They also challenge traditional social structures, such as the nuclear family, identifiable races or ethnic groups. So-called natural barriers to motherhood and pregnancy are quite often social barriers: 'natural' limits on childbearing age, 'natural' matching of skin colour, and 'natural motherhood' defined as the owner of genetic material. Now that technology has defied nature, we might ask what these 'natural limits' stand for. They often, but not always, enhance current sexist, racist or 'agist' social practices; they keep intact existing social hierarchies and defend vested interests. Rather than condemning the technology that bares social injustice and prejudice, we might use the opportunity to contemplate how technology could help solve these problems.

Besides people arguing for restrictions and bans in the name of nature, we have also noticed voices celebrating every pregnancy materializing through means of IVF. This unabated support for any new reproductive technique and its applications is often motivated by a revulsion of government regulation and a strong preference for a free reproductive marketplace. Proponents of technology invoke 'logic' rather than 'nature' to defend unrestrained application of all reproductive methods. If IVF is allowed, then why bar older women from using it? If abortion is legal, then why not permit the use of foetal eggs? If IVF enables choosing the colour of your child, why put a ban on transracial impregnation? However, the free market mechanism, like a regulated system, is also likely to reproduce gender, race and class inequalities and perpetuate existing power relations. An unregulated reproductive market would indeed allow white couples to get black babies, but not surprisingly, there would be little demand for such transaction. Egg donation might enable women past menopause to become pregnant, but this new opportunity could also usher us into a new trend stimulating older women to carry babies for younger women so that the latter can remain fully employed during their most fertile years. 'Granny mums,' like black women, might be exploited by white yuppies to serve as breeders. Of course, egg donation can make a 33-year-old woman who suffers from early menopause very happy, yet it might also be a euphemism for 'egg selling': teenagers desperately needing money might want to sell their eggs, knowingly neglecting the risks involved in hormone injections.

The ostensibly incompatible arguments in favour of legislation and in favour of the free market may both be deployed to reinforce current social injustices or discriminatory practices. Invoking nature, logic or common sense, people may defend or attack almost any technique or reproductive practice. Ironically, the debate appears torn by two sides whose prerogatives may not in fact be very different. The debate has gradually evolved from a model in which scientists and doctors were pitched against religious leaders or feminists, to a debate in which two stances on the issue are artificially opposed. But where does this leave feminist and religious voices? Not one single newspaper article relating of these three incidences, includes the voice of feminists; they appear neither in the news articles, nor on the Op-Ed or editorial pages. Yet significantly, both 'sides' in the British public debate seem to have absorbed feminist arguments in the process. Those favouring tighter regulation invoke arguments that women should be protected from exploitation, and not be reduced to barrels or deliverers of genetic material. Those arguing against regulation and for the reproductive market-place, frequently pepper their rhetoric with terms like 'choice,' 'a woman's right of disposal,' and 'equality.' Feminist voices seem to have vanished beyond recognition, appropriated by dominant discourses to support prevailing arguments.

The complexity of the debate on new reproductive technol-ogies has clearly outgrown the binary frameworks offered by traditional discourses. The fragmentation of motherhood is accompanied by a disintegration of voices who initially took the pulpit; feminist responses to the new technologies are equally splintered by the various special interests that have arisen as a result of these technologies – interests of old, young, black, white, infertile, rich, poor, physically able and other women. As reflected in the *Guardian* article, the interests of women not just vary considerably, they sometimes appear incompatible. It becomes increasingly pointless to concentrate on one factor that informs or structures the public debate on the new technologies; gender, race, class, age and other factors are inextricably intertwined in the discussion. Moreover, the debate on postmenopausal pregnancies, transracial impregnation and the use of foetal eggs cannot be separated from the debates on genetic engineering, basic health insurance, abortion, prenatal care, racism and deregulation of public services.

In fact, there are so many issues and interests involved in the debate on new reproductive technologies, that the notion of public consent is increasingly problematic. While the newspapers deploy a traditional binary framework to reflect and shape discussion, the HFEA attempts to distillate public consensus in quite a different manner. The Authority realizes that, without a clear backing by the public, recommendations or guidelines will not stand. As a statutory body, the Authority is supposed to constantly navigate between the public's desire for treatment, its urge for norms and regulations, its anxiety for unknown consequences, its wish to protect reproductive rights, and its own social and racial prejudices. At the heart of the HFEA's work is the argument over what is normal or abnormal, what is socially desirable or undesirable. In order to meet a variety of interests, the Authority has started soliciting comments from a large number of groups, individuals and organizations. With regard to the question of sex preselection, the HFEA sent out 2000 copies of a consultative document, asking people to formulate their opinion on this matter. On the issue of using ovarian tissue from aborted foetuses, the Authority wants to expand this debating model. In an interview with the *Independent*, HFEA chairman Sir Colin Campbell states: 'The issues are very difficult and a formal document cannot give all explanations. So we want to hold meetings were people can ask their questions. We are going to be very active in ensuring people can talk about this.'[23]

A public debate in which the public is actively involved – that sounds like a model much needed to funnel the current plethora of voices arguing the new technologies. A model that gives people with different interests, backgrounds, social and rhetorical capacities the power to equally participate in the public debate. Relying on a free market of public meanings may not be the most democratic venue to arrive at articulating legal or legislative definitions of new reproductive technologies. Many voices, particularly those of feminists, tend to be overlooked or appropriated. Fragmentation of the debate facilitates the marginalization or erasure of oppositional voices. If we compare this latest discussion to previous stages of the debate, we may realize how advanced technologies and their countless applications have changed the nature of the debate, yet that debating strategies, goals or parameters of discussion have never been adjusted accordingly. The binary frameworks imposed by (institutional) discourses are rarely challenged, and subversive or alternative modes of discourse have been scantily wielded. More importantly, the very objective of the public debate to arrive at a consensus has never been subjected to scrutiny. The idea that public consent is a condition for successful legislation is based on the assumption that consensus can be reached, or put in a negative sense, can be manufactured.

Consensus seems indeed to have been reduced to a telephone poll, and legislators appear to feel comforted if a majority of respondents supports their decision. The public debate has metamorphosed into a public referendum where complicated issues that require a coherent approach are instead presented as clearcut itemized proposals. The tendency of scientists to urge for rapid decisions leads to the idea that 'consensus' is a mere yes or no to specific technical developments or applications. The notion of 'consensus' appears to be based on the exclusion of factors that view new reproductive technologies in a broader social, political, economic and cultural context. If left to the free market of science and journalism, there is a fair chance that the manufacturing of public consent will always tag along after the manufacturing of babies.

But how can we assure the general public a meaningful voice in redirecting the developments in science and medicine, some of which may definitely alter the 'nature' of life as we know it? The new technologies have indeed potentially irreversible social consequences; as a result, the debate on how society adapts to those changes should not be left to scientists, ethicists, or any (self-) appointed group. By the same token, the debate should not be channelled solely through conventional discursive formats, because they tend to reduce the perception of social issues to mere technical or ethical matters. As of 1994, the public debate on new reproductive technologies has become so complex and stratified that it requires the involvement of many different groups and individuals. In addition, it requires a serious reconsideration of the discourses and language through which these technologies are communicated. A postmodern culture, which is characterized by the stratification of social groups, the fragmentation of issues, the 'newsification' of science and the narrativation of knowledge may even require a redefinition of the very concept of public debate. It seems rather peculiar that in this time and age, advanced technology and communication equipment has never been deployed to upgrade the paradigms of debating.

Conclusion

Imagine the following scene from a television programme: a well known talkshow host confronts his studio audience with, what he calls, the 'moral dilemmas doctors face in health care.' Because of budget constraints, a hospital staff has to make stringent cuts in their regular services – commonly paid for by insurance companies – which include fertility treatment up to three IVF cycles. The talkshow host presents the following 'dilemma.' A 33-year-old woman, suffering from early menopause, requests egg donation and oocyte transplantation; having failed two previous attempts at IVF, the hospital bill amounts to 45 000 dollars. In the same hospital, a premature baby, born to a drug-addicted black mother when she was thirty-two weeks into her pregnancy, needs intensive care for at least six weeks, the bill topping 45 000 dollars. After explaining the details of the situation, the talkshow host turns to his studio audience and asks: 'If you had only 45 000 dollars to spend, which treatment would you prefer? Press button A if you choose to help the infertile woman, press button B if you prefer intensive care for the baby.'

The above scene is fabricated, but the format of the television programme is not. The infotainment show was broadcast on Dutch public television in 1992.[1] A studio audience was invited to 'assist' doctors and policy-makers making decisions and thus educate the audience at large about 'ethical and moral issues in health care.' The show, which alternated filmed hospital scenes with interviews, was sponsored by the Dutch Department of Health and Welfare. Translating ethical decisions in health care into a quiz-like performance, the audience was seemingly engaged in a public discussion that concerns every citizen: how should taxpayers' money be spent wisely and effectively?

The idea that a 'choice' squeezed from a small group of selected individuals could substitute a public debate on issues of reproductive technologies and health care appears, on the face of it, quite dubious. However, the entertainment format is not very different from the framework that is commonly used by mainstream and popular news media to inform their audiences about reproductive technologies. The kind of 'public consent' that is enforced by the news media resembles the public's participatory role in the infotainment show; the audience is assigned a passive role as they can express their opinion only by pressing one of two buttons. 'Choice' is not just a blatant misnomer in this context, the term is intensely problematic on three accounts. First, it pretends to offer citizens a range of options from which they can choose, yet in reality this range is nothing but a prepackaged, decontextualized set of propositions. Second, it purports to represent a public debate while the activity of debating is apparently reduced to the outcome of a decision. And third, with regard to pregnancy and the cultural imperative to motherhood, the notion of 'choice' invokes a deceptive feminist backing of this type of argument. I will dilate upon each of these three points.

The public debate on new reproductive technologies is often presented as a disjoint set of propositions. Isolated incidences of paid surrogacy, postmenopausal mothers and transracial impregnation invigorate heated discussions which are narrowly focused on a single, specified case. Issues of reproductive control appear seemingly unrelated – slices of everyday reality. In the preceding chapters, I have demonstrated important continuities between scientific 'discoveries,' newspaper accounts, objections to technology, legal decisions and legislative moves. My 'map' of the public debate has been an attempt to disclose the social, cultural and discursive forces that shape public meanings and inform public consent. The dissemination of sophisticated technology appears to be contingent upon the cultural diffusion of normative images concerning woman's reproductive role. In the course of fifteen years, we have witnessed how IVF and related techniques have evolved from controversial methods into 'natural' means enabling infertile women to produce 'their own' offspring. The subsequent stages distinguishable in the debate – the stages of normalization, naturalization, legalization and legislation – illustrate a cohesive argumentative pattern; this pattern shows the promotional effort in favour of the new technologies as well as the vocal opposition against their implementation, the clashing of meanings as well as the mutual incorporation of arguments.

In the course of my analysis, I have also emphasized the interrelation between the public debate on the new technologies and other debates concerning issues of reproductive control, such as abortion, prenatal care and so-called foetal rights. The 'web of meanings' I set out to (re)create aimed at baring intersections between various issues. This particular purpose – to unravel the connections and continuities between discussions – is not unique or uncommon. In recent years, several feminist academics and journalists have sketched the unarticulated ideological patterns underlying reproductive power arrangements. Jennifer Terry, for instance, in a 1989 article in the *Socialist Review*, insightfully relates the 'logic of neoeugenics' with the foetal rights agenda and the politics of surrogacy.[2] Katha Pollitt, in a 1990 article in *The Nation*, rightly combines the interests of health officials in protecting foetal rights and the ousting of women out of the competitive job market.[3] Susan Faludi, in her book *Backlash* (1990), skilfully pairs journalistic skills with academic insights to demonstrate how myths ranging from the 'infertility epidemic' to the 'man shortage' have undermined the minimal emancipatory progress women have made in both the public and private sphere since the 1970s.

What Terry's, Pollitt's and Faludi's reports on the female condition in postmodern culture have in common, is that they capitalize on the implications of contemporary social and reproductive practices. By reassembling the jigsaw puzzle of reproductive politics, they articulate connections and ramifications which might otherwise remain invisible in the apparent discontinuity of isolated discussions. The analysis presented in this book both adheres to and differs from the approach favoured by Terry, Pollitt and Faludi. Like these authors, my analysis aimed at contextualizing each individual discussion in the field of reproductive technologies; by juxtaposing texts from science, journalism and popular fiction I have attempted to extrapolate critical evaluations of the socioeconomic underpinnings of reproductive practices. Yet unlike aforementioned feminist authors, I have focused more explicitly on the use of arguments and the deployment of narrative strategies in the wake of gradually blurring discourses. In other words, I have been particularly interested in how arguments are strategically posed and how facts are established. Mapping the public debate on new reproductive technologies, I wanted to identify some distinct types of discourse and explore the lines along which they compete. These lines or axes can be typified as erosive; in postmodern culture, the distinctions between dominant and oppositional discourses on the one hand, and amongst institutional types of discourse on the other hand, have dissolved.

Rather than defining discursive categories as sites of oppression, I have attempted to explicate the power relations that condition and limit dialogic possibilities in a public debate. The most obvious implication of this shift is that more attention is paid to the rhetorical manoeuvres and discursive strategies used in debating. In order to resist and subvert current practices of debating, which are increasingly staged as prepackaged, hand-me-down 'choices between two alternatives,' it is imperative to implicate the invisible web of arguments ensuing from previous stages of facticity construction. Historicizing and contextualizing the debate might foster the awareness that a public debate is more than the sum of media-ted 'decisions'.

Public debates, at least in their popular perception, are commonly framed as disagreements between two interested parties, prompted by technology and shaped by the narrative conventions of journalism. The infotainment show aimed at stimulating public participation seems to imply that neither the news media nor medical technology play a role in the staged drama; they are merely mediating the public's desires. In this fictive yet realistic example, technology and news media remain invisible as directional forces which shape public consensus. Yet, as has become abundantly clear in the preceding chapters, technology is not a neutral force but it explicitly transforms the very nature of the debate. Optical instruments and the corresponding expert narratives invisibly direct the public's perception of science and technology. By the same token, the framing of reproductive issues in news media almost imperceptibly affects the conditions for meaning production. The self-effacing role of journalism and science discourse, as I have argued in this book, constantly needs to be reevaluated, because these discourses determine who can participate in the public discussion, what they can say and how they can say it.

If we would restrict the scope of a public debate to those voices which frequently populate the news media, we would infer that new reproductive technologies solely concerned doctors, scientists, religious groups, politicians, and a certain group of feminists. Yet there are many more groups who appear to have a stake in the debate but whose view is rarely solicited: the poor, the elderly, ethnic minorities, various women's groups, patients, and so forth. Ideally, a public debate should involve anyone, including those who do not have a professional, political, or pecuniary interest in the matter. Since public debates staged by news media and scientists unequally proportion authority and space, we should think of expansive forums to supplement the restricted participation of the general public. In her book on public controversies in scientific research, Diana Button (1988), for instance, advocates the involvement of a large representation of citizen groups and individuals in tackling difficult science policy decisions, such as genetic engineering or reproductive medicine.[4] These forums should not just fish for affirmative or negative responses to particular applications of the new technologies, but encourage individual participants to contemplate on the longterm implications for society and for the relationships between social groups.[5]

In addition, public forums might stimulate the use of expansive forms of argument – alternative modes of making sense. In the preceding analysis, I have deliberately included works of fiction in my description of the public debate to show how fictive discourse can be effectively used to insert critical, reflective or expansive views on the new technologies. In a similar vein, a public platform might stimulate the production of a number of different stories on the new technologies. Rather than eliciting clearcut opinions on these issues, they could encourage a variety of responses in which people could express their anxieties, hopes, critical analyses or sketches of alternative reproductive arrangements. Why not invite novelists or film makers to submit a work of art concerning reproductive practices? Why not ask an anthropologist to register and interpret the reactions of women who experienced infertility in different cultures? A writer of children's books could produce a manuscript on the basis of interviews with children who are born through IVF.

A public debate should actively promote the production of diverging views, and encourage dissent rather than pushing towards consent. The manufacturing of public consent, if understood solely within the parameters set by the institutional discourses of news media and science, is indeed little less than forced consent; the coercive, reductive frameworks of 'choice' press for an outcome, not a discussion. Rather than requesting a position for or against older mothers, paid surrogate pregnancy, transracial impregnation and the endless variations and applications of the new technologies, we might want to focus on the process of debating; the urge to reach consent should not outflank the activity of discussion. For the long term, it might be more important to evaluate the social and cultural arrangements underlying the need for technological fixes, instead of the technologies themselves. A public debate should make people think, not make them choose. In order to change the nature of a public debate, we should first expand its limited borders and allow other voices, other arguments, other modes of expression.

This expansive proposal for a public debate, however, does not mean that 'mainstream' institutional discourses should be departed or neglected as a potential arena to construct alternative meanings of reproduction. On the contrary, as I have illustrated in my analysis, few feminists have managed to articulate critical views using conventional forms of discourse. As a result, the reproductive service industry is not invariably depicted as a successful, unproblematic enterprise in mainstream science and journalism discourse; occasionally, meanings contravening public consent can be read in respectable science journals and quality newspapers.[6] Even though dissenting voices in mainstream discourse are rarely presented as 'facts', their presence is extremely important. The problem, however, is that they are rarely picked up by, and disseminated into, other discourses, because they defy common sense. One of the critical tasks in a public debate is to recognize dissent and distribute knowledge that refutes commonly shared myths and beliefs.

Journalists and scientists are not in any sense conspirators, consciously attempting to inoculate a forced consensus upon an innocent audience. They are not suspicious actors who jointly push a potentially lucrative definition of reproductive technology to the forefront of public discussion. Rather, the cultural authority that is assumed through science and journalism has a profound effect outside these discourses. The gradual merger of scientific and journalistic narratives in respectable medical journals and mainstream news media has pushed a favourable view of the new technologies to the centre of the debate, marginalizing critical assessments. Yet the attribution of power to journalism and science discourse should be partly sought in the popularity of these discourses outside their institutional domains. I think it is important to include blurred genres like newsletters, infotainment shows, and popular or tabloid news media in the definition of a public debate, since these formats particularly show the distinct impact of scientific and journalistic authority outside their 'proper domains.' If we focus on tracing how meanings evolve and how they change in specific public arenas, it might give insight in how power works, instead of where it is located.

Finally, which role have feminist arguments played in this public debate on new reproductive technologies between 1978 and 1994? How have feminist meanings affected the dominant definition of motherhood and the reproductive body? And, not unimportantly, how can they strategically position themselves in a postmodern public debate, which is characterized by fragmentation and narrativation? At its initial stage, a group of radical feminists put a significant mark on the debate. In retrospect, the choice to formulate an unyielding view of medical science and technology seems understandable in the context of the political-social climate of the 1980s. The advent and unprecedented promotion of the new technologies enhanced anxiety and fear that these technologies would be used to further control woman's reproductive autonomy. In the wake of the 'backlash' against feminism, as convincingly described by Faludi, radical opposition to all technologies in the mid-1980s was hardly surprising.

Radical feminists positioned themselves outside mainstream discursive arenas; consequently, they made themselves prone to cooptation and inclusion by the very discourses they actually resisted. Arguments launched by feminists in earlier stages of the debate are easily picked up and twisted to fit almost opposite meanings. Terms like 'choice' and the 'right to decide,' as well as arguments like the fear for exploitation have been recycled in mainstream discourses. Indeed, this group of feminists alerted many women to possible long term implications that the new technologies might have on the status and function of women as mothers. Yet they were also eager to represent all feminists, thereby suiting themselves in a bipolar model of 'male scientists' and 'female victims of technology.' The definition of 'women' as a uniform category appeared problematic, as other feminists expressed their 'dissenting' opinion – dissenting from both public consensus and from other feminists.

Radical feminists operated from the assumption that the discourses of science and news media are dominated by pro-technology males, and are impenetrable by feminists univocally opposing these practices. As Judith Butler (1990) argues in her theory of gender construction, feminist critique 'ought to explore the totalizing claims of a masculinized signifying economy, but also remain self-critical with respect to the totalizing gestures of feminism' (13). The critical task for feminism, Butler contends, is not to establish another generalizing category of gender, but to locate strategies of subversion and tactics of intervention in the constitution of the female subject. Just as 'gender' has become inapt as a constitutive category of identity construction, the allocation of feminist meaning production to exclusively feminist channels has become illusory. As dominant and feminist meanings convolute, we can no longer identify a mainstream public debate and a feminist debate running on its sidelines. Feminist contributions to the public debate on new reproductive technologies can be located at the centre as well as on the margins; each voice is constructed and informed by its discursive disposition. There is no ontology of gender, nor an ontology of discourse; discourses themselves are neither inherently repressive, nor inherently emancipatory.

A public debate is thus a multifarious, complex phenomenon, which cannot be explained by easy bipolar categories of groups or discourses. Feminists should not expect to have a self-evident consensus among their ideological allies on this issue. As we have seen particularly in the most recent stages of the debate, feminist views on the application of new reproductive technologies vary widely, depending on specific cultural, local and social circumstances. Imposing a 'dissenting' opinion on other feminists in fact fosters another type of manufacturing consent. What holds for the public debate in general also holds for feminists partaking in this debate: maybe the focus should be shifted from the outcome of a debate to the process of signification, debating and decision making. Cultivating discord and articulating differences in the assessments of the new technologies will expand the number of opportunities for feminists to practice criticism. Feminists have a longstanding tradition of exposing the borders that are used to exclude, condemn and hierarchize. These borders, as well as the logic that promotes and maintains them, need to be made visible, so that contiguities and connections in the production of knowledge can be publicly orchestrated.

A question almost inevitably arising from preceding arguments in favour of an expansive definition of a public debate, concerns the viability of feminist politics. Does the dissolution of a gendered centre or object of criticism complicate or even prohibit feminist political action? Or, in other words, will the lack of a unified feminist strategy against reproductive technologies necessarily yield to prevailing medical definitions? Will feminist resistance against discriminatory reproductive politics and policies get lost in the disparity of the debate, which takes place in many different discourses?

The contemporary public debate characterized by fragmentation of social, physical, cultural and discursive categories should not be viewed as an environment inherently hostile to feminist concerns. The widening of gendered interests in reproduction to include race, class and age appears to prohibit a normative and flattening image of feminism. The acknowledgment of differentiated feminist interest does not weaken but strengthen feminism. Diversity might facilitate the formation of specific, localized coalitions of feminist perspectives. The condition to present a unified feminist standpoint with regard to the new technologies is in fact untenable, since such a viewpoint presumes the prevalence of gender differences over other categories such as race and class.

My intention in mapping the public debate on new reproductive technologies was to chart the variety of meanings that have proliferated in the past fifteen years. Concomitantly, I have produced my own symbolic landscape of the debate, coloured specific areas on this map and created a framework for understanding the relation between textual vehicles, social practices and ideological positions. Despite the fact that such map makes readers aware of certain links and relations, this approach also leaves many blank spaces on the map. Yet the assumption of its essential incompleteness could also be regarded as an asset. Defining a public debate as an open ended area of meaning construction permits the possibility of continuous contestation. The acknowledgment of a number of contestants and a wide range of discourses – rather than just the domains of medicine and media – in fact resets the parameters of a public debate. The inclusion of fiction and borderline genres next to science journals and news media accounts, urges a reconsideration of the underlying distribution of meaning, and a questioning of the very frameworks for making sense. It also expands the number of options in the way dominant meanings can be subverted, counteracted and resisted. The public debate offers more space for manufacturing dissent than we think, if we only recognize and exploit these openings.

Notes

Introduction

1. For an elaborate description of the differences between the USA and Britain, see Maureen McNeil, 'New Reproductive Technologies. Dreams and Broken Promises' in *Science as Culture* 3:17 (1993) pp. 483–506.
2. For a concise, excellent introduction to this approach, see Joseph Rouse, 'What Are the Cultural Studies of Scientific Knowledge?' in *Configurations* 1 (1992) pp. 1–22. See also *Culture, Media, Language: Working Papers in Cultural Studies 1972–1979*, ed. Stuart Hall (London: University of Birmingham, Centre for Contemporary Cultural Studies, 1979) and Stuart Hall, 'The Emergence of Cultural Studies and the Crisis of the Humanities' in *October* 53 (Summer 1990) pp. 11–23.

1 Mapping the Public Debate on New Reproductive Technologies

1. The term 'new reproductive technologies' is used in contrast to the 'old' reproductive technologies, which were the technologies that helped control and regulate woman's fertility, such as the contraceptive pill, intra-uterine devices and abortion. For an elaborate description of the new technologies, see Lynda Birke, Susan Himmelweit and Gail Vines, *Tomorrow's Child. Reproductive Technologies in the 90s* (London, Virago Press, 1990).
2. Cf. Anne Burfoot, 'The Normalisation of a New Reproductive Technology' in *The New Reproductive Technologies*, eds. Maureen McNeil, Ian Varcoe and Steven Yearly (London: Macmillan, 1990). Burfoot uses the method of citation analysis to show the increasing acceptance of reproductive medicine as an established field of medical knowledge.
3. See, for instance, Machelle M. Seibel, 'A New Era in Reproductive Technology' in *New England Journal of Medicine*, 31 March 1988, pp. 828–34.
4. Philip Elmer-Dewitt, 'Making Babies' in *Time*, 30 September 1991, pp. 56–63.
5. *The Surrogate Mother* is a Brazilian television soap, which was broadcast on major European stations in 1993 and 1994; *Vital*

Signs (1991) is a medical thriller written by Robin Cook, featuring Marissa Blumenthal, an infertile medical doctor, as a protagonist. (See also Chapter 5.)

6. Cf. Rosalind Petchesky, *Abortion and Woman's Choice. The State, Sexuality and Reproductive Freedom* (New York: Longman, 1984) p. 33.

7. Jürgen Habermas has outlined his theory of the public sphere in several of his books, but particularly in his *The Theory of Communicative Action*, vol. 1 *Reason and the Rationalization of Society* (Boston: Beacon Press, 1984).

8. See Nancy Fraser, *Unruly Practices. Power, Discourse and Gender in Contemporary Social Theory* (Minneapolis: University of Minnesota Press, 1989), particularly chapter 6 'What's Critical about Critical Theory? The Case of Habermas and Gender,' pp. 113–43.

9. For a fuller discussion of the convalescence of the private and public sphere, see Sarah Franklin, 'Postmodern Procreation. Representing Reproductive Practice' in *Science as Culture*, 3:17 (1993) p. 545.

10. Edward S. Herman and Noam Chomsky, *Manufacturing Consent. The Political Economy of the Mass Media* (New York: Pantheon, 1988) p. 302.

11. For an extensive explanation of the term 'normalization' see Michel Foucault, *The History of Sexuality, Vol. 1. An Introduction.* (New York: Vintage, 1980) pp. 77–131.

12. As Foucault points out in *The Archaeology of Knowledge* (New York: Pantheon, 1972), every utterance is constrained by its context: 'Exchange and communication are positive forces at play within complex but restrictive systems; it is probable that they cannot operate independently of these' (225).

13. Cf. Petchesky, *Abortion and Woman's Choice*, p. 26.

14. For a discussion of the differences between 'foetalists' and 'feminists,' see Janice G. Raymond, 'Fetalists and Feminists: They are not the Same,' in *Made to Order. The Myth of Reproductive and Genetic Progress*, eds. Patricia Spallone and Deborah Lynn Steinberg (Oxford: Pergamon Press, 1987). See also Susan Faludi, *Backlash. The Undeclared War Against American Women.* (New York, Crown, 1991), particularly chapter 14.

15. In reality, Angela Carder did not survive the Caesarian section that was forced upon her by the Washington judge, and neither did her 25-week-old foetus. In the segment of *LA Law* based on this case, however, the baby stayed alive.

16. In her book *Reproducing the Future. Anthropology, Kinship and the New Reproductive Technologies* (Manchester: Manchester University Press, 1992) Marilyn Strathern illuminates the unarticulated

relations between cultural practices, kinships and the new technologies.
17. Cf. Foucault, *The Archaeology of Knowledge*, pp. 107–12.
18. Cf. Richard Terdiman, *Discourse/Counter-discourse. The Theory and Practice of Symbolic Resistance in Nineteenth Century France* (Ithaca: Cornell University Press, 1985). Terdiman regards conflict to be an intrinsic feature of discourse, as he argues that discourse and counterdiscourse cannot exist concurrently but only conjuncturally: 'The inscription of conflict is no longer conceived as a contamination of the linguistic, but as its properly defined function' (37).
19. For an elaborate discussion on authority in medical discourse, see also Paula Treichler, 'What Definitions Do: Childbirth, Cultural Crisis, and the Challenge to Medical Discourse,' in *Rethinking Communication*, ed. Brenda Dervin (London: Sage, 1989) pp. 424–53.
20. For a description of the parallel debate on abortion and the new technologies, see Barbara Katz Rothman, *Recreating Motherhood. Ideology and Technology in a Patriarchal Society* (New York: Norton, 1989), particularly the chapter 'Redefining Abortion,' pp. 106–22.
21. In *Discipline and Punish* (New York: Vintage, 1979) Michel Foucault defines 'need' as a 'political instrument, meticulously prepared, calculated, and used' (26).
22. See also Nancy Fraser's discussion of what she calls 'the politics of need interpretation'; she assumes that claims of need are nested in contested networks of in-order-to-relations. (*Unruly Practices*, p. 163.)
23. Cf. Anne Karpf, *Doctoring the Media. The Reporting of Health and Medicine* (London: Routledge, 1988), particularly Chapters 4, 5, 6 and 8.
24. As Roland Barthes explains in *Mythologies* (New York: Hill and Wang, 1972) myths are instrumental in the process of signification, as they materialize concurrently in many different discursive forms.
25. For an excellent overview of these recent shifts in feminist theory, see Sarah Franklin and Maureen McNeil, 'Science and Technology: Questions for Cultural Studies and Feminism' in *Off-Centre. Feminism and Cultural Studies*, eds. Sarah Franklin, Celia Lury and Jacky Stacey (London: Harper Collins, 1991) pp. 129–46.
26. In Chapter 4 of *Doctoring the Media*, Anne Karpf describes the campaigns of 'natural childbirth groups' in Britain in the 1970s. She notices that home births, in Britain, decreased from forty-four per cent in 1946 to twelve per cent in 1970.

27. In her most recent book *Whose Science? Whose Knowledge?* (Ithaca: Cornell University Press, 1991) Sandra Harding still advocates the argument that increased participation of women in science will effect the dominant paradigms and methods of inquiry, but she also acknowledges that it is not the only or best possible mode of feminist criticism (pp. 112–15).

28. Cf. Donna Haraway, 'Situated Knowledges: the Science Question in Feminism and the Privilege of Partial Perspective' in *Feminist Studies* 14.3 (Fall 1988) p. 575.

29. Donna Haraway's 'A Manifesto for Cyborgs' was originally published in *Socialist Review* 80 (1985). For further reference, I will use the reprint of this article in *Feminism/Postmodernism*, ed. Linda Nicholson (New York: Routledge, 1990) pp. 190–233.

30. Cf. Judy Wajcman, *Feminism Confronts Technology* (University Park: Pennsylvania State University Press, 1991), who elaborates on the merger of medical science and technology in Chapter 1 'Feminist Critiques of Science and Technology' (pp. 1–26).

31. In *Beyond Conception. The New Politics of Reproduction*. (Granby: Bergin and Garvey, 1989), Patricia Spallone convincingly argues that the incorporation of molecular biology into medicine has changed the face of what was formerly called 'eugenics'; the merger neutralized the suspect legacy of eugenics.

32. Cf. Donna Haraway, *Primate Visions. Gender, Race, and Nature in the World of Science* (New York: Routledge, 1989), particularly pp. 12–15 of the Introduction.

33. For a fuller discussion of the waning distinction between text and context, see Katherine Hayles, 'Text out of Context: Situating Postmodernism within an Information Society' in *Discourse* 9 (Spring 1987) pp. 24–36.

34. In *Patterns of Dissonance* (Cambridge: Polity Press, 1991) Rosi Braidotti observes that feminist criticism in postmodern culture represents a conflation of the 'reactive moment of reading and textual commentary and the active moment of production' (280).

2 Reading Science, Journalism and Fiction as Culture

1. June Goodfield in *Science and the Media* (Washington: AAAS, 1981) states that the only journalists who approached Rorvik's account critically were Robin Cook and Harriet Van Horne. Robin Cook, who was in 1978 science journalist for the *Boston Globe*, is now America's famous author of medical fiction. Harriet Van Horne of the *New York Post* refuted Rorvik's claim, reported as 'news' on the front page of her own paper, in her column.

2. As Goodfield contends in *Science and the Media*: 'The very notion of being a professional implies an acceptance of the moral

responsibility for the consequences of one's work which affect both the other members of the profession and society at large' (63).

3. Cf. Barbara Foley, *Telling the Truth. Fact and Fiction in the Documentary Novel.* (Ithaca: Cornell University Press, 1986), particularly Chapters 2 and 3.

4. See, for instance, David Harvey, *The Condition of Postmodernity* (Oxford: Basil Blackwell, 1989), and James Clifford and George Marcus, *Writing Culture. The Poetics and Politics of Ethnography* (Berkeley: University of California Press, 1986), particularly Clifford's introduction to this volume.

5. Joseph Rouse lucidly explains the differences between the social constructivist approach to science and the cultural studies approach in 'What are the Cultural Studies of Scientific Knowledge?' in *Configurations* 1 (1992) pp. 1–22.

6. See, for instance, Jeanne Fahnestock, 'Accommodating Science. The Rhetorical Life of Scientific Facts,' in *Written Communication* 2.2 (1986) pp. 275–96.

7. The democratization movement of the 1960s had a profound impact on mainstream news media. For a description of how Vietnam affected the news media, see Daniel C. Hallin, *The Uncensored War. The Media and Vietnam* (Berkeley: University of California Press, 1986). Gaye Tuchman in *Making News. A Study in the Construction of Reality* (New York: The Free Press, 1978) elaborates on the relations between the women's movement and the media. The influence of student protestors on the news media is discussed by Todd Gitlin in *The Whole World is Watching. Mass Media and the Making and Unmaking of the New Left* (Berkeley: University of California Press, 1980).

8. The call for objectivity, the origin of which can be traced back to the 1880s, had a similar effect on the discursive practices of both science and journalism. Michael Schudson, in *Discovering the News. A Social History of American Newspapers* (New York: Basic Books, 1978) describes in Chapter 4 how objectivity gradually became ideology in science and journalism at the turn of the century.

9. Martin S. Brander, 'The Scientist and the News Media' in *New England Journal of Medicine*, 12 May 1983, pp. 1170–73.

10. Social scientists have found that researchers are more likely to cite papers that have been publicized in the news media. They concluded that coverage of medical research in the lay press amplifies the transmission of medical information from scientific articles to the research community. See, for instance, David Phillips, 'Importance of the Lay Press in the Transmission of Medical Knowledge to the Scientific Community' in *New England Journal of Medicine*, 17 October 1991, pp. 1180–83.

11. Cf. Christopher Dornan, 'Some Problems in Conceptualizing the Issue of "Science and the Media"' in *Critical Studies in Mass Communication* 7 (1990) 48–71. Dornan found that mainstream journalism has become strikingly harmonious with science discourse in academic journals and other specialized publications. He observes that the two discourses seem to share a mutually beneficial interest in upholding each other's authority.
12. Cf. Louis Quéré, *Des Miroirs Equivoques* (Paris: Edition Aubier Montaigne, 1982), particularly Chapter 5, 'L'information comme science-fiction' (pp. 153–75).
13. Cf. Quéré, *Des Miroirs Equivoques*, p. 155.
14. For a fuller description of New Journalism as an expansive genre, see John Pauly, 'The Politics of New Journalism' in *Literary Journalism in the Twentieth Century*, ed. Norman Sims (Oxford: Oxford University Press, 1990) pp. 110–29.
15. Cf. Jean-François Lyotard, *The Postmodern Condition: A Report on Knowledge* (Manchester: Manchester University Press, 1984) particularly pp. 41–53.
16. For a specific discussion on journalism as a form of storytelling, see, for instance David L. Eason, 'Telling Stories and Making Sense' in *Journal of Popular Culture* 15.2 (Fall 1981) pp. 125–9; Michael Schudson, 'The Politics of the Narrative Form: The Emergence of News Conventions in Print and Television' in *Deadalus* 3.4 (Fall 1982) pp. 97–112; and Barbie Zelizer, 'Achieving Journalistic Authority through Narrative' in *Critical Studies in Mass Communication* 7 (1990) pp. 366–76.
17. See, for instance, Carl R. Bybee, 'Constructing Women as Authorities: Local Journalism and the Microphysics of Power' in *Critical Studies in Mass Communication* 7 (1990) pp. 197–214.
18. Cf. Michael Schudson, 'National News Culture and the Rise of the Informational Citizen' in *America at Century's End*, ed. Alan Wolfe (Berkeley: University of California Press, 1991) pp. 265–82. Schudson considers this 'newsification' trend to be one of the underexposed themes in media studies: 'Most observers of the media have complained that the serious news institutions have been turning news into entertainment, but the larger trend is that entertainment has turned into news' (274).
19. See David Altheide and Robert P. Snow *Media Worlds in the Postjournalism Era* (New York: De Gruyter, 1991) particularly Chapter 1 'The Media as Culture' (pp. 1–14).
20. The Human Genome Project was approved and funded by the American Congress in 1990, and is administered by the Department of Energy and the Department of Health and Human Services.

21. Cf. James J. Bono, 'Science, Discourse, and Literature: the Role/
Rule of Metaphor in Science' in *Literature and Science. Theory and
Practice*, ed. Stuart Peterfreund (Boston: Northeastern University
Press, 1990) pp. 59–89.
22. Cf. Barbara Foley, *Telling the Truth*, Chapters 2 and 3.
23. On the dialogic nature of the novel, see Mikhail Bakhtin, *The
Dialogic Imagination* (Austin: University of Texas Press, 1981) and
Speech Genres and Other Essays (Austin: University of Texas Press,
1986).
24. Sarah Lefanu, in *Feminism and Science Fiction* (Bloomington:
Indiana University Press, 1989), argues that the science fiction
genre is particularly open to borrowing from other discourses,
'from physics and fairy tales, from philosophy, folklore, and myth'
(99).
25. Cf. Gayle L. Ormiston and Raphael Sassower, *Narrative
Experiments. The Discursive Authority of Science and Technology*
(Minneapolis: University of Minnesota Press, 1989). According
to Ormiston and Sassower, the creation of a labyrinth of
narratives allows the reader to unravel 'how the use, the
deployment, and the active interpretation of a text fabricates
the conditions for understanding that text and any meaning – or
authority – attributed to it' (89).
26. For a description of the term webbing, see 'Otherworldly
Conversations; Terran Topics; Local Terms' in *Science as Culture*
3:14 (1992) p. 79.
27. For practical reasons, I have excluded audiovisual materials from
my analysis, although I realize that these texts are becoming
increasingly important contributions to the public debate.
However, it was virtually impossible to track down all television
series or films in which reproductive technologies play a
significant role. In this book, I will pay attention to audiovisual
texts only if there is an explicit reference to a movie in the written
accounts that are the objects of my study.
28. I am much obliged to the staff and documentalists of the women's
Global Network for Reproductive Rights for allowing me to use
their archive, and helping me kindly with my research. (Address:
GNRR, Nieuwezijds Voorburgwal 32, 1012 RZ Amsterdam, The
Netherlands)

3 Constructing the Need for New Reproductive Technologies

1. J. Rock and M.F. Menkin, 'In Vitro Fertilization and Cleavage
of Human Ovarian Eggs' in *Science* 100 (1944) pp. 105–7.
2. B.G. Brackett, H.M. Seitz, and L. Mastroianni, 'In Vitro

Fertilization: Animal and Human' in *Advances in Planned Parenthood VII. Proceedings of the Ninth Annual Meeting of the AAPPP*, eds. A.J. Sobrero and R.M. Harvey (Amsterdam: Excerpta Medica, 1972) pp. 157–66.

3. P.C. Steptoe and R.G. Edwards, 'Birth after Reimplantation of a Human Embryo', *The Lancet*, 12 August 1978, p. 366.

4. Cf. Annette Burfoot, 'The Normalisation of a New Reproductive Technology', in *The New Reproductive Technologies*, eds. Maureen McNeil, Ian Varcoe and Steven Yearly (London: Macmillan, 1990) pp. 58–73. This citation analysis focuses particularly on Robert Edwards's scientific career.

5. It took another year before Edwards and Steptoe reported their procedures at the Royal College of Obstetricians and Gynaecologists conference in London, in 1979. The procedures and techniques were finally published in 1980. Cf. P.C. Steptoe, R.G. Edwards and J.M. Purdy, 'Clinical Aspects of Pregnancies Established with Cleaving Embryos Grown In Vitro' in *British Journal for Obstetrics and Gynaecology* 87 (1980) pp. 737–56.

6. Cf. Anne Karpf, *Doctoring the Media* (New York: Routledge, 1988) in which she vividly relates how reporters invented cunning schemes to enter the hospital.

7. Cf. Dorothy Nelkin, *Selling Science. How the Press Covers Science and Technology* (New York: Freeman, 1987). Nelkin labels this frame, which is often used by news reporters to relate a story of an incomprehensible advancement in science, the 'Ghee Whiz! A Miracle!' frame (p. 10).

8. 'The First Test-Tube Baby', *Time*, 30 July 1978, pp. 62–8.

9. Among the IVF clinics best known in the USA are the 'Institute of Fertility Assistance' in Ann Arbor, Michigan, and the 'Infertility Center of New York,' led by the infamous Noel Kane, who became known in 1987 as the 'Baby M-broker.'

10. Ian Johnston et al., 'In Vitro Fertilization: The Challenge of the Eighties' in *Fertility and Sterility* 36.6 (December 1981) pp. 699–705.

11. Another illustrative example of this type of argument can be found in W. Feichtinger, P. Kemeter and S. Szalay, 'The Vienna Program of In Vitro Fertilization and Embryo Transfer – A Successful Clinical Treatment,' *European Journal of Obstetrics, Gynaecology, and Reproductive Medicine* 15 (1983) pp. 63–70. In this article we can read the comment: 'With an established uniform schedule for clinical use, this model could solve the problems of endless waiting lists presently existing in IVF centres' (69).

12. As Lyotard argues in *The Postmodern Condition*: 'The question (overt or implied) is no longer "Is it true?" but "What use is it?" In the context of the mercantilization of knowledge, more often

than not this question is equivalent to "Is it saleable?" and in the context of power-growth: "Is it efficient?" '(51).

13. Stephen L. Curson et al., 'Early Experience with the GIFT procedure' in *Journal of Reproductive Medicine* 31.4 (April 1986) pp. 219–23.

14. For instance, A. Trounson and A. Conti, 'Research in Human In Vitro Fertilisation and Embryo Transfer' in *British Medical Journal* 285 (1982) pp. 244–48, mentions as the major concern of opponents of in vitro fertilization 'the manipulation and survival of human embryos and the concept of a human person and when this begins' (248).

15. Embryo Transfer requires the help of a so-called ovum donor: the couple unable to conceive is assisted by another woman who is artificially inseminated with the husband's sperm. The fertilized egg is then transferred to the infertile woman who carries it to term.

16. Beverly Metz, 'Stock Breeding Technique Applied to Human Infertility' in *Journal of the American Medical Association* 250.10 (September 1983) p. 1257.

17. 'Embryo Transfer: Patent Pending' in *Fertility Assistance*, April 1984, p.1.

18. Sucsy's statement strikingly resembles the rhetoric of an advertisement for Advanced Fertility Services in *The New York Times* (28 September 1986) which reads: 'Sometimes it takes more than love to have a baby. If you are having problems starting a family of your own, or suspect that you are infertile, than contact the Advanced Fertility Services.'

19. Claudia Wallis, 'Making Babies: the New Science of Conception' in *Time*, 10 September 1984, pp. 46–56.

20. This is the 'official' medical definition of infertility; however, the definition has changed over time, limiting the period of 'unprotected intercourse' from two years to one; in addition, many researchers and doctors have observed that the very term 'unprotected intercourse' may be interpreted widely different, varying on the intensity and intentional timing of intercourse during the twelve menstrual cycles.

21. W. Cates, T. Farley, and P. Rowe (on behalf of the World Health Organization), 'Worldwide Patterns of Infertility' in *The Lancet*, 14 September 1985, pp. 596–8.

22. Cf. 'The National Survey of Family Growth Cycle III', National Center for Health Statistics. Quoted in Susan Faludi, *Backlash. The Undeclared War Against American Women* (New York: Crown, 1991) p. 471.

23. I found this statistic repeated over and over again as evidence to support the infertility epidemic, even into the 1990s, despite the

fact that the number was officially contradicted by the Office of Technology Assessment in 1987. The statistic 'one out of six' is used invariably as evidence to support the 'need' for new(er) variations of the new technologies.

24. G. Johnson, 'Infertile or Childless by Choice? A Multipractice Survey of Women Aged 35 and 50' in *British Medical Journal* 294 (March 1987) pp. 804–6.

25. Aral So and W. Cates, 'The Increasing Concern with Infertility – Why Now?' in *Journal of the American Medical Association* 250 (1983) pp. 2327–31.

26. US Congress, Office of Technology Assessment, 'Infertility: Medical and Social Choices', Washington DC, 1988.

27. Joseph Palca, 'US In Vitro Fertilization in Limbo According to OTA' in *Nature* 333 (June 1988) p. 388.

28. The Office of Technology Assessment report states that the number of people seeking treatment has increased from 600 000 in 1968 to 1.6 million in 1984. US spending on medical treatment to 'combat infertility' amounted to one billion dollar in 1987.

29. Cf. Edward Albee, 'AIDS: The Victim and the Press' in *News and Knowledge* ed. Thelma McCormack (New London, Connecticut: Jai Press, 1986) pp. 135–57.

30. Cf. Geoffrey Howe et al., 'Effects of Age, Cigarette Smoking, and Other Factors on Fertility' in *British Medical Journal* 290 (1985) pp. 1697–700; see also Allen Wilcox, Clarice Weinberg and Donna Baird, 'Caffeinated Beverages and Decreased Fertility' in *The Lancet* 24–31 December 1988, pp. 1453–56.

31. The article 'New Focus on Sperm Brings Fertility Successes' in *The New York Times* (13 September 1990, p. C1) provides a comprehensive overview of the several causes of male infertility that have been researched in the past ten years.

32. Cf. 'Fecundity, Fertility, and Reproductive Health in the United States, 1982' data from the *National Survey of Family Growth*, National Center for Health Statistics, Hyattsville, Md. (May 1987) p. 52.

4 Feminist Assessments of New Reproductive Technologies

1. The first conference on reproductive technologies, organized by feminist health workers, took place in Leeds, in March 1984. At the second International Interdisciplinary Congress on Women in Groningen, The Netherlands, in April 1984, the Feminist International Network on Reproductive Technologies (FINN-RET) was founded spontaneously. In 1985, at an 'emergency

conference' in Sweden, FINNRET changed its name to Feminist International Network of Resistance to Reproductive and Genetic Engineering (FINNRAGE).

2. For instance, the British journals *Women's Studies, International Forum* and *Seeds of Change*, although British based, were international in scope, and contributors to these journals, as well as to *Test-Tube Women*, were both American and European.

3. Jana Halmner, 'A Womb of One's Own' in *Test-Tube Women. What Future for Motherhood?* eds. Rita Arditti, Renate Duelli Klein and Shelley Minden (London: Pandora Press, 1984) pp. 438–48.

4. Renate Duelli Klein, 'Taking the Egg from the One and the Uterus from the Other' in *Seeds of Change* 4 (1984) pp. 92–7.

5. Maria Mies, 'Why Do We Need All This? A Call Against Genetic Engineering and Reproductive Technology' in *Women's Studies International Forum* 8.6 (1985) pp. 1–8.

6. Illustrative in this respect is Mies's claim: 'Capital needs it, men need it and both need us as buyers of this technology, as otherwise there would be an end to the so-called growth. Are you, are we, really captives of patriarchal capital?'(2).

7. Allen L. Otten, 'Artificial Birth Methods are Attacked by Some Feminists Fearing Male Control' in *Wall Street Journal*, 15 April 1985.

8. Cf. Roland Barthes, *Mythologies*, p. 130.

9. Cf. Marjo van Soest, 'Specialiteit: Springstoffen tegen Vrouwenuitbuiters' in *De Groene Amsterdammer*, 16 March 1988, pp. 3–5.

10. Rita Arditti, for instance, reports of an international conference held in Bonn, in April 1985, which was attended by 2000 women who collectively condemned the new reproductive technologies as 'an attempt to take over women's bodies' unique potential to create human life.' Cf. Rita Arditti, 'Reproductive Engineering and the Social Control of Women' in *Radical America* 19:6 (1986) pp. 9–26.

11. Anita Direcks and Helen Becquaert Holmes, 'Miracle Drug, Miracle Baby' in *New Scientist* 112 (1986) pp. 53–5.

12. I refer to Klein's and Corea's assessment of the new technologies as 'radical' and to Mies's definition as 'Marxist.' The use of these terms is both problematic and inadequate, since they erase the nuances between their different views and because there is a negative connotation attached to these words.

13. Naomi Pfeffer, 'Not So New Technologies' in *Trouble and Strife* 5 (Spring 1985) pp. 46–50.

14. Marge Berer, 'Breeding Conspiracies. Feminism and New Reproductive Technologies' in *Trouble and Strife* 9 (Summer 1986) pp. 29–35.

15. Ann Snitow, 'The Paradox of Birth Technology. Exploring the Good, the Bad, and the Scary' in *Ms* magazine (December 1986) pp. 42–51.
16. Two important collections of articles, published in 1987, combine a number of academic disciplinary views on the issue of the new technologies: *Reproductive Technologies. Gender, Motherhood and Medicine* ed. Michelle Stanworth (Minneapolis: University of Minnesota Press) and *Made to Order. The Myth of Reproductive and Genetic Progress* eds. Patricia Spallone and Deborah Lynn Steinberg (Oxford: Pergamon Press).
17. For an elaborate discussion on how the views of these two groups of feminists diverge, see Bette Vandewater, 'Meanings and Strategies of Reproductive Control: Current Feminist Approaches to Reproductive Technology' in *Issues in Reproductive and Genetic Engineering* 5:3 (1992) pp. 215–30.
18. *Dawn* is the first part of Octavia Butler's trilogy titled *Xenogenesis*. The subsequent volumes, *Adulthood Rites* and *Imago*, were published respectively in 1988 and 1989. For the remainder of this chapter, I will exclusively refer to *Dawn*, which was first published in 1987.
19. 'Margaret Atwood Reflects on her Success' in *The New York Times*, 14 April 1990, p. B12.
20. Margaret Atwood, *The Handmaid's Tale* (New York: Ballantine, 1985) pp. 152–7.
21. For a fuller discussion of this concept, see José Van Dyck and Lies Wesseling, 'The Issue of Responsibility in Margaret Atwood's *The Handmaid's Tale*' in *Against Patriarchal Thinking. A Future without Discrimination* ed. Maja Pelikaan (Amsterdam: Free University Press, 1992) pp. 243–51.
22. The movie *The Handmaid's Tale*, directed by Volker Schlöndorff, was released in 1990. The film script was written by Harold Pinter with the help of Margaret Atwood.
23. For a description of these scenes, see Octavia Butler, *Dawn*, respectively page 93 and page 221.
24. Stephanie A. Smith, in her article 'Morphing, Materialism, and the Marketing of Xenogenesis' in *Genders* 18 (1993) pp. 67–86, argues that while Butler's trilogy is marketed by a mainstream publisher, this strategy has also compromised her ideas. For instance, on the cover of *Dawn*, Lilith is depicted as a lily-white female, ignoring the essential racial critique in Butler's story.
25. Theresa de Lauretis, in 'Eccentric Subjects: Feminist Theory and Historical Consciousness' in *Feminist Studies* 16:1 (1990), describes this historical moment as the realization that feminists are 'excluded from the established discourse of theory yet imprisoned within it or else assigned a corner of their own but denied

specificity.' See also Theresa De Lauretis, *Technologies of Gender. Essays on Theory, Film, and Fiction* (Bloomington: Indiana University Press, 1987).
26. Cf. Norma Wikler, 'Society's Response to the New Reproductive Technologies: The Feminist Perspectives' in *Southern California Law Review* 59 (1986) pp. 1043–57.

5   From Cure to Commodity: The Naturalization of IVF

1. Judge Sorkow's decision was reversed by the New Jersey Supreme Court. Justice Wilentz, writing for the unanimous Court, found the surrogacy contract to be invalid, and allowed custody to Mary Beth Whitehead, while sustaining Stern's grant of custody as the biological father.
2. While 'success rates' usually suggest pregnancy, this does not mean that all pregnancies result in live births. 'Pregnancy wastage' – medical jargon that rhetorically clouds failure or miscarriage – should be subtracted from previously claimed pregnancies. Some medical researchers claim only those pregnancies to be successful, when the foetus is carried beyond viability term, which is twenty-four weeks.
3. Richard J. Lilford and Maureen E. Dalton, 'Effectiveness of Treatment for Infertility' in *British Medical Journal* 295 (1987) 155–6.
4. Philip J. Hilts, 'U.S. Urged to Aid In Vitro Research' in *The New York Times* 2 December 1989, p. A1.
5. Joseph Palca, 'US In Vitro Fertilization in Limbo According to OTA' in *Nature* 333, 2 June 1988, p. 388.
6. 'Outpatient In Vitro Fertilization Economical' in *Ob.Gyn. News*, 15–31 December 1987, p. 10.
7. For instance, in 1989 the British newspaper the *Guardian* reports the birth of a baby in Liverpool after the first successful application of Intra Vaginal Culture (IVC). IVC is a variation of IVF whereby eggs and sperm are 'incubated' for 48 hours in a small plastic tube in the vagina, thus cutting the costs of a 'normal' IVF procedure. Cf. 'Birth Brings New Hope to the Infertile', the *Guardian*, 30 September 1989.
8. Richard E. Blackwell et al., 'Are We Exploiting the Infertile Couple?' in *Fertility and Sterility* 48 (November 1987) pp. 735–9.
9. Cf. Claudia Wallis, 'Making Babies: the New Science of Conception', *Time*, 10 September 1984, p. 53.
10. Bridget Lovell, 'In Vitro Fertilisation. The Birth of Michael' in *Nursing Times*, 29 October 1986, pp. 27–30.
11. Sue Halpern, 'Infertility: Playing the Odds' in *Ms* magazine (January–February 1989) pp. 147–56.

12. Cf. Carl R. Bybee, 'Constructing Women as Authorities: Local
     Journalism and the Microphysics of Power' in *Critical Studies in
     Mass Communication* 7.3 (September 1990) pp. 197–214.
13. Cf. Gaye Tuchman, *Making News. A Study in the Construction of
     Reality* (New York: The Free Press, 1978). In Chapters 6 and 7,
     Tuchman explains her concept of 'symbolic annihilation'
     referring to ways in which women are rendered invisible in the
     news, or banned to the margins in the construction of reality.
14. Machelle M. Seibel, 'A New Era in Reproductive Technology. In
     Vitro Fertilization, Gamete Intrafallopian Transfer and Donated
     Gametes and Embryos' in *New England Journal of Medicine* 318 (31
     March 1988) pp. 828–34.
15. For instance, an article titled 'Reassuring Study of In Vitro
     Babies' (*The New York Times*, 11 August, 1989, A17) reports that
     IVF babies conceived in a laboratory are 'as healthy and
     mentally alert as those conceived normally.' An article 'Your A-Z
     Guide to Health' (*US News and World Report*, 18 June 1990) claims
     that 'test-tube kids generally had higher IQ-scores than normal
     kids.'
16. Cf. Martha Kirejczyk and Irma van der Ploeg, 'Pregnant
     Couples: Medical Technology and Social Constructions around
     Infertility and Reproduction' in *Issues in Reproductive and Genetic
     Engineering* 5.2 (1992) pp. 113–25.
     Kirejczyk and Van der Ploeg argue that the observed
     symmetry between male and female experiences of IVF reveal a
     powerful norm in medical discourse: it does not just erase the
     inequal burden of IVF on women, but it also functions as a
     regulating mechanism which privileges the heterosexual couple as
     the natural recipients of IVF treatment, to the exclusion of
     lesbian or single women.
17. For a fuller analysis of the power of medical visualizing
     techniques, see Carol A. Stabile, 'Shooting the Mother: Fetal
     Photography and the Politics of Disappearance' in *Camera Obscura*
     28 (1992) pp. 179–205.
18. Cf. Christine Crowe's analysis of the term 'pre-embryo' in 'Whose
     Mind over Whose Matter? In Vitro Fertilisation and the
     Development of Scientific Knowledge' in *The New Reproductive
     Technologies*, eds. Maureen McNeil, Ian Varcoe and Steven
     Yearly (London: Macmillan, 1990) pp. 27–57.
19. Philip Elmer-Dewitt 'Making Babies' in *Time*, 30 September
     1991, pp. 56–63.
20. For an insightful discussion of the changing function of visualizing
     techniques in popular news media, see Barbara Duden,
     'Visualizing Life' in *Science as Culture* 3:17 (1993) pp. 562–600.

21. In the article 'Making Babies' in *Time* we can find ten quotes from medical experts, two of whom are female. The 'couple that has hit the jackpot' appears in the last paragraph, thus ending the story on a very positive note.

22. The 1984 'infertility epidemic' is recanted in 1991; curiously, *Time* now uses the number 'one out of twelve' instead of 'one out of six' to prove the extent of the epidemic.

23. Cf. 'Making Babies'; the American government cut funding for IVF clinics under pressure from conservative anti-abortion groups, which had very powerful lobbies to Congress in the late 1980s (p. 62).

24. The same argument can be found in Richard E. Blackwell et al., 'Are We Exploiting the Infertile Couple' in *Fertility and Sterility* 48.5 (November 1987) pp. 735–9.

25. For an interesting discussion of how the media have helped promote the idea of progress in reproductive medicine, see Janice Raymond, 'The Marketing of New Reproductive Technologies: Medicine, the Media, and the Idea of Progress' in *Issues in Reproductive and Genetic Engineering* 3:3 (1990) pp. 253–61.

26. Peculiarly, Robin Cook has practised all three discourses: after obtaining his Ph.D. in medicine and a few years of clinical practice, he became a science journalist for the *Boston Globe*, and finally turned to writing medical thrillers. He is the author of best-selling novel *Coma*.

27. Movies, like television series, now feature the primacy of the intra-body gaze. In the movie *Look Who's Talking* (released in 1990) for instance, the viewer is guided by the camera into the woman's womb; the camera takes on the position of the foetus, and thus witnesses the birth from the point of view from the baby.

28. This line is quoted from the dedication page of *Vital Signs*.

29. Cf. Robin Cook, *Vital Signs*, pp. 196–201.

30. One scene from *Vital Signs* literally echoes a line from *Time* magazine: the description of the sign in the waiting area of the Boston Women's Clinic reading 'You only fail when you give up trying' (37).

31. In *The Dialogic Imagination* (Austin: University of Texas Press) Mikhail Bakhtin describes how, throughout the entire development of the novel, the intimate interaction of fictional with other rhetorical genres (journalistic, philosophical, political) has never ceased. See particularly pp. 341–47. In 'The Problem of Speech Genres' (*Speech Genres and other Late Essays*, Austin: University of Texas Press, 1986) Bakhtin specifically explores how utterances are transformed and recycled in what he calls 'the chain of communication' (91).

32. Amanda Cross (a pseudonym for Carolyn Heilbrun) and Sara Paretsky have both published numerous feminist detective novels; their protagonists are invariably courageous, smart, professional women who solve sophisticated crimes.
33. See, for instance, Karen Malpede, 'Scenes 2 and 7 from "Better People: A Surreal Comedy about Genetic Engineering"' in *Issues in Reproductive and Genetic Engineering* 4:2 (1991) pp. 161–8; and Mary O'Brien, 'Elly' in *Issues in Reproductive and Genetic Engineering* 3:2 (1990) pp. 137–141. This fictional contribution is introduced by an editor's note.
34. Renate D. Klein, 'IVF Research: A Question of Feminist Ethics' in *Issues in Reproductive and Genetic Engineering* 3:3 (1990) pp. 243–51 and Somer Brodribb, 'Les Immateriaux: A Feminist Critique of Postmodernism' in *Issues in Reproductive and Genetic Engineering* 5:3 (1992) pp. 257–64.
35. Lisa Woll, 'The Effect of Feminist Opposition to Reproductive Technology: a Case Study in Victoria, Australia' in *Issues in Reproductive and Genetic Engineering* 5:1 (1992) pp. 21–38.

6 From Need to Right: The Legalization of Genetic Motherhood

1. This number includes news articles, editorials and news analyses; I have not been able to trace any Op-Ed pieces concerning this case.
2. Catherine Gewertz, 'Surrogate Mother in Custody Fight Accused of Welfare Fraud' in *LAT*, 16 August 1990, p. A3.
3. Cf. Valerie Hartouni, 'Breached Births: Reflections on Race, Gender, and Reproductive Discourse in the 1980s' in *Configurations* 2:1 (1994) p. 75.
4. Catherine Gewertz, 'Surrogate Gives Birth to Boy, Custody Fight' in *LAT*, 20 September 1990, p. A3.
5. Catherine Gewertz, 'Genetic Parents Granted Temporary Custody' in *LAT*, 22 September 1990, p. A30.
6. 'Give the Baby to the Genetic Parents. Orange County Surrogate Case Finds the Courts Deeply Involved Again' editorial in *LAT*, 22 September 1990, p. B6.
7. Catherine Gewertz, 'Surrogate-born Baby Now with Genetic Parents' in *LAT*, 23 September 1990, p. A1.
8. For a more elaborate reflection on the comparison between slave women and surrogate mothers, see Hilde Lindemann Nelson, 'Scrutinizing Surrogacy' in *Issues in Reproductive Technology I. An Anthology*, ed. Helen Bequaert Holmes (New York: Garland, 1992) pp. 297–302.

9. Catherine Gewertz, 'Consultant Says Surrogate is Child's Mother' in *LAT*, 10 October 1990, p. B1.
10. Catherine Gewertz, 'Surrogate Says She Secretly Aimed to Keep the Baby' in *LAT*, 11 October 1990, p. A3.
11. Catherine Gewertz, 'Surrogate Parent Trial Nears End; Judge is Likened to Solomon' in *LAT*, 18 October 1990, p. A3.
12. Valerie Hartouni, in 'Breached Births' elaborates on the cultural narratives about 'the way black women are.' Analysing the trial manuscript, Hartouni highlights the part of Johnson's interrogation in which the lawyer suggests that she was probably out to keep the baby because she 'fetishized whiteness' (83).
13. Cf. Zillah R. Eisenstein, *The Female Body and the Law* (Berkeley: University of California Press, 1988) who argues that in legal discourse, the natural law is the law of reason: 'The supposed objectivity of the law is often established through the "laws of nature" . . . Rationality and the laws of nature are encoded as part of the objectivist standpoint' (49).
14. Sonni Efron, 'Attorneys Turn Surrogate Mother Case into Trial by Media' in *LAT*, 22 October 1990, p. A3.
15. For a detailed description of the 'media blitz' concerning the Calvert vs. Johnson case, see M.L. Stein, 'Media Crush in California' in *Editor and Publisher* 20 (12 October 1990), p.46.
16. Catherine Gewertz, 'Genetic Parents Given Sole Custody of Child' in *LAT*, 23 October 1990, p. A1.
17. 'Child's Interest is Paramount' editorial in *LAT*, 23 October 1990, p. B6.
18. Martin Kasindorf, 'And Baby Makes Four. Johnson vs. Calvert Illustrates about Everything That Can Go Wrong in Surrogate Births' in *LAT Magazine*, 20 January 1991, pp. 11–34.
19. Mark Calvert is quoted as saying that he 'really wanted a child that had [Crispina's] innocence, sweetness, her demeanor' (14). In contrast to the typical white, middle-class surrogate mother, Anna Johnson is said to have signed the surrogate contract 'out of complex motivations that seemed dominated by pure spite toward the better-fixed couple' (12).
20. This quote is taken from Judge Parslow's ruling in the courtroom on October 22, cited in the *LAT*, 23 October 1990.
21. Cf. Eisenstein, *The Female Body and the Law*, pp. 48–9.
22. A few headlines from the *San Diego Tribune*'s coverage of the case are indicative of the frame used by this newspaper: 'Surrogate Admits Deception' (16 October 1990), 'Surrogate Mom's Boasts Told' (17 October 1990), and 'Did Ruling for Genetic Parents Give Birth to a "Breeder Class?"' (23 October 1990).
23. Two articles from the *Wall Street Journal* particularly give space to dissenting (feminist) opinions: Amy Dockser Marcus, 'Techno-

logical, Social Changes May Spur to Widen Definition of
Parenthood. Surrogate Mothers, Stepfamilies, and Lesbian
Couples Filing More Custody Cases' (18 September 1990, p.
B1) and Michelle Harrison, 'The Baby with Two Mothers' (24
October 1990, p. A14). Michelle Harrison was the expert witness
called upon to testify for Anna Johnson. In the *Christian Science
Monitor* another critical article appeared: Scott Armstrong,
'California Surrogacy Case Raises New Questions about
Parenthood' (25 September 1990, p. 1).

24. Richard Paddock and Rene Lynch, 'Surrogate Has No Rights to
Child, Court Says' in *LAT*, 21 May 1993, p. A1, cont. A27.

25. 'Surrogacy Case: A Good Ruling', editorial in *LAT*, 24 May
1993, p. B6.

26. Rene Lynch and Matt Lait, 'Supreme Court Lets Ruling Stand
in Surrogacy Case' *LAT*, 5 October 1993, p. A3.

27. For a comprehensive overview of publications on contract
pregnancy, see Helen Bequaert Holmes, 'Contract Pregnancy:
An Annotated Bibliography' in *Issues in Reproductive Technology I.
An Anthology*, ed. Helen Bequaert Holmes (New York: Garland,
1992) pp. 381–422.

28. Cf. Christine Overall, *Ethics and Human Reproduction: A Feminist
Analysis* (Boston: Allen Unwin, 1987); Lori Andrews, *Between
Strangers: Surrogate Mothers, Expectant Fathers and Brave New Babies*
(New York: Harper and Row, 1989).

29. Examples of positive experiential accounts of surrogate mother-
hood: Elizabeth Kane, *Birth Mother: America's First Legal Surrogate
Tells the Story of her Change of Heart* (San Diego: Harcourt Brace
Jovanovic, 1988), and Maggie and Linda Kirkman, *My Sister's
Child: Maggie and Linda Kirkman - Their Own Story* (New York:
Penguin Books, 1988). Examples of negative experiential tales are
Mary Beth Whitehead [with Loretta Schwartz-Nobel], *A Mother's
Story. The Truth about the Baby M Case* (New York: St. Martin's,
1989) and Renate D. Klein, *Women Speak Out about Their
Experiences with Reproductive Medicine* (London: Pandora Press,
1989).

30. See for instance *Feminist Perspectives in Medical Ethics*, eds. Helen B.
Holmes and Linda M. Purdy (Bloomington: Indiana University
Press, 1992) and *Surrogate Motherhood: Politics and Privacy*, ed.
Larry Gostin (Bloomington: Indiana University Press, 1988).

31. Alexander M. Capron, 'Whose Child Is This?' in *Hastings Center
Report* 21:6 (1991) pp. 37–8; and Rita Arditti, 'Who's the Mother?
Ask the Infertility Industry!' in *Sojourner* (December 1990) pp.
10–11.

32. Katha Pollitt 'When is a Mother Not a Mother?', *The Nation* (3
December 1990) pp. 840–4.

33. Laura M. Purdy, 'Another Look at Contract Pregnancy' in *Issues in Reproductive Technology I. An Anthology*, ed. Helen B. Holmes (New York: Garland, 1992) pp. 303–20.

7 From Legalization to Legislation: Race and Age as Determining Factors

1. Concerning the anonymity of donors, the HFEA decided to keep a confidential register, which permits children to obtain the name of their genetic parent after the age of eighteen. With regard to the number of gametes implanted per cycle, the HFEA decided that three would be the maximum. Access to infertility services for lesbian couples was settled just before the HFEA was installed. Pre-sex selection of embryos was rejected by the HFEA in 1993. Nevertheless, the first pre-sex selection clinic opened in London in 1993; it could not be restricted by the HFEA because its practices do not involve the use of donated genetic material.
2. D. Schwartz and M.J. Mayaux, 'Female Fecundity as a Function of Age. Results of Artificial Insemination in 2193 Nulliparous Women with Azoospermic Husbands' in *New England Journal of Medicine* (18 February 1982) pp. 404–6.
3. Alan H. DeCherney and Gertrud S. Berkowitz, 'Female Fecundity and Age', *New England Journal of Medicine* (18 February 1982) pp. 424–26.
4. Mark V. Sauer, Richard J. Paulson, and Rogerio A. Lobo, 'A Preliminary Report on Oocyte Donation Extending Reproductive Potential to Women over 40' in *New England Journal of Medicine* (25 October 1990) pp. 1157–60.
5. Gina Kolata, 'Menopause is Found No Bar to Pregnancy' in *The New York Times* (24 October 1990) p. A1.
6. 'Bottomley Warns on Test-Tube Children', the *Guardian* (28 December 1993) p. 1.
7. 'Under the Spotlight: The Italian Doctor Who Breeds Publicity' in *The Times* (28 December 1993) p. 3.
8. 'Pioneer with God's Gift' in the *Guardian* (28 December 1993) p.3.
9. 'Doctor Calls for Ethics Code on Mothers at 50' and 'The Man Who Defied Nature' both in the *Daily Telegraph* (28 December 1993) p. 3.
10. Simon Jenkins, 'Only the Parents Can Decide' in *The Times* (27 December 1993) editorial page.
11. The *Daily Mirror* of 28 December 1993 features six pages of articles on postmenopausal pregnancy: 'Look Who's Talking' (p.1); 'Don't Deny the Granny Mums this Joy, Europe Tells Virginia' (p.1); 'Now He's Hatching Out. Three? Four? Fertility

Doc Will Give You as Many Babies as You Want with Laser Op' (p. 4–5); 'Why Birth is a Right' (p.6); and 'Deliver Us From Hysteria (editorial, p.7).

12. 'White Baby Born to Black Mother' in *The Times* (31 December 1993) p. 1.
13. 'Genetic Engineering Row Over White Egg For Black Woman' in the *Daily Telegraph* (31 December 1993) p. 1.
14. 'Watchdog Report on Designer Baby' in *The Times* (1 January 1994) p. 1.
15. 'Mother Still Knows Best' in the *Observer* (2 January 1994), p. 7.
16. 'Couples Barred From Choosing Race of Babies' in the *Independent* (1 January 1994) p. 3.
17. 'White Baby Born to Black Mother' in *The Times* (31 December 1993) p. 1.
18. 'Unnatural Childbirth' in *The Times* (31 December 1993), editorial page.
19. Kenan Malik, 'Children of a Confused Society' in the *Independent* (3 January 1994), Op-Ed page.
20. 'New Fertility Treatment Facing Ban' in *The Times* (3 January 1994), p. 1.
21. 'The Internal Mother Will Always Be There' in the *Independent* (3 January 1994), editorial page.
22. 'Birth Pangs' in the *Guardian* (5 January 1994) p. 4.
23. 'Who Decides How Babies Are Made?' in the *Independent* (7 January 1994), p. 19.

Conclusion

1. NCRV, a Dutch public television station, broadcast the programme 'Bekentenissen' on 8, 15, 22 and 29 December 1992. The programme format drew quite a lot of criticism from viewers.
2. Cf. Jennifer Terry, 'The Body Invaded: Medical Surveillance of Women as Reproducers' in *Socialist Review* 3 (July 1989) pp. 13–43.
3. Cf. Katha Pollitt, 'A New Assault on Feminism' in *The Nation* (26 March 1990) pp. 409–18.
4. Cf. Diana Button, *Worse Than Disease. Pitfalls of Medical Progress.* (Cambridge: Cambridge University Press, 1988). See particularly Chapter 10, 'The Role of the Public' (pp. 319–49).
5. Several such platforms have already been initiated, but as of yet they are experimental in nature; in The Netherlands, for instance, a national Ethics Platform was launched in April 1994.
6. See for instance W. Cates, T.M. Farley and P.J. Rowe, 'Worldwide Patterns of Infertility: Is Africa Different?' in *The*

Lancet (14 September 1985) pp. 596–98; this article proves that infertility in Africa is a much more serious problem than in other regions of the world. For a 'dissenting' opinion on American women experiencing infertility treatment see Ellen Hopkins, 'Tales from the Baby Factory' in *The New York Times* (15 March 1992); this article is very critical of the price women have to pay for infertility treatment.

Bibliography

Albert, Edward. 'AIDS: The Victim and the Press.' *News and Knowledge*. Ed. Thelma McCormack. Studies in Communications 3. London (Conn.): Jai Press, 1986. 135–57.

Altheide, David and Robert P. Snow. *Media Worlds in the Postjournalism Era*. New York: De Gruyter, 1991.

Andrews, Lori B. *Between Strangers: Surrogate Mothers, Expectant Fathers and Brave New Babies*. New York: Harper and Row, 1989.

Arditti, Rita. 'Reproductive Engineering and the Social Control of Women.' *Radical America* 19:6 (1986): 9–26.

Arditti, Rita. 'Who's the Mother? Ask the Infertility Industry!' *Sojourner* (December 1990): 10–11.

Arditti, Rita, Renate Duelli Klein, and Shelley Minden, eds. *Test-Tube Women. What Future for Womanhood?* London: Pandora Press, 1984.

Atwood, Margaret. *The Handmaid's Tale*. New York: Ballantine, 1985.

Bakhtin, Mikhail M. *The Dialogic Imagination*. Ed. Michael Holquist, transl. Caryl Emerson and Michael Holquist. Austin: University of Texas Press, 1981.

Bakhtin, Mikhail. *Speech Genres and Other Late Essays*. Eds. Caryl Emerson and Michael Holquist. Austin: University of Texas Press, 1986.

Barthes, Roland. *Mythologies*. Trans. Jonathan Cape. New York: Hill and Wang, 1972. Trans. of *Mythologies*. Paris: Editions du Seuil, 1957.

Birke, Lynda, Susan Himmelweit, and Gail Vines. *Tomorrow's Child. Reproductive Technologies in the 90s*. London: Virago Press, 1990.

Bono, James J. 'Science, Discourse and Literature: The Role/Rule of Metaphor in Science.' *Literature and Science. Theory and Practice*. Ed. Stuart Peterfreund. Boston: Northeastern University Press, 1990.

Braidotti, Rosi. *Patterns of Dissonance. A Study of Women in Contemporary Philosophy*. Cambridge: Polity Press, 1991.

Braidotti, Rosi. 'On Contemporary Medical Pornography.' *Tijdschrift voor Vrouwenstudies* 47 (1991): 356–72.

Brander, Martin S. 'The Scientist and the News Media'. *New English Journal of Medicine* (12 May 1983): 1170–73.

Brodribb, Somer. 'Les Immateriaux: A Feminist Critique of Postmodernism.' *Issues in Reproductive and Genetic Engineering* 5:3 (1992): 257–64.

Burfoot, Anne. 'The Normalisation of a New Reproductive Technology.' *The New Reproductive Technologies*. Eds. Maureen McNeil, Ian Varcoe, and Steven Yearly. London: Macmillan, 1990. 58–73.

Butler, Judith. *Gender Trouble. Feminism and the Subversion of Identity*. New York/London: Routledge, 1990.

Butler, Octavia. *Dawn*. New York: Warner Books, 1987. Volume I of *Xenogenesis*. 3 vols. 1987–1989.

Button, Diana B. *Worse than Disease. Pitfalls of Medical Progress*. Cambridge: Cambridge University Press, 1988.

Bybee, Carl R. 'Constructing Women as Authorities: Local Journalism and the Microphysics of Power.' *Critical Studies in Mass Communication*, 7.3 (1990): 197–214.

Capron, Alexander M. 'Whose Child is This?' in *Hastings Center Report* 21:6 (1991): 37–38.

Clifford, James, and George E. Marcus, eds. *Writing Culture. The Poetics and Politics of Ethnography*. Berkeley: University of California Press, 1986.

Condit, Celeste M. *Decoding Abortion Rhetoric: Communicating Social Change*. Urbana: University of Illinois Press, 1990.

Cook, Robin. *Vital Signs*. London: Macmillan, 1991.

Cranny-Francis, Anne. *Feminist Fiction. Feminist Uses of Generic Fiction*. Cambridge: Polity Press, 1990.

Crowe, Christine. 'Whose Mind over Whose Matter? Women, In Vitro Fertilization and the Development of Scientific Knowledge.' *The New Reproductive Technologies*. Eds. Maureen McNeil, Ian Varcoe and Steven Yearley. London: Macmillan, 1990.

Dahlgren, Peter, and Colin Sparks, eds. *Journalism and Popular Culture*. London: Sage, 1992.

de Lauretis, Teresa. *Technologies of Gender. Essays on Theory, Film, and Fiction*. Bloomington: Indiana University Press; London: Macmillan,1987.

de Lauretis, Teresa. 'Eccentric Subjects: Feminist Theory and Historical Consciousness.' *Feminist Studies*, 16.1 (Spring 1990): 115–50.

Dervin, Brenda, ed. *Rethinking Communication*. London: Sage, 1989.

Dornan, Christopher. 'Some Problems in Conceptualizing the Issue of "Science and the Media".' *Critical Studies in Mass Communication*, 7 (1990): 48–71.

Duden, Barbara. 'Visualizing "Life".' *Science as Culture* 3:17 (1993): 562–600.

Eason, David L. 'Telling Stories and Making Sense.' *Journal of Popular Culture* 2 (Fall 1981): 125–9.

Eisenstein, Zillah R. *The Female Body and the Law*. Berkeley: University of California Press, 1988.

Fahnestock, Jeanne. 'Accommodating Science. The Rhetorical Life of Scientific Facts.' *Written Communication* 3.3 (July 1986): 275–96.

Faludi, Susan. *Backlash. The Undeclared War Against American Women*. New York: Crown, 1991.

Firestone, Shulamith. *The Dialectic of Sex. The Case for Feminist Revolution*. New York: Bantam, 1970.

Fiske, John. 'Popularity and the Politics of Information.' *Journalism and Popular Culture*. Eds. Peter Dahlgren and Colin Sparks. London: Sage, 1992. 45–63.

Foley, Barbara. *Telling the Truth. Fact and Fiction in the Documentary Novel*. Ithaca: Cornell University Press, 1986.

Foucault, Michel. *The Archaeology of Knowledge and the Discourse on Language*. Transl. A.M. Sheridan Smith. New York: Patheon, 1972. Transl. of *L'archeologie du Savoir* and *L'ordre du Discours*. Paris: Editions Gallimard, 1969.

Foucault, Michel. *Discipline and Punish. The Birth of the Prison*. Transl. Alan Sheridan. New York: Vintage, 1979. Transl. of *Surveiller et Punir; Naissance de la Prison*. Paris: Editions Gallimard, 1975.

Foucault, Michel. *The History of Sexuality. Volume 1: An Introduction*. Transl. Robert Hurley. New York: Vintage, 1980. Transl. of *Histoire de la Sexualité*. Paris: Editions Gallimard, 1976.

Franklin, Sarah. 'Deconstructing "Desperateness": The Social Construction of Infertility in Popular Representations of New Reproductive Technologies.' *The New Reproductive Technologies*. Eds. Maureen McNeil, Ian Varcoe and Steven Yearly. London: Macmillan, 1990. 200–29.

Franklin, Sarah. 'Postmodern Procreation: Representing Reproductive Practice.' *Science as Culture* 3:17 (1993): 522–61.

Franklin, Sarah, and Maureen McNeil. 'Science and Technology: Questions for Cultural Studies and Feminism.' *Off-Centre. Feminism and Cultural Studies*. Eds. Sarah Franklin, Celia Lury, and Jackie Stacey. London: HarperCollins, 1991. 129–46.

Franklin, Sarah, Maureen McNeil, and Jackie Stacey, eds. *Off-Centre. Feminism and Cultural Studies*. London: HarperCollins, 1991.

Fraser, Nancy. *Unruly Practices. Power, Discourse, and Gender in Contemporary Social Theory*. Minneapolis: University of Minnesota Press, 1989.

Gallagher, Janet. 'Fetal Personhood and Women's Policy.' *Women, Biology, and Public Policy*. Ed. Virginia Shapiro. London: Sage, 1985. 91–116.

Gitlin, Todd. *The Whole World Is Watching. Mass Media and the Making and Unmaking of the New Left*. Berkeley: University of California Press, 1980.

Goodfield, June. *Science and the Media*. Washington: American Association for the Advancement of Science, 1981.

Gostin, Larry, ed. *Surrogate Motherhood: Politics and Privacy*. Bloomington: Indiana University Press, 1990.

Habermas, Jürgen. *The Theory of Communicative Action Vol. 1. Reason and the Rationalization of Society.* trans. Thomas McCarthy. Boston: Beacon Press, 1984.

Hall, Stuart, ed. *Culture, Media, Language: Working Papers in Cultural Studies 1972–1979.* London: University of Birmingham, Centre for Contemporary Cultural Studies, 1980.

Hall, Stuart. 'The Emergence of Cultural Studies and the Crisis of the Humanities.' *October* 53 (Summer 1990): 11–23.

Hallin, Daniel C. *The Uncensored War. The Media and Vietnam.* Berkeley: University of California Press, 1986.

Haraway, Donna. 'Situated Knowledges: the Science Question in Feminism and the Privilege of Partial Perspective.' *Feminist Studies* 14.3 (Fall 1988): 575–99.

Haraway, Donna. *Primate Visions. Gender, Race, and Nature in the World of Science.* New York/London: Routledge, 1989.

Haraway, Donna. 'The Biopolitics of Postmodern Bodies: Determinations of Self in Immune System Discourse.' *Differences* 1 (Winter 1989): 3–43.

Haraway, Donna. 'A Manifesto for Cyborgs: Science, Technology, and Socialist Feminism in the 1980s.' *Feminism/Postmodernism.* Ed. Linda Nicholson. New York: Routledge, 1990. 190–233.

Haraway, Donna. *Simians, Cyborgs, and Women. The Reinvention of Nature.* London: Free Association Books, 1991.

Haraway, Donna. 'Otherworldly Conversations; Terran Topics; Local terms.' *Science as Culture* 3:14 (1992): 64–98.

Harding, Sandra. *The Science Question in Feminism.* Ithaca: Cornell University Press, 1986.

Harding, Sandra. *Whose Science? Whose Knowledge? Thinking from Women's Lives.* Ithaca: Cornell University Press, 1991.

Hartouni, Valerie. 'Containing Women: Reproductive Discourse in the 1980's.' *Techno-Culture.* Eds. Andrew Ross and Constance Penley. Minneapolis: University of Minnesota Press, 1991. 27–56.

Hartouni, Valerie. 'Breached Births: Reflections on Race, Gender and Reproductive Discourse in the 1980s.' *Configurations* 1 (1994): 73–88.

Harvey, David. *The Condition of Postmodernity.* Oxford: Basil Blackwell, 1989.

Hayles, Katherine. 'Text out of Context: Situating Postmodernism within an Information Society.' *Discourse* 9 (Spring 1987): 24–36.

Herman, Edward S. and Noam Chomsky. *Manufacturing Consent. The Political Economy of the Mass Media.* New York: Pantheon, 1988.

Holmes, Helen Becquaert. 'Contract Pregnancy. An Annotated Bibliography.' *Issues in Reproductive Technology I. An Anthology.* Ed. Helen B. Holmes. New York: Garland, 1992. 381–422.

Holmes, Helen B. and Laura M. Purdy, eds. *Feminist Perspectives in Medical Ethics.* Bloomington: Indiana University Press, 1992.

Jacobus, Mary, Evelyn Fox Keller, and Sally Shuttleworth, eds. *Body/ Politics. Women and the Discourse of Science.* New York: Routledge, 1990.

Kane, Elizabeth. *Birth Mother: America's First Legal Surrogate Mother Tells the Story of Her Change of Heart.* San Diego: Harcourt, Brace, Jovanovich, 1988.

Karpf, Anne. Doctoring the Media. *The Reporting of Health and Medicine.* New York: Routledge, 1988.

Keller, Evelyn Fox. *A Feeling For Organism. The Life and Work of Barbara McClintock.* New York: Freeman, 1983.

Keller, Evelyn Fox. *Reflections on Gender and Science.* New Haven: Yale University Press, 1985.

Keller, Evelyn Fox. 'The Gender/Science System: or, is Sex to Gender as Nature is to Science?' *Feminism and Science.* Ed. Nancy Tuana. Bloomington: Indiana University Press, 1989. 32–44.

Kirejczyk, Martha, and Irma van der Ploeg. 'Pregnant Couples: Medical Technology and Social Constructions around Fertility and Reproduction.' *Issues in Reproductive and Genetic Engineering* 5:2 (1992): 113–25.

Kirkman, Maggie and Linda. *My Sister's Child: Maggie and Linda Kirkman – Their Own Story.* Ringwood: Penguin Books, 1988.

Klein, Renate Duelli. *Infertility: Women Speak Out About Their Experiences of Reproductive Medicine.* London: Pandora Press, 1989.

Klein, Renate Duelli. 'IVF Research: A Question of Feminist Ethics.' *Issues in Reproductive and Genetic Engineering* 3:3 (1990): 243–51.

Latour, Bruno, and Steve Woolgar. *Laboratory Life: The Social Construction of Scientific Facts.* London: Sage, 1979.

Lefanu, Sarah. *Feminism and Science Fiction.* Bloomington: Indiana University Press, 1989.

Lyotard, Jean-François. *The Postmodern Condition: A Report on Knowledge.* Transl. Geoff Bennington and Brian Massumi. Manchester: Manchester University Press, 1984. Transl. of *La Condition Postmoderne: Rapport sur le Savoir.* Paris: Editions de Minuit, 1979.

Malpede, Karen. 'Scenes 2 and 7 from "Better people: A surreal Comedy about Genetic Engineering".' *Issues in Reproductive and Genetic Engineering* 4:2 (1991): 161–8.

Martin, Emily. *The Woman in the Body.* Boston: Beacon Press, 1987.

Martin, Emily. 'Science and Women's Bodies: Forms of Anthropological Knowledge.' *Body/Politics. Women and the Discourse of Science.* Eds. Mary Jacobus, Evelyn Fox Keller, and Sally Shuttleworth. New York: Routledge, 1990. 69–82.

McNeil, Maureen. 'New Reproductive Technologies. Dreams and Broken Promises.' *Science as Culture* 3:17 (1993): 483–506.

McNeil, Maureen, Ian Varcoe, and Steven Yearly, eds. *The New Reproductive Technologies.* London: Macmillan, 1990.

Montgomery, Scott L. 'Codes and Combat in Biomedical Discourse.' *Science as Culture* 2.12 (1991): 341–90.

Myers, Greg. *Writing Biology. Texts in the Social Construction of Knowledge.* Madison: University of Wisconsin Press, 1990.

Nelkin, Dorothy. *Selling Science. How the Press Covers Science and Technology.* New York: Freeman, 1987.

Nelson, Hilde Lindemann. 'Scrutinizing Surrogacy.' *Issues in Reproductive Technology I. An Anthology.* Ed. Helen B. Holmes. New York: Garland, 1992. 297–302.

Nicholson, Linda, ed. *Feminism/Postmodernism.* New York: Routledge, 1990.

O'Brien, Mary. 'Elly.' *Issues in Reproductive and Genetic Engineering* 3:2 (1990): 137–41.

Ormiston, Gayle L., and Raphael Sassower. *Narrative Experiments. The Discursive Authority of Science and Technology.* Minneapolis: University of Minnesota Press, 1989.

Overall, Christine. *Ethics and Human Reproduction: A Feminist Analysis.* Boston: AllenUnwin, 1987.

Pauly, John. 'The Politics of New Journalism.' *Literary Journalism in the Twentieth Century.* Oxford: Oxford University Press, 1990. 120–9.

Petchesky, Rosalind Pollack. *Abortion and Woman's Choice. The State, Sexuality, and Reproductive Freedom.* New York: Longman, 1984.

Petchesky, Rosalind Pollack. 'Foetal Images: The Power of Visual Culture in the Politics of Reproduction.' *Reproductive Technologies. Gender, Motherhood, and Medicine.* Ed. Michelle Stanworth. Minneapolis: University of Minnesota Press, 1987. 57–80.

Phillips, David. 'Importance of the Lay Press in the Transmission of Medical Knowledge to the Scientific Commentry'. *New England Journal of Medicine* (17 October 1991): 1180–7

Piercy, Marge. *Woman on the Edge of Time.* New York: Fawcett Crest, 1976.

Pollitt, Katha. 'A New Assault on Feminism.' *The Nation*, 26 March 1990: 409–18.

Poster, Mark. *The Mode of Information. Poststructuralism and Social Context.* Chicago: University of Chicago Press, 1990.

Purdy, Laura M. 'Another Look at Contract Pregnancy.' *Issues in Reproductive Technology I. An Anthology.* Ed. Helen B. Holmes. New York: Garland, 1992. 303–20.

Quéré, Louis. *Des Miroirs Equivoques. Aux Origines de la Communication Moderne.* Paris: Editions Aubier Montaigne, 1982.

Raymond, Janice G. 'Fetalists and Feminists: They are not the Same.' *Made To Order. The Myth of Reproductive and Genetic Progress.* Eds. Patricia Spallone and Deborah Lynn Steinberg. Oxford: Pergamon Press, 1987. 58–66.

Raymond, Janice G. 'The Marketing of New Reproductive Technologies: Medicine, the Media, and the Idea of Progress.' *Issues in Reproductive and Genetic Engineering* 3:3 (1990): 253–61.

Rorvik, David. *In His Image. The Cloning of a Man.* Philadelphia: J.B. Lippincott, 1978.

Ross, Andrew, and Constance Penley, eds. *Techno-Culture.* Minneapolis: University of Minnesota Press, 1991.

Rothman, Barbara Katz. *Recreating Motherhood. Ideology and Technology in a Patriarchal Society.* New York: Norton, 1989.

Rouse, Joseph. 'What Are the Cultural Studies of Scientific Knowledge?' *Configurations* 1 (1992): 1–22.

Sargent, Pamela. *Cloned Lives.* New York: Fawcett Gold Metal, 1976.

Schudson, Michael. *Discovering the News. A Social History of American Newspapers.* New York: Basic Books, 1978.

Schudson, Michael. 'The Politics of Narrative Form: the Emergence of News Conventions in Print and Television.' *Deadalus* 3.4 (Fall 1982): 97–112.

Schudson, Michael. 'National News Culture and the Rise of the Informational Citizen.' *America at Century's End.* Ed. Alan Wolfe. Berkeley: University of California Press, 1991. 265–82.

Spallone, Patricia. 'Reproductive Technology and the State: The Warnock Report and its Clones.' *Made to Order. The Myth of Reproductive and Genetic Progress.* Eds. Patricia Spallone and Deborah Lynn Steinberg. Oxford: Pergamon Press, 1987. 166–83.

Spallone, Patricia. *Beyond Conception. The New Politics of Reproduction.* Granby, Massachusetts: Bergin and Garvey, 1989.

Spallone, Patricia, and Deborah Lynn Steinberg, eds. *Made To Order. The Myth of Reproductive and Genetic Progress.* Oxford: Pergamon Press, 1987.

Stabile, Carol A. 'Shooting the Mother: Fetal Photography and the Politics of Disappearance.' *Camera Obscura* 28 (1992): 179–205.

Stanworth, Michelle. *Reproductive Technologies. Gender, Motherhood, and Medicine.* Minneapolis: University of Minnesota Press, 1987.

Strathern, Marilyn. *Reproducing the Future. Anthropology, Kinship, and the New Reproductive Technologies.* Manchester: Manchester University Press, 1993.

Terdiman, Richard. *Discourse/Counter-Discourse. The Theory and Practice of Symbolic Resistance in Nineteenth Century France.* Ithaca: Cornell University Press, 1985.

Terry, Jennifer. 'The Body Invaded: Medical Surveillance of Women as Reproducers.' *Socialist Review* 3 (July 1989): 13–43.

Treichler, Paula. 'What Definitions Do: Childbirth, Cultural Crisis, and the Challenge to Medical Discourse.' *Rethinking Communication.* Ed. Brenda Dervin. London: Sage, 1989. 424–53.

Treichler, Paula. 'Feminism, Medicine, and the Meaning of Childbirth.' *Body/Politics. Women and the Discourse of Science.* Eds. Mary Jacobus, Evelyn Fox Keller, and Sally Shuttleworth. New York: Routledge, 1990. 113–38.

Tuana, Nancy, ed. *Feminism and Science.* Bloomington: Indiana University Press, 1989.

Tuchman, Gaye. *Making News. A Study in the Construction of Reality.* New York: The Free Press, 1978.

Vandewater, Bette. 'Meanings and Strategies of Reproductive Control: Current Feminist Approaches to Reproductive Technology.' *Issues in Reproductive and Genetic Engineering* 5:3 (1992): 215–30.

Van Dyck, José and Lies Wesseling. 'The Issue of Responsibility in Margaret Atwood's "The Handmaid's Tale".' *Against Patriarchal Thinking. A Future without Discrimination?* Ed. Maja Pelikaan. Amsterdam: Free University Press, 1992. 243–51.

Wajcman, Judy. *Feminism Confronts Technology.* University Park: Pennsylvania State University Press, 1991.

Whitehead, Mary Beth and Loretta Schwartz-Nobel. *A Mother's Story. The Truth about the Baby M Case.* New York: St. Martin's Press, 1989.

Wikler, Norma J. 'Society's Response the New Reproductive Technologies: Feminist Perspectives.' *Southern Californian Law Review* 59 (1986): 1043–57.

Wolfe, Alan. ed. *America at Century's End.* Berkeley: University of California Press, 1991.

Woll, Lisa. 'The Effect of Feminist Opposition to Reproductive Technology: A Case Study in Victoria, Australia.' *Issues in Reproductive and Genetic Engineering* 5:1 (1992): 21–38.

Woolgar, Steve. *Science: The Very Idea.* London: Travistock Publications, 1988.

Zelizer, Barbie. 'Achieving Journalistic Authority through Narrative.' *Critical Studies in Mass Communication* 7 (1990): 336–76.

Zelizer, Barbie. *Covering the Body. The Kennedy Assassination, the Media, and the Shaping of Collective Memory.* Chicago: University of Chicago Press, 1992.

Index

abortion 13, 23, 31, 32, 162
abortion pill *see* RU486
Altheide, David 51
American Fertility Society 42, 70
American Medical Association 23,
     26, 141
Andrews, Lori B. 171
Antinori, Severino 1, 5, 177, 180,
     181, 184
Arditti, Rita 90, 99, 172
Atwood, Margaret 104–9, 112, 113,
     114

Baby M case 119–20, 146, 150, 171
Backlash (Susan Faludi) 197
Barthes, Roland 95
Berer, Marge 100–1
Beyond Conception (Patricia
     Spallone) 141
blocked Fallopian tubes 2, 12, 62,
     72, 77, 97, 130, 138, 139
Braidotti, Rosi 27
Brave New World (Aldous
     Huxley) 52, 66, 88
British Medical Association 26,
     180, 181
British Medical Journal 41, 79, 122,
     123
Brown, Louise 1, 6, 62–5, 69, 71,
     151
Burfoot, Anne 10
Butler, Judith 202
Butler, Octavia 104, 109–14, 116,
     142
Button, Diana 199
Bybee, Carl 127

Caesarian section 19, 27, 62, 95
Calverts *v.* Johnson case 151–71,
     172, 185
Capron, Alexander 172
Carder, Angela, case of 18
childbirth, definition of 22

Chomsky, Noam 15–21
clinical gaze 26, 132–3, 139, 143,
     145
Cloned Lives (Pamela Sargent) 67–9
Condit, Celeste 32
contraceptives 23, 27, 52, 114–16
contract pregnancy 171–3
Cook, Robin 119, 138, 142
Corea, Gena 90, 94, 98, 99, 100,
     102, 103, 107, 109, 141
countermyth 90–8, 115
counterdiscourse 20, 22, 56, 95, 117
Cranny-Francis, Anne 55–6
Cross, Amanda 142
cultural studies of science 5, 43
cyborg 29

Daily Mail 50, 64
Daily Mirror 182–3
Daily Telegraph 181, 182, 184
Dawn (Octavia Butler) 104,
     109–14, 142
DES 97, 136–7
Dialectic of Sex (Shulamith
     Firestone 87, 88
Direcks, Anita 96–8
discourse and authority 20, 31, 42,
     50, 55, 128, 137, 168
discourse, boundaries of 38, 43, 44,
     51, 53, 121
discourse, definition of 19
discourse, hierarchy of 20, 38, 40,
     43, 45, 55, 56, 74, 113, 117, 137,
     144

Edwards, Robert 61–5, 69, 71, 80,
     132
Efron, Sonni 161
Embryo Transfer (ET) 9, 75–76

Faludi, Susan 197, 201
feminism 33, 34

Feminist International Network on New Reproductive Technologies (FINNRET) *see* FINNRAGE *below*

Feminist International Network of Resistance to Reproductive and Genetic Engineering (FINNRAGE) 90–2, 94, 96, 99–101, 115, 141, 146

Feminist Studies 145

Fenton, James 188

Fertility and Sterility 42, 70–4, 76, 123, 124, 159

Fertility Assistance 42, 75

Firestone, Shulamith 87–9, 90, 102, 114

Fiske, John 45, 59

Foley, Barbara 35

Foucault, Michel 16, 19, 30, 37

Frankenstein (Mary Shelley) 66, 180

Franklin, Sarah 9, 70, 132

Fraser, Nancy 15

Gamete Intrafallopian Transfer (GIFT) 9, 74, 76, 122, 131, 150

Gewertz, Catherine 157–63, 165

Global Network of Reproductive Rights (GNRR) 58

Goldfarb, James 149

Goodfield, June 36, 37

Guardian 180, 181, 182, 188, 191

Habermas, Jürgen 14–16

Halmner, Jana 91

Halpern, Sue 126–8, 142, 144

Handmaid's Tale (Margaret Atwood) 104–9, 112, 115

Haraway, Donna 28–33, 35, 57

Harding, Sandra 27

Hartouni, Valerie 32, 83, 153, 172, 186

Herman, Edward 15–21

Holmes, Helen B. 96–8

Human Fertilisation and Embryology Act 132, 176

Human Fertilisation and Embryology Authority 176–8, 180

Human Genome Project 11–12

Huxley, Aldous 52, 66, 88

Independent 175, 185, 187, 188

infertility 12, 70–3, 77

infertility and age 178

infertility and class 83, 102, 106, 160, 172

infertility and ethnicity 83, 102, 106, 160, 172

infertility, definition of 72–3

infertility, female *see* blocked Fallopian tubes

infertility, male 81–2, 130

infertility, myth of 178

infertility, unexplained 72

info-science journals 41, 42, 54

In His Image (David Rorvick) 35–6, 52

in vitro fertilization (IVF) 9–13, 16, 24, 15, 61–5, 77, 96–8, 123–43, 178–9, 190

Issues in Reproductive and Genetic Engineering (IRGE) 145–6

Jenkins, Simon 175, 182

Johnson, Anna *see* Calverts v. Johnson case

Journal of Reproductive Medicine 74

Journal of the American Medical Association 75, 79

Karpf, Anne 24

Kasindorf, Martin 163, 165

Keller, Evelyn Fox 27

Klein, Renate Duelli 90, 91–3, 94, 95, 98, 100, 101, 109, 141, 146

LA Law 19

Lancet 62, 63, 65, 78, 132

laparoscopy 26, 61, 65, 121, 132, 143

Latour, Bruno 35, 38–9

Los Angeles Times 149, 151–70

Lyotard, Jean-François 37, 51

Malik, Kenan 175, 187

Martin, Emily 28, 31

medical gaze *see* clinical gaze

Medical News 42
metaphor 31, 53, 57, 77, 80, 124–6, 130
Mies, Maria 93–4, 95, 98, 109
Montgomery, Scott 53
motherhood, fragmentation of 150, 191
motherhood, genetic 150, 168, 170, 173, 177, 187
motherhood, gestational 150, 160–1, 164, 170–1, 173, 177, 187
motherhood, legal definition of 168, 174
motherhood, social 150
motherhood, surrogate 13, 119, 158, 164, 171, 173
Ms magazine 101, 126–7, 142
Myers, Greg 42–4, 59
myth 24, 25, 36, 62, 78–9, 82–4, 95, 130

narrativation 50, 84, 121, 132, 134, 144
Nation 149, 172, 197
National Enquirer 50, 51
Nature 79, 123
Nelkin, Dorothy 45, 47
New England Journal of Medicine 32, 40, 41, 46, 119, 120, 129–36, 137, 138, 139, 142, 143, 178–9
New Scientist 96, 98
Newsday 165
newsification 51, 193
newsletter 42, 54, 75
New York Times 47, 48, 50, 105, 122, 123, 179
Newsweek 47, 50, 51, 61
1984 (George Orwell) 66
normalization 16
Nursing Times 125, 126, 127

Ob.Gyn.News 123
Observer 185
Office of Technology Assessment 79
Ormiston, Gayle L. 57, 114
Orwell, George 66
Overall, Christine 171

Paretsky, Sara 142
Petchesky, Rosalind 12, 31, 116
Pfeffer, Naomi 99–100, 101, 103, 107
Piercy, Marge 87–9, 111, 113, 114
Pollitt, Katha 149, 172, 197
postmenopausal pregnancy 177–8, 179, 182–3, 187–9, 191
public consent 15–24, 34, 192–4, 196
public debate 3, 5, 6, 7, 13, 14–27, 44, 57, 59, 128, 160, 178, 191–4, 196–204
public debate, mapping of 23, 34, 57–8, 60, 196–7
public sphere 14, 63
Purdy, Laura 172

Quéré, Louis 49, 56

religion 74, 76, 80, 84, 131, 182
reproductive tourism 4, 180
Rock, John 52
Roe *v.* Wade 23
Rorvik, David 35–7, 52, 53
RU486 (abortion pill) 13

San Diego Tribune 169
Sargent, Pamela 67
Sassower, Raphael 57, 114
Schudson, Michael 51
Science 61
science article, rhetorical devices of 39
Shelley, Mary 66
Silent Scream (Rosalind Petchesky) 31
Snitow, Ann 101–2, 103, 116
Snow, Robert 51
social constructivism 38, 43
Socialist Review 197
Spallone, Patricia 32, 141
Stanworth, Michelle 103
Steptoe, Patrick 61–6, 69, 71, 80, 132
Strategic Defense Initiative (SDI) 11
Strathern, Marilyn 9, 19
success rates 122, 129

Terry, Jennifer 197
test-tube baby 1, 2, 62–4, 87, 132, 151
Test-Tube Women (Rita Arditti et al.) 90–3, 100
Time magazine 47, 50, 51, 61, 65, 66, 68, 77–84, 91, 92, 119, 120, 124, 134–39, 142, 143, 149, 161
Times, The 50, 175, 180–2, 183, 184–5, 187–8
transracial impregnation 178, 184–9, 191
Treichler, Paula 22, 168
Trouble and Strife 99

ultrasound 26, 31, 132, 134, 135, 143

Vital Signs (Robin Cook) 119, 120, 138–42
Voluntary Licensing Authority 176

Wall Street Journal 94–5, 109, 114
Warnock Report 32, 176
Woll, Lisa 146
Women on the Edge of Time (Marge Piercy) 87, 88, 111
Women's Studies International Forum 93, 145
Woolgar, Steven 35, 38–43, 48
'World of the Unborn, The' (BBC TV series) 132

Zelizer, Barbie 54
Zygote Intrafallopian Transfer (ZIFT) 9